W9-CZM-499

CONTEMPORARY SOUTHERN WOMEN FICTION WRITERS

THE MAGILL BIBLIOGRAPHIES

The American Presidents, by Norman S. Cohen, 1989

Black American Women Novelists, by Craig Werner, 1989

Classical Greek and Roman Drama, by Robert J. Forman, 1989

Contemporary Latin American Fiction, by Keith H. Brower, 1989

Masters of Mystery and Detective Fiction, by J. Randolph Cox, 1989

Nineteenth Century American Poetry, by Philip K. Jason, 1989

Restoration Drama, by Thomas J. Taylor, 1989

Twentieth Century European Short Story, by Charles E. May, 1989

The Victorian Novel, by Laurence W. Mazzeno, 1989

Women's Issues, by Laura Stempel Mumford, 1989

America in Space, by Russell R. Tobias, 1991

The American Constitution, by Robert J. Janosik, 1991

The Classic Epic, by Thomas J. Sienkewicz, 1991

English Romantic Poetry, by Brian Aubrey, 1991

Ethics, by John K. Roth, 1991

The Immigrant Experience, by Paul D. Mageli, 1991

The Modern American Novel, by Steven G. Kellman, 1991

Native Americans, by Frederick E. Hoxie and Harvey Markowitz, 1991

American Drama: 1918–1960, by R. Baird Shuman, 1992

American Ethnic Literatures, by David R. Peck, 1992

American Theater History, by Thomas J. Taylor, 1992

The Atomic Bomb, by Hans G. Graetzer and Larry M. Browning, 1992

Biography, by Carl Rollyson, 1992

The History of Science, by Gordon L. Miller, 1992

The Origin and Evolution of Life on Earth, by David W. Hollar, Jr., 1992

Pan-Africanism, by Michael W. Williams, 1992

Resources for Writers, by R. Baird Shuman, 1992

Shakespeare, by Joseph Rosenblum, 1992

The Vietnam War in Literature, by Philip K. Jason, 1992

Contemporary Southern Women Fiction Writers, by Rosemary M. Canfield Reisman and Christopher J. Canfield, 1994

Cycles in Humans and Nature, by John T. Burns, 1994

Environmental Studies, by Diane M. Fortner, 1994

Poverty in America, by Steven Pressman, 1994

The Short Story in English: Britain and North America, by Dean Baldwin and Gregory L. Morris, 1994

CONTEMPORARY
SOUTHERN WOMEN
FICTION WRITERS
An Annotated Bibliography

by
ROSEMARY M. CANFIELD REISMAN
and
CHRISTOPHER J. CANFIELD

Magill Bibliographies

The Scarecrow Press, Inc.
Metuchen, N.J., & London
and
Salem Press
Pasadena, CA & Englewood Cliffs, N.J.
1994

British Library Cataloguing-in-Publication data available

Library of Congress Cataloging-in-Publication Data

Reisman, Rosemary M. Canfield.
    Contemporary southern women fiction writers : an annotated
bibliography / by Rosemary M. Canfield Reisman and
Christopher J. Canfield.
        p.   cm.—(The Magill bibliographies.)
    Includes bibliographical references and index
    ISBN 0-8108-2832-4 (acid-free paper)
    1. American fiction—Southern states—Bibliography.   2.
Women and literature—Southern states—Bibliography.   3.
American fiction—Women authors—Bibliography.   4.
American fiction—20th century—Bibliography.   5. Southern
states in literature—Bibliography.   I. Canfield, Christopher
J.   II. Title.   III. Series.
Z1251.S7R44   1994
[PS261]
016.813'54099287'0975—dc20   93-6549

EDITORIAL STAFF

Publisher
FRANK N. MAGILL

Advisory Board
KENNETH T. BURLES
DAWN P. DAWSON

Series Editor
JOHN WILSON

Production Editor
CYNTHIA BRESLIN BERES

Copy Editor
PHILIP WONG

For Vernie Alton and Lois Slee Moody

CONTENTS

CONTEMPORARY SOUTHERN WOMEN FICTION WRITERS

ACKNOWLEDGMENTS

Rosemary Reisman wishes to thank the Troy State University Library staff, especially Nell Bassett, for her cheerful efficiency; her student assistant, Tina Menees, for her dedication and persistence; and the Wake Forest University Library staff, for their kindness to a stranger in their midst. She would also like to thank Troy State University for their generous one-quarter sabbatical, which enabled her to conduct the research for this book.

INTRODUCTION

The indebtedness of the writers presented here to their predecessors, those women who struggled against the patriarchal traditions of the South to gain a voice, is clear. Few, if any, fail to acknowledge the influence of Katherine Anne Porter, Eudora Welty, Flannery O'Connor, or Carson McCullers. They single out these authors from the men writing at the same times, often identifying one or more of these women as the source of empowerment for their own creations. This next generation of writers seems proud to carry forward the flag of their literary mothers.

Yet most, if not all, of the writers considered in this bibliographical study of *Contemporary Southern Women Fiction Writers* would object, at some level, to being included. They would object not so much to the prospect of further scholarship on their writings as to the subcategorizations required to promote that scholarship. A writer wants to be thought of as a writer, without qualifiers—that which these predecessors fought to make possible.

In a perfect world, of course, we would have been able to eliminate the qualifiers. We had to grapple with their meanings at every turn ourselves. None of our "rules" stood without exception. "Contemporary" came to mean for us that the writer (as of this volume's publication) is currently producing works of fiction, that she had produced works recently, or that her previous works are receiving increased academic or general attention. Some of the authors have considerable legacies, while others have only recently begun to gain notice. "Fiction Writers" delineated our primary interest in novelists and short-story writers, requiring the exclusion of sometimes substantial works in other fields from many of these writers—from plays to poetry, criticism to biography.

More potentially insulting than problematic is the gender label. Grouping "Women" writers is easy enough on the surface. Yet more than a few of these authors would argue (and have) that they can stand shoulder-to-shoulder with their male counterparts. Literature, however, is not an athletic event. These authors do not need and do not appreciate the special treatment, particularly if it tempts dismissal of their works as "women's writing." Plainly, no such condescension is meant here. It is an unfortunate dilemma that in order for women writers to achieve greater respect they first have had to receive separate consideration. The same has been true for minority authors. The goal of this study is to facilitate the kind of discussion that may soon resolve this dilemma.

Finally, and most convoluted, is the category "Southern." Flannery O'Connor has been quoted as saying that "the woods are full of regional writers, and it is the great horror of every serious Southern writer that he will become one of them." The statement expresses the fear of many of these authors, stated emphatically in interview after interview. The writers of any gender in the South fit less and less the various clichés that have both plagued and benefited them. First, many "Southern" writers live in cities such as San Francisco, New York, or Boston and have done so for all their years since early childhood. They may write about epiphanies associated with, for example, seeing their first calving, but they generally do so from distant memory or background reading. Second, those who still live in the geographic South may be far from the literary South of old. Atlanta burned and has, of late, been rebuilt in the image of the universal city rather than the particular town of the remembered South. The urban South often has more in common with the urban North than with any of the surrounding rural areas. Third, even those writers with one version of the right credentials—rural upbringing, family barely budging from one spot of land for generations, resistance to education's homogenizing tendency, and a commitment to stay where reared—especially if born after 1950, are as likely to include images from television and pop culture in their Southern world as they are images from farming and country music. The aristocratic version of the South is equally as muddled these days.

The South is, in many ways, no longer what it used to be. Somehow, though, its literary reputation continues and prospers anew. The Center for the Study of Southern Culture at the University of Mississippi recently published its massive (1,634-page) *Encyclopedia of Southern Culture* (1989), including a large section on the region's literature. Similar organizations, from the University of South Carolina's Institute for Southern Studies to the University of North Carolina's proposed Center for the Study of the American South, ensure that the South will not be forgotten or fully absorbed into the nation at large. More specific to literature is the growing number of journals devoted to the Southern voice. *The Southern Literary Journal, The Southern Review*, and *Southern Quarterly*, to name the most prominent, encourage scholarship on writers of national reputation as well as those likely to be overlooked in less specialized criticism. Southern university presses have a history of supporting "regional" writers. Through the early 1990's, small private publishing houses, such as Louis Rubin's Algonquin Books of Chapel Hill, have carved out a significant market, bringing national attention to authors without New York addresses.

The general entries of this bibliography also demonstrate the vitality of the study of Southern literature. While including resources of historical importance, such as W. J. Cash's *The Mind of the South* (1941), the entries also display a wealth of recent scholarship. Particularly important are two collections of essays on the newest generation of women writers. Peggy Whitman Prenshaw's *Women Writers of the Contemporary South* (1984) and Tonette Bond Inge's *Southern Women Writers: The New Generation* (1990) have begun a wave of study that we predict will swell in the coming decades.

Thus, the study of the region and its literature flourishes, despite the difficulties of saying exactly what that study is about. Without a shared or proven definition, critics, readers, and even the writers themselves are somehow able to nod in agreement about who is and who is not a Southern writer. Even those who fight their Southern heritage have to acknowledge its influence. Alice Adams, for example, said, "I couldn't wait to get out [of the South] the first time and I couldn't wait to get out [after returning twenty years later]." Still, Adams and reviewers acknowledge the profound impact that her upbringing had on her and her writing. Adams lives in San Francisco and has through 1992 written more about that setting than about the South. Yet every new word she types must necessarily derive (even if in rebellion) from the words and rhythms of her North Carolina and Virginia youth.

This annotated bibliography is compiled with full knowledge of the pitfalls of categorization. We accept the risks in the hope that our choices, be they obvious or questionable, will promote discourse. What common elements unite these greatly varied women authors? What particular traits make them "Southern" writers? Only further scholarship and discussion will more clearly answer those questions. Our goal is simply to assist those efforts.

There are more practical considerations in our choices than the philosophical ones already discussed. Take, for example, the list of writers included. Many fine Southern women authors certainly will have been excluded. The size and scope of this book limited the number of subjects. Once we had a short list of writers we felt had to be included (Anne Tyler and Alice Walker come immediately to mind), we began the more difficult task of expanding the list to our final twenty-eight.

Should we choose them on the basis of academic material available on their works, or on the degree of popular success they have found, or maybe on the basis of sustained performance even if relatively unsupported by secondary materials? In the end, we used all the above and more in deciding on the final list. We believe the women here represent a significant range of accomplishment—some whose work has begun to receive greater appreciation, some who have been neglected after past promise was judged unfulfilled, and a few who have begun to feel the pressure of high expectations.

In compiling the entries, we started with some basic guidelines. In theory, we hoped to average twenty to twenty-five annotated citations per author. Those citations would come from generally accessible books at the first level, well-known scholarly journals and/or general interest magazines after that. If necessary, we would delve into more obscure scholarly works, followed by newspaper and magazine reviews. As much biographical information (especially interviews) would be noted as possible. There was never any illusion of the bibliographies being exhaustive. Rather, we hoped they would be representative and assist a general student or even a specialist scholar in hunting down secondary sources pertinent to a particular interest or thesis.

In practice, the selection of critical materials varied greatly from writer to writer. At one extreme, secondary citations on Alice Walker alone could have filled this book. We chose to limit selections almost exclusively to books with significant references to her works. At the other extreme, a young writer such as Vicki Covington is lucky to have a page of limited references. In that case, we listed reviews and incidental references in sources we admit may be difficult for the general student to find. Our conviction is that researchers interested in such a writer are in greater need of this bibliography than those interested in Alice Walker. Including Covington or Mary Ward Brown expands the horizons, we hope, even if violating some of our "rules" on accessibility of sources.

In the citation of reviews, we made no effort to be complete. Those writers represented by a large sampling of secondary sources might have no reviews cited. Others, for whom reviews were the principal source of discussion of their writings, might have a great number of reviews listed. We chose reviews based on the ways they represented general response to the work, on the prominence of the reviewers or publications, or on the unique perspective a particular review might provide. In no case did we list all the reviews of a single author's work or works. Researchers should consult book review digests and indexes for more complete listings.

Our annotations for all the citations are intended to serve a number of purposes. First, we hoped to indicate what books or aspects of a writer's style and themes are noted in the particular study. Second, we intended to indicate the tone and point of view of the critic, either through our own characterization or through selected quotation. Last, and most selectively, we sought to weigh the relative merit of the source, but only if we believed that such an appraisal would prove significantly helpful.

A disclaimer about currency is in order for a study of this kind. The lag time between when the research is done and when the bibliography is finally published can be considerable. We have made every effort to include the most recent studies available. Many of the authors herein are constantly producing new novels and stories, however, and their critics are racing to provide new commentary. Indexes and reference works we consulted undoubtedly will be full of new secondary material on these authors by the time our work is in print. Therefore, we urge students and researchers to supplement our work with further trips to the review references discussed above, the Modern Language Association Bibliography, and the host of other catalogs and computer search services that the modern library has to offer. May your study stimulate as much reflection and enthusiasm in you as ours has in us.

GENERAL STUDIES

Ammons, Elizabeth. *Conflicting Stories: American Women Writers at the Turn into the Twentieth Century*. New York: Oxford University Press, 1991.
Although this study deals only with writers from the 1890's to the 1920's, it provides excellent background for a study of contemporary women writers. The extended discussion of Ellen Glasgow, in particular, points out that writer's lifelong conflict with the ideal of the obedient and restricted "Southern Lady."

Armstrong, Nancy. *Desire and Domestic Fiction: A Political History of the Novel*. New York: Oxford University Press, 1987.
Argues that the rise of that middle-class genre, the novel, was closely associated with the need to set forth an ideal for womanhood that did not involve birth or wealth, but behavior in the domestic area. Eventually, men, too, were defined by their conduct at home, not in the world at large. Since women generally had authority over the day-to-day conduct of the home, however, they were seen by writers as also having considerable power. Women writers, in particular, saw that women had developed effective political strategies in order to consolidate that power within their assigned sphere.

Bain, Robert, Joseph M. Flora, and Louis D. Rubin, Jr. *Southern Writers: A Biographical Dictionary*. Baton Rouge: Louisiana State University Press, 1979.
A reliable though dated reference work. Includes assessments of writers' importance in literary history, as well as full biographical data and listings of their works published through the mid-1970's.

Balakian, Nona, and Charles Simmons, eds. *The Creative Present: Notes on Contemporary American Fiction*. Garden City, N.Y.: Doubleday, 1963.
An anthology of essays by various writers. Balakian's introduction is of particular interest. Argues that common qualities among contemporary writers are an interest in technique and their skepticism

as to the existence of truth. They find certainty only in their belief that both the integrity of the self and meaningful connections with others are important. Essays by others discuss works of Eudora Welty and Carson McCullers.

Bell, Bernard W. *The Afro-American Novel and Its Tradition*. Amherst: University of Massachusetts Press, 1987.
A history of the African-American novel, from its roots in African myths and folktales to modernism and postmodernism. Instead of approaching works from any one theoretical position, whether psychological, political, or linguistic, the author looks at texts in terms of cultural history, as a means of surviving as a people and of developing a sense of racial identity. The volume is organized chronologically. Within each chapter, writers are grouped within literary schools. There is a separate discussion of "The Women's Rights Movement" in chapter 7. Contemporary women writers treated include Toni Morrison, Alice Walker, and Margaret Walker. Voluminous notes and lengthy index. In addition to secondary sources, the bibliography lists works by forty-one black writers.

Berry, J. Bill, ed. *Home Ground: Southern Autobiography*. Columbia: University of Missouri Press, 1991.
Papers presented at a 1989 conference entitled "Home Ground: Parents and Children in Southern Autobiography" and demonstrating "the power of the material to define group as well as individual experience." The title "Home Ground" suggests the synthesis apparent in these papers between a sense of family and a sense of place. Participants take various approaches, ranging from the purely critical to the primarily personal. Unfortunately, none of the five "personal narratives" was written by a woman.

―――――――, ed. *Located Lives: Place and Idea in Southern Autobiography*. Athens: University of Georgia Press, 1990.
Includes both essays about autobiography and personal essays illustrating that genre. Of particular interest are discussions of the relationship between voice and place, the distinctive characteristics of autobiographical writing by black women and by white women, and the relationships between Southern autobiography and Southern fiction. Even in the personal essays, all written by men, the reflections on family structures and traditions are pertinent to studies of women writers. A bibliography is appended to the initial essay.

Betts, Doris. "Introduction." In *Southern Women Writers: The New Generation*, edited by Tonette Bond Inge, pp. 1-8. Tuscaloosa: University of Alabama Press, 1990.

A brief, incisive essay that suggests that generalizations about Southern writing do not take into account the diversity of the South in terms of region and viewpoint. Betts points out various patterns in contemporary writing by women, as well as in criticism of women's writing. Common elements she does identify are the use of language as a mask, tough realism, and faith in the possibility of love.

_____. "Many Souths and Broadening Scale: A Changing Southern Literature." In *The Future South: A Historical Perspective for the Twenty-first Century*, edited by Joe P. Dunn and Howard L. Preston, pp. 158-187. Urbana: University of Illinois Press, 1991.

Traces twentieth century changes in attitudes toward the South and toward Southern literature. Cites evidence to prove that instead of ending in the 1950's, the Southern Renaissance gained new strength from the social changes of the 1960's, which gave new opportunities to black and women writers. Betts points also to changes in intellectual climate, which have encouraged the academic study of Southern writers and the development of strong writing programs at Southern colleges and universities, as well as a grass-roots commitment to cultural programs. Includes a lengthy list of contemporary Southern writers, as well as interesting incidental comments. A perceptive and illuminating essay.

Bradbury, John M. *Renaissance in the South: A Critical History of the Literature, 1920-1960*. Chapel Hill: University of North Carolina Press, 1963.

An encyclopedic survey of the period. While critics agree as to the continuing vitality of Southern literature, they have acknowledged only the achievements of the traditionalists, originally noted and approved by the New Critics. The canon should be broadened to include different viewpoints, such as those of the liberals, and different genres, such as problem novels. The South has its "realistic, as well as romantic, historical novelists, its humorists, even its existentialists." Each chapter concentrates on a different type of Southern literature. Since the canon was later broadened, as Bradbury urged, his discussion of types that are still much in evidence is invaluable. A useful appendix lists writers by states.

Bruck, Peter, ed. *The Black American Short Story in the Twentieth Century: A Collection of Critical Essays.* Amsterdam: B. R. Gruner, 1977.
Although collections by Toni Cade Bambara and Alice Walker are listed in the bibliography, none of the thirteen essays in this volume focuses on a woman writer. The brief introductory essay by the editor discusses matters such as audience and themes.

Cash, W. J. *The Mind of the South.* New York: Alfred A. Knopf, 1941.
Recognized as one of the most accurate analyses of the Southern mind ever written. Argues that Southern society is based on myths held in common by white Southerners of every intellectual level and of all social classes. Stresses the romanticism and sentimentality of the Southern outlook, its conservatism, its contradictory hedonism and Calvinism, and its tradition of violence. Cash's volume is essential reading for an understanding of Southern culture and Southern literature.

Christian, Barbara. *Black Women Novelists: The Development of a Tradition, 1892-1976.* Westport, Conn.: Greenwood Press, 1980.
The recent appearance of numerous novels by black women writers suggests the existence of a long-standing tradition that nourished their craft and their hopes. This work traces that tradition historically. The few novels by black women writers that were published between 1860 and 1960 were especially important in refuting the stereotypes of black women evident in most literature. The vision of these writers has been further developed in the works of Paule Marshall, Toni Morrison, and Alice Walker. The volume ends with some interesting suggestions as to the future direction of fiction by black women.

Clayton, Bruce. *The Savage Ideal: Intolerance and Intellectual Leadership in the South, 1890-1914.* Baltimore: The Johns Hopkins University Press, 1972.
Like C. Vann Woodward, Clayton challenges W. J. Cash's assumption that the white South was dominated by a single set of beliefs, a "Savage Ideal" enforced by social pressure. Clayton examines the lives and thought of a number of Southerners who worked to change public opinion in the decades before World War I. Unfortunately, most of them ignored the black population in their efforts to effect a true democracy in the South. An important historical work, basic

for understanding the figure of the liberal in Southern literature.
Lengthy bibliographical essay.

Cornillon, Susan Koppelman, ed. *Images of Women in Fiction: Feminist
Perspectives*. Bowling Green, Ohio: Bowling Green University
Popular Press, 1972.
Twenty-three essays about such topics as the fictional portrayal of
women by both men and women writers, the special problems that
women writers have in practicing their craft, and the significance of
feminist criticism. Extensive annotated bibliography of both primary
and secondary works. Provides a comprehensive overview of
feminist issues.

Cowie, Alexander. *The Rise of the American Novel*. New York:
American Book, 1948.
A critical history on the evolution of the American novel through the
nineteenth century, with a short final chapter on possible directions
in the twentieth century. Though obviously dated, this work presents
useful information on early Southern fiction. A lengthy chapter on
"The Domestic Sentimentalists and Other Popular Writers," many of
whom were Southern women, is particularly helpful. The bibliography is limited to general works on the American novel, not to
specific writers.

Davenport, F. Garvin, Jr. *The Myth of Southern History: Historical
Consciousness in Twentieth-Century Southern Literature*. Nashville:
Vanderbilt University Press, 1967.
A study of Southerners' views of their own history. In an introduc-
tory chapter, it traces the development of the myth through the
nineteenth century. In the works of the Southern Agrarians, the myth
is seen as a humanizing corrective to industrialization. Pointing to the
real facts of Southern history, however, William Faulkner and Robert
Penn Warren use the myth for symbolic purposes, in examinations
of universal good and evil. A final chapter, entitled "Black Man's
Burden," analyzes the use of the myth by Martin Luther King, Jr.
Although women writers are ignored in this study, Davenport's
perceptions should be applied to their works as well. Lengthy
bibliography.

Davidson, Cathy N., and E. M. Broner, eds. *The Lost Tradition:
Mothers and Daughters in Literature*. New York: Frederick Ungar,
1980.

To remedy a critical omission, the editors of this volume have collected twenty-four essays on links between mothers and daughters, as reflected in various literary forms, including autobiography and the oral tradition. Covers a period of four thousand years. Although there is no general introduction to the volume, introductions to the six major sections can be read for a historical perspective on the subject. Of particular interest are the later sections "Mother as Medusa," which analyzes unhealthy relationships, and "The New Matrilineage," which emphasizes the importance of mothers in preserving and transmitting family history and cultural heritage. The bibliography lists relevant primary works by genre and suggests secondary sources for further reading.

Degler, Carl N. *At Odds: Women and the Family in America from the Revolution to the Present*. New York: Oxford University Press, 1980.
A comprehensive study relating two topics previously treated in isolation, the history of the family and the history of women. Argues that the tension between family demands and women's desire for full equality is not the product of the feminist movement but is inherent in the modern family structure, which developed almost two centuries ago. Concludes by pointing out the seriousness of the problem now faced by women who want both families and fulfillment outside the home, but does not attempt to predict what changes will take place. Voluminous notes.

Douglas, Ann. *The Feminization of American Culture*. New York: Alfred A. Knopf, 1978.
Argues that modern American mass culture is an outgrowth of the sentimental excesses of the United States of the nineteenth century. Renouncing any struggle for real power, which could effect changes in society, ministers and women attempted to influence and to manipulate, employing whatever dishonest means were necessary to do so. Margaret Fuller and Herman Melville attempted to warn their contemporaries against this trend; both saw that Americans were substituting easy and superficial sentimentality for intellectual rigor, honesty, and progress.

Ellison, Emily, and Jane B. Hill. "Introduction." In *Our Mutual Room: Modern Literary Portraits of the Opposite Sex*, edited by Emily Ellison and Jane B. Hill, pp. i-xxvi. Atlanta: Peachtree, 1987.
Explains the premise of the collection: When writers imagine the thoughts and feelings of members of the opposite sex, the resulting

literature can be illuminating. The editors comment briefly upon each of the selections in this volume, almost all of which are segments of novels. Gail Godwin, Josephine Humphreys, and Anne Tyler are among the writers included.

Emanuel, James A., and Theodore L. Gross, eds. *Dark Symphony: Negro Literature in America*. New York: Free Press, 1968.
Anthology of fiction, poetry, and essays by thirty-four black writers. The volume is divided chronologically into four sections: "Early Literature"; "The Negro Awakening," placed in the 1920's; the "Major Authors" of the 1930's, Langston Hughes, Richard Wright, Ralph Ellison, and James Baldwin; and "Contemporary Literature," which includes lesser writers from the 1930's and the three decades that followed. Each section is preceded by a useful introduction, with an overview of developments, decade by decade, and references to important writers and works that are not included in the anthology. The bibliography includes description of holdings at various institutions, periodical and references sources in African-American literature, and primary and secondary listings by period and by author.

Evans, Mari, ed. *Black Women Writers (1950-1980): A Critical Evaluation*. Garden City, N.Y.: Anchor Press/Doubleday, 1983.
Intended to be a comprehensive guide to the fifteen black writers selected for inclusion. Most of the sections contain an initial essay by a writer, in response to the editor's questionnaire; two critical essays on that writer's works, representing different viewpoints; and definitive biographical and bibliographical information. A few of the initial essays were either omitted, by the author's request, or submitted in different format. Some bibliographies contain secondary sources; others do not. An uneven work, which can, however, be helpful.

Ferguson, Mary Anne, ed. *Images of Women in Literature*. Boston: Houghton Mifflin, 1973.
This anthology for the general reader includes works by both men and women, organized according to seven stereotypical views of women, which Ferguson sees as prevailing throughout literature. In her introduction, the editor discusses the origins of the stereotypes and explains their implications, with additional examples from works not in the collection. Eudora Welty and Alice Walker are both

represented in the volume, and an extensive list of further readings, categorized according to stereotype, includes works of other Southern women writers.

Fiedler, Leslie A. *Love and Death in the American Novel.* New York: Criterion Books, 1960.
A landmark work. Although Fiedler's primary focus is the immaturity of American male writers in their attitudes toward love, sex, life, and death, the discussion of William Faulkner and his influence on later Southern women writers is notable.

Forkner, Ben, and Patrick Samway. "Introduction." In *Stories of the Modern South,* edited by Ben Forkner and Patrick Samway, expanded ed., pp. xi-xxvi. New York: Viking Penguin, 1986.
A good overview of the history of short fiction in the South, pointing out that the genre had long been popular, even though the "great period of the Southern short story" began in the 1940's, after the Southern Renaissance was well under way. The editors also deal with the issue of what makes literature specifically Southern. There are brief comments on the stories included in the anthology, which includes works by Doris Betts, Ellen Gilchrist, Jayne Anne Phillips, Elizabeth Spencer, Anne Tyler, and Alice Walker, among others.

Fox-Genovese, Elizabeth. "Of Quilts and Cape Jasmines: Elements of a Common Southern Culture." *Humanities in the South* 75 (Spring, 1992): 1-4.
A brief but incisive essay on cultural interaction between blacks and whites. Even before emancipation, masters and slaves began to share traditions. The development of written black literature was delayed, however, until blacks were freed and therefore allowed to become literate. In the twentieth century, although writers such as Zora Neale Hurston, Toni Morrison, and Alice Walker have begun to tell the story of their people in their own language, their works continue to reflect the common heritage of Southerners, in turn "reinterpreting and broadening the sense of what it means to be American."

French, Warren, ed. *The Fifties: Fiction, Poetry, Drama.* Deland, Fla.: Everett/Edwards, 1970.
A number of essays on various subjects and writers. The introduction by the editor summarizes the decade with reference to the popularity of J. D. Salinger; two other long essays discuss the Beat generation

and the achievements of black writers during the period. Other essays concentrate on particular writers and specific works. Among those of interest to students of contemporary Southern literature are Mark Leaf's essay on the Snopes family and the evolving South; Kenneth Frieling's, on Flannery O'Connor; and David G. Pugh's, on Elizabeth Spencer's *The Voice at the Back Door*. The annotated bibliography, though dated, can serve as a checklist.

Frye, Joanne S. *Living Stories, Telling Lives: Women and the Novel in Contemporary Experience*. Ann Arbor: University of Michigan Press, 1986.
A well-written work of feminist criticism. The author points out that traditionally it was male writers who spoke for their female characters, while most of the women writers voicing the views of their own sex were dismissed as trivial. Now, Frye contends, women writers can speak for women. The essays in this book examine the use of first-person narration by a number of writers, suggesting that it is an effective and empowering technique. Voluminous notes, helpful bibliography and index.

Fryer, Judith. *The Face of Eve: Women in the Nineteenth-Century American Novel*. New York: Oxford University Press, 1976.
Analysis of views of women in nineteenth century novels. Suggests importance of the American edenic myth to development of views of women, then describes four categories of women seen in nineteenth century fiction: "The Temptress," "The American Princess," "The Great Mother," and "The New Woman." The only work by a woman that is treated at length is Kate Chopin's *The Awakening*, discussed in the final pages, where Fryer indicates that the suicide of Edna Pontellier is her response to rejection from her world. Good bibliography.

Gayle, Addison, Jr., ed. *The Black Aesthetic*. Garden City, N.Y.: Doubleday, 1971.
A collection of essays by writers as varied as W. E. B. Du Bois, LeRoi Jones, Langston Hughes, Darwin T. Turner, and Ishmael Reed. All discuss black critical theory in terms of "the black artist's war against the society," as the editor points out in his well-reasoned introduction. Comments on such issues as appropriate objectives, the role of anger, and the question of adaptation to the reader are

applicable to women writers of any race. Seven essays focus specifically on fiction. Helpful index.

Gibson, Mary Ellis. "Introduction." In *New Stories by Southern Women*, edited by Mary Ellis Gibson, pp. 3-12. Columbia: University of South Carolina Press, 1989.
Discusses the definition of "Southern women writers" and the tradition in which these writers are working. Gibson also makes specific comments about specific stories in the anthology. Among the twenty-one short stories included are a number by writers listed in this annotated bibliography.

Gilbert, Sandra M., and Susan Gubar. *The Madwoman in the Attic: The Woman Writer and the Nineteenth-Century Literary Imagination*. New Haven, Conn.: Yale University Press, 1979.
A major work in feminist criticism. The initial section, "Toward a Feminist Poetics," outlines the theoretical structure of the work, including such topics as "Female Creativity," "Male Images of Women," and a woman writer's attitude toward herself. Later sections apply feminist theory to the works of Jane Austen, Mary Shelley, Emily and Charlotte Brontë, George Eliot, and nineteenth century women poets, including Emily Dickinson. Voluminous, detailed notes and an excellent index.

Goldfield, David R. *Black, White, and Southern: Race Relations and Southern Culture, 1940 to the Present*. Baton Rouge: Louisiana State University Press, 1990.
A well-documented historical study of the turbulent period that is the setting of most contemporary Southern fiction. The book is organized into eleven chapters, each of which describes the direction of events in a brief time segment. After the drive for voting rights and integrated schools, in 1965 blacks were still left with economic problems. The final two chapters discuss problems and possibilities in the modern South.

Gossett, Louise Y. *Violence in Recent Southern Fiction*. Durham, N.C.: Duke University Press, 1965.
A thoughtful explanation of the prominence of violence in Southern fiction since 1930, suggesting that it serves as a means of social criticism, as well as a dramatization of the individual's alienation and spiritual uncertainty. Identifies elements in Southern culture that

result in particular forms of violence. Also points out the relationship between violence and the grotesque in Southern literature.

Grantham, Dewey S. "History, Mythology, and the Southern Lady." *The Southern Literary Journal* 3 (Spring, 1971): 98-108.
Evaluation of three books about the South, concluding with high praise for Anne Firor Scott's *The Southern Lady: From Pedestal to Politics* as a study of the inner lives of Southern women, a subject long neglected by historians.

Gwin, Minrose C. *Black and White Women of the Old South: The Peculiar Sisterhood in American Literature*. Knoxville: University of Tennessee Press, 1985.
Analyzes the mistress-slave woman relationship, as revealed in autobiographies and in twentieth century novels. Sees a pattern of connection and reconciliation arising out of a tragic social structure in which both white and black women are trapped. Separate chapters are devoted to expansion on this central idea, as it is illustrated in William Faulkner's *Absalom, Absalom!*, in Willa Cather's *Sapphira and the Slave Girl*, and in Margaret Walker's *Jubilee*. Extensive notes and lengthy bibliography of both primary and secondary sources.

Harris, Alex, ed. *A World Unsuspected: Portraits of Southern Childhood*. Chapel Hill: University of North Carolina Press, 1987.
In this unusual book, produced at Duke University's Center for Documentary Photography, eleven contemporary Southern writers were challenged to move from the world of imagination into the world of reality. Prompted by family photographs, they were asked "to tell the *true* story of their childhoods." As a result of the experiment, several of the writers conclude, with Harris himself, that even memories are made from imagination as much as from reality. The chapters vary greatly in form and in content, but all are illuminating. Women included are Josephine Humphreys, Sheila Bosworth, Robb Forman Dew, Bobbie Ann Mason, and Ellease Southerland.

Hart, James D. *The Popular Book: A History of America's Literary Taste*. New York: Oxford University Press, 1950.
Examination of changing American culture based on a study of best-sellers and an analysis of their appeal. Points out continuing

differences in the reasons for reading, from inspiration and education to pure escape. Of particular interest is the discussion of historical novels in "Their Yesterdays," particularly novels about the Old South published late in the nineteenth century, which portrayed it as an idyllic society. Checklist and chronological index of books discussed.

Hartman, Mary, and Lois W. Banner, eds. *Clio's Consciousness Raised: New Perspectives on the History of Women.* New York: Harper & Row, 1974.
Essays, primarily by historians, that deal with the status of women from the Middle Ages to the present. Several articles discuss the medical treatment of women, including the influence of birth control on their lives. Others explore incidents of exploitation, as well as the efforts of women to gain power, either in the family or in the work place. A final essay analyzes the effects of the technological revolution on women's status. The articles are particularly stimulating because the authors are willing to challenge generally accepted viewpoints, supporting their conclusions with careful documentation.

Haskell, Molly. *From Reverence to Rape: The Treatment of Women in the Movies.* New York: Holt, Rinehart and Winston, 1974.
Views films as both mirroring and influencing women's perception of themselves. In the first chapter, "The Big Lie," Haskell argues convincingly that Western society assumes women's inferiority to men and defines female stereotypes in movies. After tracing portrayals of women in film decade by decade, the author analyzes trends from 1962 to 1973, pointing out evidence of a conservative backlash against feminism in the film industry.

Hawks, Joanne V., and Sheila L. Skemp. *Sex, Race, and the Role of Women in the South.* Jackson: University Press of Mississippi, 1983.
Six essays dealing primarily with the lives of real, rather than fictional, Southern women in the nineteenth and the twentieth centuries. The writers share the view that the myth of Southern womanhood has obscured the reality, and that simplistic attempts to generalize about Southern women have obscured the diversity among them. They illustrate the fact that while women of both races (black and white) in the South were committed to their faiths and their families, the outlook and experience of black women was very different. This division has delayed the growth of a strong women's movement. Extensive notes and a useful bibliographical essay.

Heilbrun, Carolyn G. *Reinventing Womanhood*. New York: W. W. Norton, 1979.

A major feminist work in which the author outlines society's traditional expectations for women, analyzes the behavior of women of achievement, and suggests ways in which contemporary women can likewise reach worthy goals, while still fulfilling their needs to nurture. Drawing her illustrations both from literature and from life, Heilbrun concludes that if women are ever to enfranchise themselves, they must overcome their own fears and "reinvent" themselves. Selective bibliography for further study.

Hendin, Josephine. *Vulnerable People: A View of American Fiction Since 1945*. New York: Oxford University Press, 1978.

Argues that the sense of meaninglessness in modern fiction is counterbalanced by an insistence on the capacity of human beings to endure and even to triumph. Contrasts the predominance of helpless, defeated men in recent fiction with the emergence of women characters who, even if trapped, are determined to change their lives and their societies. An interesting thesis, but inadequately supported. It is surprising, for example, that only one Southern writer, Flannery O'Connor, is considered at any length.

Hernton, Calvin C. *The Sexual Mountain and Black Women Writers: Adventures in Sex, Literature, and Real Life*. Garden City, N.Y.: Anchor Press, 1987.

Written by a black man in defense of black women writers, such as Toni Morrison and Alice Walker, against accusations that they have used their literary skills to attack black men. Argues that in actuality black women writers are victims of "the sexist bigotry of black males," who continue to dominate the black literary establishment in the same way that white males do the white literary establishment. Illustrates his analysis with references to the works of Alice Walker, Ann Petry, and a number of other fiction writers and poets. In an interesting chapter, he discusses the feminism of Langston Hughes. Selected bibliography.

Hill, Samuel S., Jr., et al. *Religion and the Solid South*. Nashville: Abingdon Press, 1972.

Six thoughtful essays on religion in the Deep South, five of which were presented at an interdisciplinary symposium held at Duke University in 1969. In his two essays, Hill attempts to account for such antithetical attitudes as commitment to Christianity and commitment to white culture and white supremacy. Of particular interest to the student of literary works by women are Anne Firov Scott's essay, "Women, Religion, and Social Change in the South, 1830-1930," and Hill's final chapter, which attempts to find a theological basis for persistent Southern attitudes toward religion, including the proper role of women in the church. Notes suggest further readings.

Hoffman, Frederick J. *The Art of Southern Fiction: A Study of Some Modern Novelists.* Carbondale: Southern Illinois University Press, 1967.
A major study of later Southern Renaissance. Introductory chapters define the Southern attitude and note the characteristics of Southern fiction, including its emphasis on place. Divides Southern writers into three groups: those who are primarily descriptive, those who describe and evaluate their traditions, and those who move beyond the setting to a universal moral fable. Discusses Eudora Welty, Carson McCullers, James Agee, Flannery O'Connor, and William Styron at length. Brief but perceptive comments on numerous other writers and on specific works are indexed.

Holman, C. Hugh. *The Roots of Southern Writing: Essays on the Literature of the American South.* Athens: University of Georgia Press, 1972.
Scholarly essays on various subjects. "The Southerner as American Writer," "The Novel in the South," "The View from the Regency Hyatt," and "Three Views of the Real" are recommended as background reading.

Hooks, Bell. *Ain't I a Woman: Black Women and Feminism.* Boston: South End Press, 1981.
A study of the black female experience, based on the assumption that sexism is no less important than racism in denying black women their independence and their sense of identity. Discusses the unique situation of black women in regard to the Civil Rights movement and the growth of feminism, when allegiance to their own race placed them within the enslaving patriarchal structure of black society. Although many black women fear feminism, it is only through allegiance to a feminist movement, purged of racism and devoted to liberty, they can reach their full potential.

Howe, Florence, ed. *Tradition and the Talents of Women*. Urbana: University of Illinois Press, 1991.
A collection of essays in honor of the influential feminist scholar Mary Anne Ferguson, ranging in subject matter from self-knowledge and relationships between women to the significance of customs and language. Although very few contemporary Southern women writers are discussed, the essays suggest a wide range of possibilities for ongoing criticism.

Hubbell, Jay B. *The South in American Literature: 1607-1900*. Durham, N.C.: Duke University Press, 1954.
A standard, comprehensive study of Southern literature, covered by historical periods. The final segment of the volume, "Epilogue: The Twentieth Century," summarizes developments from 1900 to 1953 and suggests prophetically that Southern writers will produce works that, like those of Faulkner, are critical of their society, while at the same time being solidly based in their own traditions. The lengthy bibliography is divided into general works, specific topics, and individual writers.

Huf, Linda. *A Portrait of the Artist as a Young Woman: The Writer as Heroine in American Literature*. New York: Frederick Ungar, 1983.
Examines the problems faced by women artists by discussing six novels, ranging in date from 1855 to 1963, in which the heroine is an artist. The introduction points out five ways in which artist-heroine novels differ from artist-hero novels, all related to the concept of the ideal woman as being self-effacing, rather than committed to self-fulfillment. In the final chapter, "The Artist Heroine Today," Huf comments that protagonists in contemporary fiction still encounter opposition from society and from nonsupportive husbands, but that they now have a good chance of success because they will not sacrifice themselves to others but insist on placing their art first, as artist-heroes have always done. The bibliography includes a list of twentieth century artist-novels.

Inge, Tonette Bond, ed. *Southern Women Writers: The New Generation*. Tuscaloosa: University of Alabama Press, 1990.
A collection of fifteen essays by different critics, all of whom are women, each discussing the works and the themes of a different writer. Each essay contains biographical material. The format of the bibliography varies: In some cases, articles, interviews, and uncol-

lected short stories are included. Definitive bibliographical sources are noted where available.

Jones, Anne Goodwyn. *Tomorrow Is Another Day: The Woman Writer in the South, 1859-1936*. Baton Rouge: Louisiana State University Press, 1981.
A book of major importance. Separate chapters are devoted to Augusta Jane Evans, Grace King, Kate Chopin, Mary Johnston, Ellen Glasgow, Frances Newman, and Margaret Mitchell. The concluding chapter outlines clearly the various directions that were taken by earlier Southern women writers and thus is a helpful introduction for the study of contemporary fiction.

Jones, John Griffin, ed. *Mississippi Writers Talking*. 2 vols. Jackson: University Press of Mississippi, 1982-1983.
Relatively unstructured interviews that permit the writers considerable latitude. The interviewer-editor asks appropriate questions such as the influence of Mississippian William Faulkner on the authors' works, as well as their interpretation of the social changes in Mississippi that began during the 1960's. The main foci of the interviews, however, are the genesis and the development of specific works. Women writers in the first volume are Elizabeth Spencer and Beth Henley, in the second, Ellen Douglas and Margaret Walker. Photograph of each writer included.

Kent, George E. *Blackness and the Adventure of Western Culture*. Chicago: Third World Press, 1972.
Traces the attempt by black writers to break free from the sensibility absorbed from white American culture and to create a new sensibility, based on the folk tradition and on the black experience. After an overview of the Harlem Renaissance, the author devotes chapters to Claude McKay, Langston Hughes, Richard Wright, Gwendolyn Brooks, James Baldwin, and Ralph Ellison, pointing out and analyzing motifs that can be noted in more recent works. Includes a revealing discussion of William Faulkner as a representative of the white liberal cultural establishment, denying his real universality and noting weaknesses in his perception of black society but acknowledging that there are some episodes in Faulkner's works in which "black life is caught with some intensity and complexity."

Lawson, Lewis A. *Another Generation: Southern Fiction Since World War II*. Jackson: University Press of Mississippi, 1984.
Demonstrates the continuing vitality of the Southern Renaissance. The introductory chapter, "Twentieth-Century Southern Fiction," is an excellent overview of the evolution of this genre from the end of the Civil War to the 1930's, when a romantic view of the past was replaced by a more realistic view of problems in the South, such as race relations and "the disintegration of the self." Many of the best works were written by women and about women. In this volume, Lawson looks at six writers of the post-Faulkner generation, two of whom are women, who offer "alternatives to despair." The chapter on Flannery O'Connor concentrates on her Catholic perspective; that on Harriette Arnow, on the protagonist of *The Dollmaker*, who is seen as a Christlike, self-sacrificing heroine. Appended is a list of Southerners publishing first novels after World War II.

MacKethan, Lucinda H. *Daughters of Time: Creating Woman's Voice in Southern Story*. Athens: University of Georgia Press, 1990.
A series of three lectures on "the process of self-creation" seen in written works by Southern women. Although they live in a patriarchal society that expects them to be self-sacrificing and silent, women in the South have expressed themselves in letters, autobiographies, and fiction. Although the major focus of this volume is on Ellen Glasgow, Zora Neale Hurston, and Eudora Welty, in the final chapter the author concentrates on Alice Walker's *The Color Purple* and Lee Smith's *Fair and Tender Ladies*. These works are typical of contemporary fiction in showing relationships between Southern women, either mothers and daughters or sisters, as enabling them to define themselves.

May, Keith M. *Characters of Women in Narrative Literature*. New York: St. Martin's Press, 1981.
Discusses women figures who express not only the author's view of reality but also the possibilities among which women must choose as they forge their own identities. Analysis of Moll Flanders, Emma Bovary, and Anna Karenina is followed by a chapter on turn-of-the-century "New Women," such as those found in Ibsen and Shaw. The final chapter looks at writers as recent as Iris Murdoch and Muriel Spark. May's comments on Carson McCullers' work and on her assessment of her fellow Southern writers is especially interesting.

Meeker, Richard K. "The Youngest Generation of Southern Fiction Writers." In *Southern Writers: Appraisals in Our Time*, edited by R. C. Simonini, Jr., pp. 162-171. Charlottesville: University Press of Virginia, 1964.
An examination of Southern writers born about 1920 that attempts to identify characteristics of that generation. Argues that while they continue to show love of language and preoccupation with evil, they are less concerned with family, regional pride, and past history than their predecessors.

Moers, Ellen. *Literary Women*. Garden City, N.Y.: Doubleday, 1976.
A wide-ranging study of major English, American, and French women writers, emphasizing the relationship between their lives as women and their works. Argues that their literary tradition and their experience as women strengthened their works. Topics of special interest include the characteristics of heroines in works by women, the behavior of these heroines in love and in conflict, and the empowerment of the governess figure. A final chapter deals with metaphors. A highly original work, based on impressive knowledge of literary works by women of various cultures and periods.

Morrow, Mark. *Images of the Southern Writer*. Athens: University of Georgia Press, 1985.
Photographs, brief commentaries, and informal interviews with forty-eight writers, representing a half-century of Southern literature. In an introduction, Morrow explains that his omissions of writers were often caused by circumstances or by a writer's unwillingness to be photographed, as well as by financial constraints. Only thirteen women writers are included: Doris Betts, Ellen Douglas, Ellen Gilchrist, Gail Godwin, Elizabeth Hardwick, Beth Henley, Mary Lee Settle, Lee Smith, Elizabeth Spencer, Anne Tyler, Margaret Walker, Eudora Welty, and Sylvia Wilkinson. Brief foreword by Erskine Caldwell.

Naipaul, V. S. *A Turn in the South*. New York: Alfred A. Knopf, 1989.
Written by a major novelist whose primary interest is on traditional societies in the process of changing, this travel book is balanced and perceptive. Based on extensive interviews, including conversations with Anne Rivers Siddons and Eudora Welty.

Osterweis, Rollin G. *The Myth of the Lost Cause: 1865-1900*. Hamden,
Conn.: Archon Books, 1973.
This sequel to *Romanticism in the Old South* explains further
development of romantic ideas after the Civil War, when a defeated
people devised the "Legend of the Lost Cause" in order to preserve
their identity. This complex of myths dominated political, social, and
literary expression. In the South, it was a conservative force; in the
North, where it was also given credence, it provided an escape from
urban, industrialized society. The final chapter describes the
consequences of the Lost Cause Myth in the twentieth century,
including its influence over recent Southern writers. Well-developed
intellectual history. Good discursive notes.

Pearlman, Mickey, ed. *American Women Writing Fiction: Memory,
Identity, Family, Space*. Lexington: University Press of Kentucky,
1989.
Essays on ten contemporary writers. Noting that escape, often to the
wide open spaces, is a major theme in American literature written by
men and about men, the editor wished to examine that theme and
associated issues in works written by women and in works where
women writers use a female narrative voice. Four of the writers
discussed can be classified as Southern: Toni Cade Bambara, Gail
Godwin, Jayne Anne Phillips, and Mary Lee Settle. The scholars
presuppose some knowledge of the writers discussed. Bibliography
follows each essay.

Pearlman, Mickey, and Katherine Usher Henderson, eds. *Inter/View:
Talks with America's Writing Women*. Lexington: University Press
of Kentucky, 1990.
Interviews with twenty-eight women writers. Intended to serve as a
model for future interviews with women writers, avoiding questions
of a trivial biographical nature and instead stressing nongender-
related questions, such as the development of these individuals as
artists and their perceptions of the function of memory in the writing
process. Instead of transcriptions, these interviews are written as
short essays that incorporate lengthy quotations. As a result, there is
less repetition, as well as an opportunity for the interviewer to
include her own impressions and a good deal of solid factual
information. Gail Godwin, Shirley Ann Grau, and Josephine
Humphreys are included.

Peden, William. *The American Short Story: Front Line in the National Defense of Literature.* Boston: Houghton Mifflin, 1964.
Good discussion of the genesis of the American short story and delineation of trends in both writing and publishing during the 1940's and the 1960's. Although of the writers in this bibliography, only Doris Betts and Shirley Ann Grau are discussed, many of the author's points in the chapter "Jane Austens of Metropolis and Suburbia" are applicable to contemporary writers. The predictions in Peden's final chapter are especially interesting. The appendix has an extensive checklist of American short-story writers of works published between 1940 and 1963, with some helpful bibliographical notations.

Prenshaw, Peggy Whitman. "Women's World, Man's Place: The Fiction of Eudora Welty." *Eudora Welty: A Form of Thanks*, edited by Louis Dollarhide and Ann J. Abadie, pp. 46-77. Jackson: University Press of Mississippi, 1979.
An analysis of Welty's novel *Delta Wedding* that points out the matriarchal structure of her world, in which males are significant primarily through their relationship with their mothers and thus with the all-important family. Argues that even when men leave this world, in order to find themselves, they eventually return to resume their place within the family. A thought-provoking analysis of Southern society.

_____, ed. *Women Writers of the Contemporary South.* Jackson: University Press of Mississippi, 1984.
Essays by various scholars on writers who began publishing after 1945. In a thoughtful introduction, the editor points out the persistence of sense of place in contemporary literature, but reflects on changes in attitudes toward race and gender. The opening essay consists of answers to specific questions about writing obtained in interviews with Lisa Alther, Ellen Douglas, Gail Godwin, Shirley Ann Grau, Mary Lee Settle, Elizabeth Spencer, and Anne Tyler. Bibliographical checklist for each writer. Essential source.

Prenshaw, Peggy Whitman, and Jesse O. McKee, eds. *Sense of Place: Mississippi.* Jackson: University Press of Mississippi, 1979.
A collection of papers presented at a 1978 symposium in Hattiesburg, Mississippi, and representing perspectives ranging from architecture and urban planning to literature and the arts. While all

the essays deal with the theme that dominates Southern literature, a
number of them specifically discuss Southern fiction.

Pryse, Marjorie. "Introduction: Zora Neale Hurston, Alice Walker, and
the 'Ancient Power' of Black Women." In *Conjuring: Black Women,
Fiction, and Literary Tradition*, edited by Marjorie Pryse and
Hortense J. Spillers, pp. 1-24. Bloomington: Indiana University
Press, 1985.
Finds an explanation for the emergence of black women as novelists
in the tradition of storytelling as a form of magic, which for a time
released the tellers from their poverty and isolation. In addition to
these conjurers of earlier decades, mothers who initiated their
daughters into the world of the imagination, every woman writer has
"mothers" among the earlier women writers who influenced her. At
present, criticism of women by women is offering new insights and
another form of magic. A perceptive essay, preceding fourteen essays
by various critics and an "Afterword" by the other editor of the
volume.

Pullin, Faith. "Landscapes of Reality: The Fiction of Contemporary
Afro-American Women." In *Black Fiction: New Studies in the Afro-
American Novel Since 1945*, edited by A. Robert Lee, pp. 173-203.
Plymouth, England: Vision, 1980.
Following in the footsteps of Zora Neale Hurston, contemporary
black women writers have shown their audiences that far from
merely reacting defensively to "poverty, powerlessness and cultural
deprivation," blacks have developed a culture independently and
creatively. In the struggle for identity, black women have had to
surmount obstacles placed in their way not only by the white
establishment but also by black men. Their strength and their
determination are reflected in works by black women writers, who
are successfully experimenting with techniques that will enable them
to express their unique sensibilities.

Rubin, Louis D., Jr. *The Mockingbird in the Gum Tree: A Literary
Gallimaufry*. Baton Rouge: Louisiana State University Press, 1991.
Essays on various subjects by a noted scholar of Southern literature,
unified by his interest in defining Southern culture, which, he
believes, makes Southern literature distinctive. On this subject, see
the chapter, "From Combray to Ithaca: Or, The "Southernness' of
Southern Literature." Although there is extensive discussion of

William Faulkner, Thomas Wolfe, and Robert Penn Warren, among Southern women writers, only Eudora Welty is treated at length.

Rubin, Louis D., Jr., and C. Hugh Holman, eds. *Southern Literary Study: Problems and Possibilities*. Chapel Hill: University of North Carolina Press, 1975.
A publication resulting from a 1972 conference in Chapel Hill organized in order that leading scholars could consider "problems, possibilities, and future directions in southern literary study." Four major papers are included, as well as the transcripts of five panel discussions. Of the latter, "Twentieth-Century Southern Literature," "The Continuity of Southern Literary History," and "Thematic Problems in Southern Literature" are particularly relevant to the subject of contemporary literature.

Rubin, Louis D., Jr., and Robert D. Jacobs, eds. *South: Modern Southern Literature in Its Cultural Setting*. Garden City, N.Y.: Doubleday, 1961.
A collection of essays, primarily on the first generation of Southern Renaissance writers. Of particular interest is the introduction by the editors, "Southern Writing and the Changing South," and the four essays on general topics by Louis D. Rubin, Jr., Robert B. Heilman, Frederick J. Hoffman, and James Dickey. Both the introduction and Walter Sullivan's "The Continuing Renascence: Southern Fiction in the Fifties" speculate as to the direction that later Southern writers may take.

Russ, Joanna. *How to Suppress Women's Writing*. Austin: University of Texas Press, 1983.
Contends that the male establishment has used and continues to use various methods to discourage women from writing and publishing, including "informal prohibition," "belittlement of work," denial of credit for authorship, and disregarding both women's works and the tradition of which they are a part. This argument is supported by specific examples from literary and critical works and by revealing interviews.

Ryan, Mary P. *Womanhood in America: From Colonial Times to the Present*. New York: New Viewpoints/Franklin Watts, 1975.
A history that seeks to explain how American women have been systematically relegated to a subordinate status. The author identifies

the various roles that have been presented to women, ranging from "Adam's Rib" in early agrarian society to "The Sexy Saleslady" in consumer culture, all of which have imprisoned the women who were forced to act the part. A well-documented and persuasive study, with voluminous notes and a comprehensive index.

Scott, Anne Firor. *The Southern Lady: From Pedestal to Politics: 1830-1930*. Chicago: University of Chicago Press, 1970.
Examination of the difference between the image of the Southern lady and the reality. This image defined a woman's role and establish a pattern of expected behavior. Real life demanded more of Southern women, however, and thus they found themselves living two lives, one of pretense and one of reality. Details their struggle to achieve an identity defined not by society, but by themselves. An essential source for further study. Based primarily on manuscripts, documents, autobiographies, and contemporary sources. Includes a bibliographical essay.

Seidel, Kathryn Lee. *The Southern Belle in the American Novel*. Tampa: University of South Florida Press, 1985.
A study of the changing attitude toward the Southern belle, called "the symbol of the South itself," as reflected in nineteenth and twentieth century novels. Each chapter is devoted to a discussion of several novels that illustrate an aspect of the tradition. Both male and female contemporary writers are included in the study. Interestingly, the author pairs Gail Godwin with her predecessor, Ellen Glasgow, in their exploration of the intricate relationships between mothers and daughters.

Shaw, Harry E. *The Forms of Historical Fiction: Sir Walter Scott and His Successors*. Ithaca, N.Y.: Cornell University Press, 1983.
A critical examination of the historical novel. Points out that there is no clearly defined genre, but that historical novels do have a problem in common, the matter of characterization. As history, these works must show characters as representative of "social groups and historical trends"; as fiction, they must be peopled with individuals, not abstractions. To explain this problem, Shaw shows the difference between Sir Walter Scott's use of the "hero as instrument" and of the "hero as subject." These theories are applicable to contemporary historical novels such as Mary Lee Settle's *Beulah Quintet* and Margaret Walker's *Jubilee*.

Showalter, Elaine. *Sister's Choice: Tradition and Change in American Women's Writing*. Oxford, England: Clarendon Press, 1991.
A study that traces "themes, images, genres, cultural practices, and choices" in writing by American women. Throughout her work, however, the author guards against simplistic generalizations; in a multicultural American society, it is impossible to assume that there is a clear definition either of "American" literature or of "women's" literature. Indeed, as men read what women write, the many viewpoints expressed by women in their works will pass into the mainstream of literature. Useful notes and index.

Simpson, Lewis P. *The Dispossessed Garden: Pastoral and History in Southern Literature*. Athens: University of Georgia Press, 1975.
A brilliant examination of the pastoral ideal, which has dominated Southern thought and literature for more than two centuries. In the twentieth century, as memories of the Civil War faded, it was transmuted into the use of history and of memory to establish an ethical and spiritual order. This quest is illustrated by such writers as William Faulkner. In more modern times, Southern writers have abandoned that ideal, thus "dispossessing" their Garden of Eden, and instead have adopted the attitude that they had opposed for so long, as reflecting the Northern rejection of tradition and of the pastoral world. The new "covenant" is with the "existential self." This "evinces the dispossession of its visionary source, the culture of alienation." Essential background reading.

_____. "Introduction." In *Three By Three: Masterworks of the Southern Gothic*, pp. vii-xiv. Atlanta: Peachtree, 1985.
Argues that the gothic tradition, originally a reaction against eighteenth century rationalism, became in the South a dramatization of the horror of a search for identity in a world without spiritual meaning. The anthology includes works by Doris Betts, Mark Steadman, and Shirley Ann Grau.

Spacks, Patricia Meyer. *The Female Imagination*. New York: Alfred A. Knopf, 1975.
A major critical work that investigates the creative powers and practices of women writers. Argues that artists who are women must defy society's traditional expectations of women, such as passive behavior and dedication to nurturing, and must, unlike creative men, continue to rebel throughout their lives, as if they were doomed to

a perpetual adolescence. She concludes, however, that by dominating their own experience and capturing it in print, women writers do acquire a power that most other women do not attain. Although her references to recent Southern fiction are limited, Spacks's comments are applicable to almost all works by contemporary women writers.

Spender, Dale. *The Writing or the Sex? Or, Why You Don't Have to Read Women's Writing to Know It's No Good.* New York: Pergamon Press, 1989.
Seeks to establish and to explain the existence of prejudice against works by women and to suggest a remedy for the situation. In the first section of the book, the author argues that the male-dominated critical establishment serves as "gatekeepers" to keep women's works from being published or from being reviewed. Spender vehemently denies the perception of some that contemporary women writers are "getting more than their share" of attention. The second section presents a plan for women's criticism to attack this problem of unfair treatment. An interesting chapter on "Polish, Plagiarism, and Plain Theft" discusses the subordination of Sonja Tolstoy to her husband, Leo Tolstoy, and that of Zelda Fitzgerald to her husband, F. Scott Fitzgerald. The appendix includes quotations from discussions with anonymous male academicians. Numerous references and suggestions for further reading.

Strout, Cushing. *Making American Tradition: Visions and Revisions from Ben Franklin to Alice Walker.* New Brunswick, N.J.: Rutgers University Press, 1990.
Essays intended to illuminate works from different periods by comparing them in relation to common themes, as well as by tracing specific influences. Two early chapters deal with women characters who become involved with ministers and with women mediums. The concluding chapter is devoted to exploring the relationship between Ralph Ellison's *Invisible Man* and Alice Walker's *Meridian*.

Tate, Claudia, ed. *Black Women Writers at Work.* New York: Continuum, 1983.
Interviews with fourteen contemporary black writers, emphasizing the writers' perceptions of their own motivations and their assessments both of their works and of their critics. In her introduction, the editor points out that black women writers are all conscious of the restrictions placed on them in a racist and sexist world. It is these

restrictions that force their heroines either to remain weak and uncertain in relationships or to transcend their situations and arrive at understanding and high self-esteem, thus achieving a kind of triumph for race and for gender.

Voss, Arthur. *The American Short Story: A Critical Survey*. Norman: University of Oklahoma Press, 1973.
Traces the genre from its beginnings in the nineteenth century through the 1960's, with particular interest in narrative technique. Katherine Anne Porter, Eudora Welty, and Flannery O'Connor are discussed at length. Concludes that despite the limited possibilities for periodical publication and the unimpressive sales figures for collections of short stories, writers continue to produce distinguished works. Includes a brief listing of short-story writers not treated at length. Extensive bibliographical references in the end notes.

Wade-Gayles, Gloria. *No Crystal Stair: Visions of Race and Sex in Black Women's Fiction*. New York: Pilgrim Press, 1984.
A survey of the subject from the standpoint of black feminism. After chapters delineating the issues and outlining the real-life situation of black women between 1946 and 1976, the author proceeds to discuss black women as mothers and wives, black women in positions of triumph and of despair, and black women in quest of identity, with references to numerous black women fiction writers and some extensive analyses of their works. Scholarly notes and lengthy bibliography.

Wagner-Martin, Linda. "'Just the Doing of It': Southern Women Writers and the Idea of Community." *The Southern Literary Journal* 22 (Spring, 1990): 19-32.
Points out the importance of the theme of community in works of contemporary Southern women writers. Although as children, as women, or as the poor, fictional protagonists may seem to be powerless in society, they are often seen as important conveyors of family history and of the histories of their people, usually in oral form. Among the writers discussed at length are Alice Walker, Lee Smith, and Jill McCorkle; works by Elizabeth Spencer, Gail Godwin, Anne Tyler, Kaye Gibbons, and Ellen Glasgow are also mentioned. Wagner-Martin concludes that all these writers believe that women must themselves find control of their own lives, often through some

art that allows the "family past, historical past, personal past" to be redeemed "in the satisfaction and beauty and work of the present."

Weaver, Gordon, ed. *The American Short Story, 1945-1980: A Critical History.* Boston: Twayne, 1983.
The period is covered by three essays by different writers, each summarizing trends within this period. Although a number of collections by Southern women writers are listed in the general bibliography, there are surprising omissions. Among the writers treated at length are Flannery O'Connor, Caroline Gordon, and Eudora Welty. Doris Betts and Shirley Ann Grau are mentioned briefly.

Westling, Louise. *Sacred Groves and Ravaged Gardens: The Fiction of Eudora Welty, Carson McCullers, and Flannery O'Connor.* Athens: University of Georgia Press, 1985.
An attempt to define the singular viewpoint of women writers with a Southern background. Includes a consideration of issues of identity, mother-daughter relationships, these writers' perception of men, and their perception of their own sex. Concise summary chapter and helpful bibliography.

Wolfe, Margaret Ripley. "The View from Atlanta: Southern Women and the Future." In *The Future South: A Historical Perspective for the Twenty-first Century*, edited by Joe P. Dunn and Howard L. Preston, pp. 123-157. Urbana: University of Illinois Press, 1991.
An overview of the women's movement in the South. Historical evidence proves that the concept of the protected and helpless Southern lady had little foundation in real life but instead has been used to prevent Southern women from attaining the equality for which they continue to struggle. Although a number of Southern women have attained national prominence, even under conservative administrations, both statistics and current political trends show that the battle for equality is far from won.

Wyatt-Brown, Bertram. *Southern Honor: Ethics and Behavior in the Old South.* Oxford, England: Oxford University Press, 1982.
A study of the Southern code of honor, whose importance Wyatt-Brown insists has been minimized by Southern historians. In fact, honor was "the keystone of the slaveholding South's morality," not simply an invention to justify the existence of slavery. Of particular

importance for the study of contemporary Southern literature by women is the second section of the book, "Family and Gender Behavior," which deals with such matters as gender roles, self-image, and male dominance. Excellent notes and index.

Young, Thomas Daniel. *The Past in the Present: A Thematic Study of Modern Southern Fiction.* Baton Rouge: Louisiana State University Press, 1981.
A study of tradition in Southern literature by one of its most highly respected scholars. Young points out that although different Southern writers define and use tradition in different ways, all of them believe that it continues to be central in Southern life. Although many Southern writers no longer believe in a divine order, Young notes that the unbelievers and the uncertain share with the faithful a conviction that the rites and customs that were associated with the former order are still essential in the modern world. In separate chapters, these issues are applied to works by William Faulkner, Allen Tate, Robert Penn Warren, Eudora Welty, Flannery O'Connor, Walker Percy, and John Barth. A volume that is essential for the study of all twentieth century Southern writers.

ALICE ADAMS

Abrahams, William. "A Tribute to Alice Adams." *San Francisco Chronicle Review* (April 11, 1982): 1, 11.
This review of the short-story collection *To See You Again* provides an opportunity for Abrahams to laud Adams in general. "Adams' style is so felicitous, so agile, so effortlessly readable that one finishes one story and hurries on to the next and the next." Abrahams believes that this collection is representative of so much of Adams' works—serious and moving, yet with a rare but notable irony and wit. The reviewer expects great things from Adams' next decade.

Adams, Alice. "On Turning Fifty." *Vogue* (December, 1983): 230, 235.
An introspective essay by Adams that reveals her emotional adaptation to aging. "In a literal sense, of course, those of us in our fifties are not middle-aged; we have lived more than half our lives. Which is to say that I think about death much more than I did at thirty or at forty." Contains open discussion of her upbringing and motivations for writing.

Carlson, Ron. "Clobbering Her Ex." *The New York Times Book Review* (October 8, 1989): 27.
A lukewarm review of the short-story collection *After You've Gone*. Carlson argues that while Adams' narrative skill is obvious and impressive, the content of the stories leaves one unmoved. "Reading the stories becomes like reading about people in stories and not—as in the best realistic fiction—about people we know."

Chell, Cara. "Succeeding in Their Times: Alice Adams on Women and Work." *Soundings: An Interdisciplinary Journal* 68 (Spring, 1985): 62-71.
Chell examines the choices Adams' characters have and make relative to the criticism often laid on them as being too bourgeois to be feminists. According to Chell, Adams shares much with writers such as Lisa Alther, even Alice Walker. Generally (and particularly

in *Families and Survivors, Listening to Billie,* and *Rich Rewards),*
Adams' "novels deal with work that is progressively less romantic
and more practical, that moves from writing and painting to
doctoring and making furniture."

DeMott, Benjamin. "Elderly Lives and Lovers." *The New York Times
Book Review* (May 1, 1988): 11.
DeMott considers *Second Chances* "the strongest work that I have
read by this author. The strength flows partly from Ms. Adams'
capacity to evoke fellow feeling, kindness and devotion as entirely
natural inclinations of the heart." The writing seems "mannered" in
places with a few unbelievable characters, but DeMott can find no
other faults with the novel.

Feineman, Neil. "An Interview with Alice Adams." *StoryQuarterly* 11
(1980): 27-37.
A short biographical note opens this interview that precedes Adams'
"A Pale and Perfectly Oval Moon." Adams speaks of returning to the
South after twenty years: "I couldn't wait to get out the first time
and I couldn't wait to get out then." She also talks of her "ABDCE"
formula (action, background, development, climax, ending) for short
stories. Other topics include her years of struggle, the differing
pleasures of short versus long fiction, and her impending role as
creative writing instructor.

Gottlieb, Annie. "They Stumbled Blindly into Marriage." *The New York
Times Book Review* (March 16, 1975): 28-29.
Review of *Families and Survivors.* Gottlieb is very impressed with
Adams' venture with the omniscient narrator. Comparing her choice
to those of such narrators in Austen or James, Gottlieb finds the time
twists (sometimes knowing simultaneously the past, present, and
future of a character) "a solace, a source of that cutting yet soothing
perspective that, uniquely in this book, is always present." Adams is
subject to some illusions about the wonders of youth, Gottlieb
contends, but still delivers a "perceptive, ironic and kind novel about
the way we live now."

Holt, Patricia. "PW Interviews Alice Adams." *Publishers Weekly*
(January 16, 1978): 8-9.
An interview-based article written after the launching of *Listening to
Billie.* Commenting on her own life (and relationship with live-in

Robert McNee), Adams says that "it seems that relationships often flounder when one person has nothing to do and is looking to the other for total sustenance." As Holt notes, the comment reflects on Adams' characters as well. About the trends in literature, Adams sees "a movement among all writers, male or female, away from the conventional "male stud novel' toward something far more diversified and exploratory." Biographical notes.

Madrigal, Alix. "The Breaking of a Mold." *San Francisco Chronicle Review* (September 9, 1984): 11.
An interview with Adams at the time of the publication of *Superior Women*. Adams speaks of that book (her "five-pound novel"). The article, with Adams' consent, draws parallels between her women of the new novel and her own inclinations. "I wasn't as liberated as Megan, who was really ahead of her time. I wish I had been," Adams says. An interesting note is that Adams says she outlines short stories in more detail than her novels. See also the companion review of *Superior Women*. The reviewer, Mary Mackey, finds Proustian impulses in Adams' narrative voice.

Pollitt, Katha. "Good Ole Boys and Wistful Hippies." *The New York Times Book Review* (January 14, 1979): 14, 27.
Review of Adams' first collection of stories, *Beautiful Girl*. "Miss Adams writes with a seductive grace that burnishes even a slight tale," Pollitt forwards, noting "Winter Rain" as just such a story. Still, the reviewer would like more grit and depth at times in Adams' explorations of characters' inner worlds. The strongest story in that regard is "Verlie I Say unto You," in which "there is plenty of real grist for Miss Adams's powers of observation."

_____. *"Listening to Billie." Saturday Review* (March 4, 1978): 30-31.
This brief review notes Adams' "clean, spare prose and subtle choice of details." Despite the obvious negative traits of some of them, Adams maintains "a rare sympathy for almost all her characters." Pollitt finds the central character, Eliza, however, "curiously unfocused" and contradictory.

Prescott, Peter S. "Edgy Woman." *Newsweek* (February 3, 1975): 64.
A review of *Families and Survivors*. Prescott sees Adams as "less concerned with cosmic cataclysms than with the subtle, even

subliminal encounters that make men and women edgy." He notes the economy of the present-tense narrative and approves of the authorial comments throughout the work. Though the scenes and characters sometimes jumble, Prescott contends that Adams' writing more than makes up for that weakness.

Ross, Jean W. "CA Interview." In *Contemporary Authors*, New Revision Series, edited by Hal May and James G. Lesniak. Vol. 26, pp. 11-13. Detroit: Gale Research, 1989.
An interview from September, 1987. Adams, for whom success came late, speaks of her struggles, especially those against expectations of her as a woman. She finds the 1950's a horrible decade, not least because of the ways in which it kept women apart. Adams also notes the difficulties of dealing with a Southern upbringing as a woman. Contains much on her relations with *The New Yorker* and her attraction to poetry. See the entry prior to the interview for a summation of her biography and critical reception.

Schindehette, Susan. *"Return Trips."* *Saturday Review* (November/ December, 1985): 73-74.
The stories of this collection are "examples of sublime subtlety, of nuance and quiet perception—stories from a writer who is quite clearly an accomplished, absolute master of her craft." Shunning extremes of external drama, Adams chooses to study the turbulence deep beneath placid surfaces, the reviewer believes.

See, Carolyn. "Spoiled in Paradise." *The Washington Post Book World* (March 10, 1991): 1-2.
See praises *Caroline's Daughters* as "the best book Alice Adams has ever written." The review focuses on the political aspects of the novel where Adams points most sharply to the sin of greed, "selling the great gifts that we already had in the first place." Overall, the novel is, according to See, "elegant, beautiful, big."

_____. "Twenty-three Stories Form Necklace of Thought." *Los Angeles Times* (April 13, 1982): p. V6.
A review of *To See You Again*. Defying normal expectations of the "delicate" woman writer, Adams' stories "are hard and sharp and unbearably concrete—a hammer on the carpenter's thumb," as See describes them. All the stories are successful in their own ways,

collectively making the reader think hard about the profoundly simple impulses of our lives, according to the review.

Stull, William L. "Alice Adams." In *Dictionary of Literary Biography Yearbook: 1986*, edited by J. M. Brook, pp. 271-280. Detroit: Gale Research, 1987.
This lengthy discussion weaves Adams' works into biographical context. Although Adams claims San Francisco as her adopted home, Stull points out that "as a writer and as a woman, she remains a child of the South." In analyzing critical reception to Adams, the essay finds an ongoing ambiguity in her works: "It is sometimes hard to determine whether her overall attitude toward her characters is sympathetic or satirical." Short primary and secondary bibliographies.

Tyler, Anne. "An Honorable Heroine." *The New York Times Book Review* (September 14, 1980): 13, 20.
Review of *Rich Rewards*. Tyler considers Daphne "one of the most admirable female characters in recent fiction." Daphne seems in spirit attached to Adams' heroines of previous works. Tyler also admires Adams' scrutiny of the details of life as indicators of so much more. If the plot of the book comes too quickly to its ends, Tyler is understanding: "It's only right that [Daphne] be granted a happy ending."

Updike, John. "No More Mr. Knightlys." *The New Yorker* (November 5, 1984): 160-170.
A lengthy discussion of *Superior Women*. Updike praises the flow of Adams' style: "Though not short, the book feels edited, by a racing blue pencil that leaps the years." He seems to wish the pencil had slowed more often and offered even more insights into the "feminine wisdom." Updike finds traces of Jane Austen in the book's themes, especially because it looks at the plight of young women subjected to the awkward fumblings of young men pursuing romance.

Upton, Lee. "Changing the Past: Alice Adams' Revisionary Nostalgia." *Studies in Short Fiction* 26 (Winter, 1989): 33-41.
Looking through Adams' short stories, Upton finds a pattern in which Adams "allows her characters to go home again, inevitably to transform their relationships to the past and to confirm or renegotiate current choices." Upton is quick to caution against "nostalgic" being equated with "sentimental." Adams, she posits, goes further than

sentimental reflection, rather using past images to project future action. Characters who misuse their visions of their past (for example, to revise the memory purely for escapist goals) find numerous pitfalls.

Warga, Wayne. "A Sophisticated Author Gets by with Help from Her Friends." *Los Angeles Times Book Review* (November 16, 1980): 3. Spawned by *Rich Rewards'* publication, this interview covers that book's theme, Adams' life as a writer, her late success, and her future hopes. In *Rich Rewards*, Adams relates to Daphne, who has troubled relations with her family. Adams talks of being disowned by her own father: "Obviously I've got a way to go because I'm still writing about it quite a lot." Adams dismisses the agonies of writing: "It isn't that lonely and there isn't that much agony. At least not for me. Not now."

Weller, Sheila. "Timely Goes Trendy." *Ms.* (September, 1980): 18, 20. Review of *Rich Rewards*. Weller lauds Adams' old-fashioned qualities—"the Dickensian coincidence, the solemn omniscience, the sense of lives destined to intertwine"—then shows these same qualities sadly lacking in the new novel. Daphne is a character not in keeping with Adams' previous tone. She is "awfully chatty and glib," Weller laments, and the ending is "perfunctorily happy."

Wolitzer, Hilma. "Sisters Under the Skin." *Los Angeles Times Book Review* (March 10, 1991): 3, 7.
Review of *Caroline's Daughters*. Wolitzer notes some irritation at the parenthetical asides and second thoughts but otherwise expresses approval of the work, even its present-tense narrative. Although the novel deals with myriad contemporary issues, Wolitzer considers it "a roomy and tantalizing old-fashioned read."

Wood, Susan. "Stories of Love and Loss." *The Washington Post Book World* (January 21, 1979): G3.
Wood proclaims that "no other writer in recent memory has called to mind quite so clearly the work of F. Scott Fitzgerald, both in style and subject matter, as Alice Adams does" in *Beautiful Girl*. Although Adams' ordinary characters lack understanding of their lives, the author does understand them, often viewing them with a gentle, satiric eye. The voice of Adams, while difficult to define, is a consistent quality of her writing, Wood says.

LISA ALTHER

Adams, Alice. "Endjokes." *Harper's Magazine* (May, 1976): 94, 98.
Glowing appraisal of *Kinflicks*. Adams asserts the "book is so continuously funny that its wisdom takes you by surprise." Only the title warrants complaint as needing to be stronger to show "the presence of a most powerful and remarkable talent." The portrayal of awkwardness in love and life is allowed to sidestep neat answers, according to Adams, maintaining a tolerant, human outlook.

"Alther, Lisa, 1944-   ." In *Contemporary Authors*, New Revision Series, edited by Hal May and James G. Lesniak. Vol. 30, pp. 5-7. Detroit: Gale Research, 1990.
Summarizes Alther's writings and critical responses to them (up through *Other Women*). Notes a recurring use of the coming-of-age format and the strong Southern climate of the stories. Includes a short bibliography of reviews.

Cantwell, Mary. "Serious When Once She Was Funny." *The New York Times Book Review* (May 3, 1981): 9, 38.
Original Sins "has all the spontaneity of a paint-by-numbers landscape" in its portrayal of the South. Much of the material is similar to that in *Kinflicks*, only this time without much humor. Cantwell is particularly irritated (if not surprised) by the symmetrical ending of the novel.

Cochran, Tracy. "*Bedrock.*" *The New York Times Book Review* (June 3, 1990): 23.
Short review of a disappointing portrait of Vermont country life. Alther "never really brings her rural characters to life—and never achieves the humor and humanity that made 'Kinflicks' so appealing," according to Cochran.

Ferguson, Mary Anne. "The Female Novel of Development and the Myth of Psyche." *Denver Quarterly* 17 (Winter, 1983): 58-74.
Places *Kinflicks* in the company of Welty's "At the Landing" and

Erica Jong's *Fanny* as works that parallel the Psyche myth. Ginny's growth is seen through her alternating rejections of and reconciliations with her mother, all while maintaining the irony indicative of the Psyche perspective, Ferguson argues. The three works of the essay are said to mark the beginning of a particularly female version of the *Bildungsroman*.

_____. "Lisa Alther: The Irony of Return?" In *Women Writers of the Contemporary South*, edited by Peggy Whitman Prenshaw, pp. 103-115. Jackson: University Press of Mississippi, 1984.
This essay analyzes *Kinflicks* and *Original Sins* as being about "home viewed from the perspective of a native who has left and returns." The theme is common among Southerners and exhibits the more general form of comic epic, Ferguson adds. Especially noteworthy is the ironic voice of the works that make great use of "Alther's verbal wit." The approach, however, ultimately limits the reader's involvement. Ferguson hopes for "a new voice that will go beyond irony." See also in this same volume Laurie L. Brown's "Interviews with Seven Contemporary Writers" (pp. 3-22). Alther's written answers comment on aspects of her career from how she started writing to her greatest influences and attitude toward publishing success.

Gray, Paul. "Beating the Sophomore Jinx." *Time* (April 27, 1981): 71.
Gray finds *Original Sins* a more than worthy follow-up to Alther's first novel. The work "propels singular, interesting characters through a panoramic plot." This review has special respect for the way Alther manages to maintain her humorous tone while making significant comments on social issues of the 1960's and early 1970's.

_____. "Blue Genes." *Time* (March 22, 1976): 80.
Review of *Kinflicks* as "exuberant caricature." Gray finds much to entertain and shock but much less to inform. The heroine is compared to male counterparts Tom Jones and Holden Caufield. Only Mrs. Babcock reaches the audience emotionally, and she "seems to have been smuggled in from a different novel."

Hall, Joan Lord. "Symbiosis and Separation in Lisa Alther's *Kinflicks*." *Arizona Quarterly* 38 (Winter, 1982): 336-346.
Hall considers "Ginny's quest for autonomy" the main theme of the novel and one seriously developed beyond what reviews have noted

as Alther's entertainment value. Ginny wants to stop either reacting against or being drawn to her mother's views of the world. Rather, as Hall points out, Ginny must find herself as an organism interlinked to a larger ecosystem.

Karl, Frederick R. "The Female Experience." In *American Fictions, 1940-1980*, pp. 417-443. New York: Harper & Row, 1983.
Karl calls *Kinflicks* "a distinguished book" in the section discussing women's writings from 1960 to 1980. There is a wit to the novel that, unlike other coming-of-age novels, precludes illusions of heaven-sent innocence. Ginny realizes her mother cannot see her as here and now, only as an image recorded for later viewing, Karl advances. Ginny eventually breaks free from the living death of her existence by accepting the real death of so much that was familiar, the essay concludes. Discussion of the book is lengthy given the number of other works and writers mentioned in the chapter.

"*Kinflicks.*" *The New Yorker* (March 29, 1976): 112-113.
This concise review lauds the first-time novelist. The main character "can easily take her place alongside Holden Caufield as a symbol of everything that is right and wrong about a generation." Comparison to Doris Lessing is made, noting that Alther's "touch is a lot lighter."

Lehmann-Haupt, Christopher. "Books of the Times." *The New York Times* (December 10, 1984): p. C16.
Lehmann-Haupt has difficulty accepting all the miraculous changes of Caroline in *Other Women* at the hands of a therapist who seems to break more than a few of the rules. The question of her sexuality slips to the background as "the reader begins to feel manipulated." Lehmann-Haupt credits Alther for "psychological acuity" but believes there is "a fatal tendency to overstate."

Leonard, John. "Pop Goes the Novel: *Kinflicks.*" *The New York Times Book Review* (March 14, 1976): 4.
This review calls the novel an "exuberant yawp." *Kinflicks* draws on Doris Lessing for inspiration, adding its own breezy tone—"a tone that has been missing in American fiction for years," not present since Holden Caufield, Augie March, and Huckleberry Finn, Leonard proclaims.

Levine, Paul. "Recent Women's Fiction and the Theme of Personality." In *The Origins and Originality of American Culture*, edited by Tibor Frank, pp. 333-343. Budapest, Hungary: Akademiai Kiado, 1984.
Levine sees *Kinflicks* as particularly representative of much recent writing about the woman's struggle for "visibility." Ginny's first obstacle is the break with family, to assert her role as an individual, "to be, in short, the subject in her life and not the object of it." The essay compares Alther's themes to those in Godwin's *The Odd Woman* and Mary Gordon's *Final Payments*.

Rubin, Merle. "The Murky Waters of Middle Age." *Los Angeles Times Book Review* (July 29, 1990): 5.
Finds *Bedrock* touched with Alther's familiar sociological and ironic bent, yet "most of the time it is heavy-handed and needlessly repetitive." Rubin concedes to moments of showing her "knack for conveying the tempo of contemporary manners and mores" but little more.

Shapiro, Walter. "One to Miss." *Time* (May 21, 1990): 82.
Scathing review of *Bedrock*, calling the work "drivel." The characters are one-dimensional with lines below sitcom level. "Such rural New England cliches make *Newhart* seem like subtle satire, but Alther recycles them with such a tone of social superiority that the entire state of Vermont might sue for defamation."

Shechner, Mark. "A Novel of the New South." *The New Republic* (June 13, 1981): 34-36.
Unlike her first novel, *Original Sins* "is a protest novel of a conventional sort, a compound outrage and doctrine." The South comes under special attack, seen much less charitably here than in *Kinflicks*, Shechner notes. Particularly lacking is Alther's command of men, "no small matter for a writer whose subject is the ubiquity of sexual grief."

Sternhell, Carol. "At Last, a Cure for Politics." *The Village Voice* (December 18, 1984): 71.
Complicated review of *Other Women*, interweaving objections about the political ramifications of the novel with the reviewer's own political views. According to Sternhell, Alther's basic theme is that political activism is really a sign of unresolved personal conflicts, especially in the case of Caroline's parents. Otherwise, Sternhell has

trouble with the didactic nature of the writing and the predictable uses of scenery to reflect directly the ups and downs of character moods.

Vinuela, Urbano. "North Vs. South: Lisa Alther's Original Sin." In *Cross-Cultural Studies: American, Canadian, and European Literatures, 1945-1985*, edited by Mirko Jurak, pp. 223-228. Ljubljana, Yugoslavia: Eduard Kardelj University of Ljubljana, 1988. Sees Newland, Tennessee, as "a symbol of southern tradition" against "the radically new reality" of New York. Vinuela explores the challenges of the five children growing up away from home and what that represents, concluding that any reconciliation with Newland is ill-fated.

Waage, Frederick G. "Alther and Dillard: The Appalachian Universe." In *Appalachia/America: Proceedings of the 1980 Appalachian Studies Conference*, edited by Wilson Somerville, pp. 200-208. Johnson City, Tenn.: Appalachian Consortium Press, 1981. Looks at views of Lisa Alther and Annie Dillard on the contemporary Appalachian world. Through an examination of *Kinflicks*, Waage suggests the theme of the pilgrim strongly at work. Ginny's return to her dying mother brings her in contact and conflict with her Appalachian home. Ginny is "a wandering female Quixote of the lineage of Moll Flanders." Her native environment brings Ginny back in touch with the role of mystery in her life.

DAPHNE ATHAS

Athas, Daphne. "The Art of Storytelling." *The South Atlantic Quarterly* 73 (Spring, 1974): 256-260.

Starting with comments on differing views of what constitutes the "reality" of *Entering Ephesus*, Athas goes on to consider what constitutes "storytelling" in an age of journalistic expectations. Athas argues for the "recognition of artifice" in writing and for readers willing to ask for more than what is "real" in a work.

_____. "Why There Are No Southern Writers." In *Women Writers of the Contemporary South*, edited by Peggy Whitman Prenshaw, pp. 295-306. Jackson: University Press of Mississippi, 1984.

Makes many autobiographical references to Athas' entry into the South from the North. Insightful essay on changes in Southern character that make defining the Southern writer (especially the Southern woman writer) more difficult. Ultimately, Athas finds the only remaining certain index in style: "[I]f Southerness was once an obvious characteristic of writers, it is now mere evidence, detectable in style, waiting perhaps to be recognized."

"Athas, Daphne." In *Contemporary Authors*, New Revision Series, edited by Ann Evory. Vol 3, pp. 37-38. Detroit: Gale Research, 1981.

A very brief entry. Lists career history (with awards) and writings along with a few quotes from critical responses to her notable *Entering Ephesus*. "Biographical/Critical Sources" are few.

Berkman, Sylvia. "Murmurous World of the Blind." *The New York Times Book Review* (May 13, 1956): 28.

Berkman reviews *The Fourth World*. Despite Athas' obvious deep feeling for the world of the blind, the review notes, her authorial voice is seldom sentimental or preachy. The book is so real in its portrayals, some may be put off by it; "but few readers will deny the depth of the author's penetration into its shadows, the intensely dramatic impact of the scenes she has contrived there."

Campbell, Don G. *"Entering Ephesus." Los Angeles Times Book Review* (March 24, 1991): 6.
Short note on second-chance publication of the novel. Campbell believes the story "deserves retelling (although it should have been resurrected with a new title, too)." He also says the characters beg comparison to those of *Little Women.*

"Cora." *Publishers Weekly* (August 28, 1978): 389.
This review points to Athas' "penchant for poetic prose" that "often seems unduly pretentious." The characters, no matter their walk of life, are full of philosophical arguments worthy of an academic dissertation, according to the essay. Athas is credited, however, with "conveying the palpable aura of mystery and spirituality that is uniquely the spirit of Greece."

"The Doom of Differences." *Time* (June 2, 1947): 107, 109.
Review of Athas' first novel, *The Weather of the Heart.* She is called "a new writer of distinction" who shows mature insight into the emotions of her characters. What structural problems there are "will be forgiven easily by readers whose weary eyes have lately seen a lot of old formulas passing as new fiction."

Duffy, Martha. "Little Women." *Time* (September 13, 1971): 85, 87.
The reviewer sees *Entering Ephesus* as "vivid" and "like life" in that so much reality is chronicled so well. Like reality, however, there is a disjointed nature to many of the episodes. That flaw does not dissuade Duffy from recommending the book: "This is a novel."

"Entering Ephesus." *The New York Times Book Review* (October 5, 1971): 35.
A short review. Athas' "rhetoric (sometimes a bit over-rich, sometimes keenly poetic) confers on the Bishops a mythical quality, making such universals as love and death seem strangely remote." The reviewer is engaged by the dramatic growth of Urie, whose insights are fundamental "to the book's haunting tone."

Haynes, Muriel. *"Entering Ephesus." Saturday Review* (October 9, 1971): 38-39.
This review of *Entering Ephesus* calls it "a wonderfully loving, pure-spirited book with an exuberant vision." Haynes praises the voice of the novel for staying within the young characters and not allowing

adult viewpoints to intercede. Still, according to Haynes, the book never takes itself too seriously. Haynes compares it to *Little Women*, "[b]ut without the piety, without the tears."

"An Insight into Blindness." *Time* (May 14, 1956): 134, 136, 138.
While faulting its structure, the reviewer believes *The Fourth World* evokes "a world as eerie and haunting as any that this year's crop of fiction is apt to produce." There is little sentimentality in the portrayal of these children in a school for the blind. Athas' keen perception of that world excuses her for the plot improbabilities, according to the essay.

Prenshaw, Peggy Whitman. "A Conversation with Seven Fiction Writers." *Southern Quarterly* 29 (Winter, 1991): 69-93.
Roundtable discussion among North Carolina women writers. Athas' contributions are primarily about her beginnings in writing, the voice of the Southern writer, literary influences, and the importance of diverse reading. One participant alludes to the impact *Entering Ephesus* had on a friend who drove late one night to the former's home after finishing the book: The friend desperately needed to talk about the novel.

Smith, Shawn Michael. "Transcending the Great Depression." *The Christian Science Monitor* (March 26, 1991): 15.
Review of the rereleased 1971 novel *Entering Ephesus*. Smith sees relevance to "today's steadily down-turning economy" for the Depression tale. The philosophical debates of the book strike the reviewer as sometimes too forward. Otherwise, "the story captures like a firefly in a jar something of the essence of being alive."

Trilling, Diana. "Fiction in Review." *The Nation* (July 12, 1947): 51.
The Weather of the Heart is "a very remarkable attempt to put sensibility at the service of growth instead of at the service of a self-pitying retreat," this review states. Trilling lauds the trueness of spirit in the novel's dramatic moments and the freedom of the imagination. Delicate one moment, then powerful the next, Athas "can match Faulkner in the imagination of aberrant human behavior," Trilling forwards. Ends with interesting criticism of the book's marketing strategy.

TONI CADE BAMBARA

Bambara, Toni Cade. "Foreword." In *This Bridge Called My Back: Writings by Radical Women of Color*, edited by Cherríe Moraga and Gloria Anzaldua, pp. vi-viii. Watertown, Mass.: Persephone Press, 1981.

In her characteristic flood of original language constructs, Bambara evokes the power of her political fervor. The book is a collection of essays, letters, and poems on the issues of women of color. Bambara's opening essay fits right in with this book, which "needs no Forword. It is the Afterward that'll count. The Coalitions of women determined to be a danger to our enemies."

_____. "Some Forward Remarks." In *The Sanctified Church*, by Zora Neale Hurston, pp. 7-11. Berkeley, Calif.: Turtle Island, 1981.

A lively homage to a woman Bambara respects greatly (she wrote a film script on Hurston). Bambara most admires Hurston's energy and persistence: "Fun loving and bodacious, Zora was not playing." The myriad roles Hurston assumed may give insight into Bambara's constant juggling of her own priorities. Bambara also owes much to Hurston's early observations "on music and other stylistics of Blackart practice in worship."

_____. "Thinking About My Mother." *Redbook* (September, 1973): 73, 116, 118.

Bambara writes a story/essay about the impact of her mother on her life. Above all else, it seems, her mother gave her pride in her race and heritage, boldly challenging the entrenched views of her teachers on the stereotypes for all minorities. She also gave Bambara creative freedom and privacy in her inner life: "If I chose to daydream in the middle of the kitchen floor, Mama'd mop around me."

_____. "What It Is I Think I'm Doing Anyhow." In *The Writer on Her Work*, edited by Janet Sternburg, pp. 153-168. New York: W. W. Norton, 1980.

"Writing is one of the ways I participate in struggle," Bambara says in this essay on the motivations for her work. The sense of community and the writer's obligation to it loom large in Bambara's proclamations. Contains brief comments on her works to date and relates the differences between work habits required for long-term versus short-form writing: "The short story is a piece of work. The novel is a way of life."

Butler-Evans, Elliott. *Race, Gender, and Desire: Narrative Strategies in the Fiction of Toni Cade Bambara, Toni Morrison, and Alice Walker*. Philadelphia: Temple University Press, 1989.
"Drawing largely on narratology, feminist cultural theory, semiotics, and Neo-Marxist concepts of ideology, this study explores the relationship between two conflicting discourses—one an inscription of race, the other focused on gender—within the fictional narratives of three Afro-American women writers." In Bambara's case, Butler-Evans finds *The Salt Eaters* incompletely considered as a feminist text and her short stories full of "dissonance and ruptures" that often preempt "the stories' primary focus on classic realism and nationalism." Long bibliography. Much textual discussion of other critical works.

Byerman, Keith E. "Women's Blues: The Fiction of Toni Cade Bambara and Alice Walker." In *Fingering the Jagged Grain: Tradition and Form in Recent Black Fiction*, pp. 104-170. Athens: University of Georgia Press, 1985.
Both Bambara and Walker are credited with feminist ideologies, especially in telling "stories of the initiations of black girls into womanhood, defining in the process the complex meaning of being black and female in a culture that has denigrated both qualities," according to this essay. Both hope for political change. In Bambara's case, Byerman considers the novels more realistic in their expectations, realizing that it is difficult to avoid change that merely substitutes a new form of oppression for the old.

Cartwright, Jerome. "Bambara's 'The Lesson." *Explicator* 47 (Spring, 1989): 61-63.
A brief reading of the short story from *Gorilla, My Love*. Takes issue with previous "incomplete" studies of the story as being about Sylvia's disillusionment. "Rather than simply teaching a single lesson," according to Cartwright, "the story is essentially about the

value of lessons themselves, the value of learning and thinking."
Thus, the story ends with hope and direction, not despair, this essay
forwards.

Chevigny, Bell Gale. "Stories of Solidarity and Selfhood." *The Village
Voice* (April 12, 1973): 39-40.
Review of *Gorilla, My Love*. Admires the power of the stories,
especially as they evoke the inner lives of black women both young
and old. Chevigny notes the absence of male/female relationships as
a topic in the stories. Instead, Bambara chooses "those for whom
sexual conflict is past and those for whom sexual differentiation has
not yet become rigid." The reviewer calls Bambara's tone "zealously
cool, ardently tough" and wonders how soon a novel will follow.

Dance, Daryl Cumber. "Go Ena Kumbla: A Comparison of Erna
Brodber's *Jane and Louisa Will Soon Come Home* and Toni Cade
Bambara's *The Salt Eaters*." In *Caribbean Women Writers: Essays
from the First International Conference*, edited by Selwyn R. Cudjoe,
pp. 169-184. Wellesley, Conn.: Calaloux, 1990.
Dance explores the similarities in voice and experience between the
American and the Jamaican writers. Among the comparisons
presented are the similar breakdowns of the characters Velma and
Nellie, their journeys toward health, and their "need for self-
knowledge." Dance concludes that the similarities are not coincidence and deserve further study as a recognition of shared cultural
experience. Bibliography attached.

Deck, Alice A. "Toni Cade Bambara." In *Dictionary of Literary
Biography: Afro-American Writers After 1955, Dramatists and Prose
Writers*, edited by Thadious M. Davis and Trudier Harris. Vol. 38,
pp. 12-22. Detroit: Gale Research, 1985.
This lengthy entry traces Bambara's biography and literary produc-
tion. Deck groups Bambara with the politically conscious African-
American writers of the 1960's and sees her as one of the few who
continues to work in that vein to the present. The essay considers the
difficult transition for Bambara from the short story to the novel.
Includes short bibliographies of works by and about Bambara.

Evans, Mari, ed. *Black Women Writers (1950-1980): A Critical
Evaluation*, pp. 42-71. Garden City, N.Y.: Anchor Press/Doubleday,
1984.

The chapter "Toni Cade Bambara" collects one essay by Bambara and two others about her work. In her autobiographical contribution to the book, "Salvation Is the Issue," Bambara discusses the inspirations for her writing as well as her feelings for the variety of forms in which she works. She claims to have "always been partial to the short story." Ruth Elizabeth Burks's "From Baptism to Resurrection: Toni Cade Bambara and the Incongruity of Language" explores the paradox of Bambara's powerful language in the context of characters for whom language is not the key to their freedom. "Bambara eschews language, words, rhetoric, as the modus operandi for the people to attain their freedom," Burks posits. Eleanor W. Traylor analyzes a different language in her essay, "Music as Theme: The Jazz Mode in the Works of Toni Cade Bambara." Traylor believes Bambara's narratives owe much in form and content to the complex movements of jazz music. Short bibliography and biography at end.

Fisher, Jerilyn. "From Under the Yoke of Race and Sex: Black and Chicano Women's Fiction of the Seventies." *Minority Voices* 2 (Fall, 1978): 1-14.
Brief discussion of Bambara's contributions to helping blacks and Chicanas "defy the barrier of 'Anglo' and 'male' standards that have long discouraged their own creative expression." Looks particularly at Bambara's "My Man Bovanne" as an example of the young black woman rebelling against the countrified ways of her mother. Ultimately, Bambara's story shows that rebellion must bring heritage with it.

Frye, Charles A. "How to Think Black: A Symposium on Toni Cade Bambara's *The Salt Eaters*." *Contributions in Black Studies* 6 (1983-1984): 33-48.
Four scholars attend, in turn, to the question of the "black cognitive process" in Bambara's novel. Frye comments on the difficulty European-American students have in understanding the writing. Carlyn Harper looks at "the historical or collective consciousness" and the "mythic consciousness" at work in Bambara's narrative. Linda James Myers is concerned with "the utilization of an African-centered conceptual system" with little or no reference to Bambara. Eleanor Traylor provides a much closer examination of the novel, demonstrating how its lyrical qualities blend with Wright, Baldwin, and other writers of the black experience past and present.

Guy-Sheftall, Beverly. "Commitment: Toni Cade Bambara Speaks." In
Sturdy Black Bridges: Visions of Black Women in Literature, edited
by Roseann P. Bell, Bettye J. Parker, and Beverly Guy-Sheftall, pp.
230-249. Garden City, N.Y.: Anchor Press/Doubleday, 1979.
This interview covers Bambara's early life and early writings, as
well as literary influences and the advantages and barriers of the
black woman writer. Bambara comments on her gravitation to the
short story "because I'm a sprinter rather than a long-distance
runner."

Hargrove, Nancy D. "Youth in Toni Cade Bambara's *Gorilla, My
Love*." In *Women Writers of the Contemporary South*, edited by
Peggy Whitman Prenshaw, pp. 215-232. Jackson: University Press
of Mississippi, 1984.
After some broader considerations of Bambara's ability to evoke the
speech and feelings of youth throughout her work, Hargrove focuses
on the stories from this collection. "Told from the viewpoint of
young black girls, they capture how it feels as a child to undergo the
various experiences of loneliness, disillusionment, and close
relationships with others." Hargrove compares Bambara's skill in this
area to Twain, Salinger, and others.

Hull, Gloria T. "What It Is I Think She's Doing Anyhow': A Reading
of Toni Cade Bambara's *The Salt Eaters*." In *Conjuring: Black
Women, Fiction, and Literary Tradition*, edited by Marjorie Pryse
and Hortense J. Spillers, pp. 216-232. Bloomington: Indiana
University Press, 1985.
Hull rates the novel with *Native Son*, *Invisible Man*, and *Song of
Solomon* in terms of its impact on its particular decade. Using a
complicated diagram, Hull attempts to explain the interconnected
nature of the characters and the "subjective nature of time." Above
all else, Hull calls for *The Salt Eaters* to "be read and reread."

Johnson, Charles. "The Women." In *Being and Race: Black Writing
Since 1970*, pp. 103-105. Bloomington: Indiana University Press,
1988.
In a rather quick survey of many different writers, Johnson describes
Bambara's writing in *The Salt Eaters* as "relentlessly funny,"
although the novel "tends to sprawl shapelessly, occasionally losing
focus and a clear through-line of development." Johnson attributes
this latter weakness to an incomplete transition from the short story,
her more confident medium.

Lardner, Susan. "Third Eye Open." *The New Yorker* (May 5, 1980):
169-173.
Reviews *The Salt Eaters*, but not before considering her short stories.
Lardner notes the mixed qualities of Bambara's plot structures in the
short stories yet believes they all share a strength of purpose and "a
distinctive motion of the prose, which swings from colloquial
narrative to precarious metaphorical heights and over to street talk,
at which Bambara is unbeatable." Those talents are put to great use
in the novel, Lardner believes, where the "expanse of a novel has
freed Bambara to follow her diverging lines of thought with
considerable abandon." Occasionally abandoning plot lines until the
last minute, Bambara nonetheless has achieved "a book full of
marvels" in Lardner's estimation.

Macauley, Robie. "*The Sea Birds Are Still Alive*." The New York Times
Book Review (March 27, 1977): 7.
A short review of the story collection. Believes Bambara works hard
on character sketches with mixed success. Some fail because of too
much language, too many glimpses of people's lives with insufficient
focus. Others, like the title story and "Witchbird," accomplish their
goals. Macauley summarizes the effect as being "like coming into a
crowded, hot, smoky room where a dozen different voices (most of
them speaking Black English) are telling a dozen disparate tales."

Morrison, Toni. "City Limits, Village Values: Concepts of the Neigh-
borhood in Black Fiction." In *Literature and the Urban Experience:
Essays on the City and Literature*, edited by Michael C. Jaye and
Ann Chalmers Watts, pp. 35-43. New Brunswick, N.J.: Rutgers
University Press, 1981.
Looks at the emotions of black writers toward the urban life as
particular to their racial experience. Morrison briefly considers
Bambara's short stories and *The Salt Eaters* as fulfillers of the theme
that "the worst thing that can happen in a city is that the ancestor
becomes merely a parent or an adult and is thereby seen as a
betrayer." The ancestor is the "advising, benevolent, protective, wise
Black" with village values who must be in the city to make its life
livable and lovable.

Porter, Nancy. "Women's Interracial Friendships and Visions of
Community in *Meridian, The Salt Eaters, Civil Wars*, and *Dessa
Rose*." In *Tradition and the Talents of Women*, edited by Florence

Howe, pp. 251-267. Urbana: University of Illinois Press, 1991.

Using a "feminist psychoanalytic perspective," Porter discusses "how race, class, and cultural experience affect the dynamics" of friendships between black and white women in various authors' works. In *The Salt Eaters*, Bambara uses "reconstruction of cultural difference to represent not inferiority to a presumed superiority but a source of political strength" for the women joined in their political, social, and personal struggles.

Salaam, Kalamu ya. "An Interview: Searching for the Mother Tongue." *First World* 2 (1980): 48-53.

Bambara speaks of trying to regain a language that will allow expressions of different kinds of experiences and ways of thinking, much of which was stripped from the European-based English existing today. *The Salt Eaters* is also discussed in that context. Bambara believes fiction is "a perfectly legitimate way to participate in the struggle." Salaam adds a "Commentary" expanding on the issues of a new language and the role of writers in emphasizing African-American cultural presence. See also Eleanor Traylor's "*The Salt Eaters*: My Soul Looks Back in Wonder" (pp. 44-47, 64). Traylor attempts to evoke more than present a reading of the novel. The review says that "*The Salt Eaters* is a rite of transformation quite like a jam session."

Shipley, W. Maurice. "Book Review." *CLA Journal* 26 (September, 1982): 125-127.

A review of *The Salt Eaters*. Calls the book "an unqualified success" in portraying the suffering of black women. Shipley sees the book as a study of the black community, especially since Velma is both dependent on and resentful of it. The character of Minnie is especially important in dramatizing the relative proximity of sanity to insanity, Shipley says. The book considers many subjects, from mythology to politics; "the range is immense but the focus is keen," the review concludes.

Tate, Claudia. "Toni Cade Bambara." In *Black Women Writers at Work*, edited by Claudia Tate, pp. 12-38. New York: Continuum, 1983.

Extensive interview covering a full range of topics from social/ political views to advice for young writers. Bambara makes clear the agenda for much of her work when she says, "I start with the recognition that we are at war," adding that the war is ultimately over the truth. Bambara also discusses a current obsession with film-making, even more so than with the future of her writing. A biographical summary opens the interview.

Tyler, Anne. "At the Still Center of a Dream." *The Washington Post Book World* (March 30, 1980): 1-2.
Tyler warns against the many excesses of *The Salt Eaters* in this review yet concludes that it "is a powerful piece of writing. The effort spent in deciphering it is rewarded many times over." Tyler considers the language of the characters (as with Bambara's short stories, too) the most compelling aspect of the novel. Bambara chooses seemingly simple, everyday words and phrases and shows them to be "sheer poetry," Tyler contends.

Vertreace, Martha M. "The Dance of Character and Community." In *American Women Writing Fiction: Memory, Identity, Family, Space*, edited by Mickey Pearlman, pp. 155-171. Lexington: University Press of Kentucky, 1989.
This essay describes the power of community in shaping character as found in Bambara's fiction. Concentrates on short stories. Vertreace finds the women characters especially shaped by social interactions. "Bambara's women learn to handle themselves within the divergent, often conflicting, strata that compose their communities," according to the essayist. Extended bibliography at end of essay.

Wideman, John. "The Healing of Velma Henry." *The New York Times Book Review* (June 1, 1980): 14, 28.
A review of *The Salt Eaters* that notes the chances it takes as a novel and the overall success of those risks. "In its best moments, the novel recalls Faulknerian montage, the harmonic counterpoint of the poetry and prose of Jean Toomer's 'Cane,'" as well as the writings of Toni Morrison, Leslie Silko, Albert Murray, and Leon Forrest, Wideman submits. He also finds the arguments about global recovery as persuasive as those about the personal recovery of Velma.

Willis, Susan. "Problematizing the Individual: Toni Cade Bambara's Stories for the Revolution." In *Specifying: Black Women Writing the American Experience*, pp. 129-158. Madison: University of Wisconsin Press, 1987.

Willis considers Bambara one who aspires to revolution in the manner of the 1960's, yet who is made ineffectual by the political vagaries of the 1980's. Nevertheless, the essay applauds the portrayal of women as struggling against the male viewpoint of history. "The desire to formulate a feminist perspective on history accounts for the centrality of mother figures in Bambara's writing," Willis suggests.

DORIS BETTS

Alderson, Laura. "An Interview with Doris Betts." *Poets and Writers* 20 (January/February, 1992): 36-44.
More essay than interview, this article contains a wealth of information on the views of Betts, especially on the role of mentor and teacher to younger writers. Betts also talks about her forthcoming *Souls Raised from the Dead* and the planned *Wings of the Morning.* Speaking of her current attraction for the novel, Betts says, "I'm tired of the short story form. I do not believe as much in revelation and change and intense experience as I once did." Betts also provides insights on what constitutes "women's fiction."

Bain, Robert. "Doris Betts." In *Southern Writers: A Biographical Dictionary*, edited by Robert Bain, Joseph M. Flora, and Louis D. Rubin, Jr., pp. 25-26. Baton Rouge: Louisiana State University Press, 1979.
A short biographical entry, perhaps useful for the list of awards included. Bain does include a remark by reviewer Jonathan Yardley lamenting the lack of attention to Betts. Contains a list of works with publication dates.

Betts, Doris. "The Fingerprint of Style." In *Voicelust: Eight Contemporary Fiction Writers on Style*, edited by Allen Wier and Don Hendrie, Jr., pp. 7-22. Lincoln: University of Nebraska Press, 1985.
Betts's impassioned and almost mystical essay reveals many personal opinions about her own writing style. She prefers words with serious intent to those designed merely to delight; words with power, even when rough and uneducated, to those semantically correct yet reaching for nothing. To Betts, words (at their best) are magic with intimate connections to religion. Although the essay is written for scholarly audiences, the images will strike any reader.

_____. "Many Souths and Broadening Scale: A Changing Southern Literature." In *The Future South: A Historical Perspective for the Twenty-first Century*, edited by Joe P. Dunn and Howard L.

Preston, pp. 158-187. Urbana: University of Illinois Press, 1991.
An excellent summary of the arguments on all sides of the "what is 'Southern' writing?" debate. This essay quotes from and makes allusions to a large number of historic and contemporary writers. Betts calls for special skepticism with regard to what Southern writers themselves say on the topic. Social and technological influences (for example, civil rights and television) play crucial roles in the evolution of the region's writing. Yet, as Betts concludes, despite the continuing clichés, Southern writing will survive according to how well the story is told, not how well the historic location is evoked. Contains useful endnotes.

_____. "My Grandfather Haunts This Farm." *The Saturday Evening Post* 249 (January/February, 1977): 62, 85-86.
A simple, elegant elegy to her grandfather. Betts has occasion to remember him and his death thirty-five years prior. She has bought a farm and house in North Carolina that evokes her autobiographical essay. Good source for comparison to descriptions in her short stories and novels.

_____. "Tyler's Marriage of Opposites." In *The Fiction of Anne Tyler*, edited by C. Ralph Stevens, pp. 1-15. Jackson: University Press of Mississippi, 1990.
While mainly a critical look at Tyler's fiction, this essay contains enough personal reflections by Betts to be of interest. She particularly questions categorizing writers as "Southern" or "Feminist." Also contains allusions to Betts's own creative process and experiments thereon. Finally, understanding Betts's attractions to Tyler helps in understanding Betts's tendencies in her own writing.

Coleman, John C. "*The Scarlet Thread.*" In *Survey of Contemporary Literature*, edited by Frank N. Magill. Rev. and enlarged ed. Vol. 10, pp. 6647-6649. Englewood Cliffs, N.J.: Salem Press, 1977.
Coleman finds fault with the narrative structure of *The Scarlet Thread*, Betts's second novel. She forwards too many points of view, too much historical information, too much social significance at times, according to Coleman. Unlike her short works (notably the short-story collections to which Coleman gives extended attention), "Mrs. Betts is not yet fully at ease in the full scope of the novel."

Eaton, Evelyn. "A Fine Debut." *Saturday Review* 37 (July 10, 1954): 14.
A noteworthy review if, for no other reason, because it is about Betts's first published book, *The Gentle Insurrection*. Eaton finds little fault in the premiere of Betts's writing (except for "Serpents and Doves"—too ambitious). Eaton senses the "generous pessimism of indignant youth" in Betts, wondering what will come after the dark cloud has passed.

Evans, Elizabeth. "Another Mule in the Yard: Doris Betts' Durable Humor." *Notes on Contemporary Literature* 11 (March, 1981): 5-6.
A very brief review of Betts's short story "The Dead Mule." Evans finds the story typical of the kind of humor Betts employs in much of her work, the kind that "frequently turns laughter into sardonic grimaces." In the short story's case, the laughs at Buzzer Martin's failure to outwit the law are followed by sighs for the lot in life of people like the moonshiner, according to Evans.

——————. "The Mandarin and the Lady: Doris Betts' Debt to Amy Lowell." *Notes on Contemporary Literature* 6 (November, 1976): 2-5.
Using Betts's own acknowledgment of her short story's indebtedness to Amy Lowell's poem, Evans presents a reading of "The Mandarin" with "Patterns" (the poem) in mind. Both story and poem, Evans submits, are about women longing "to break the patterns that have ordered" their lives. The story goes beyond the poem in its portrayal of old age and the longings' seeming futility, the author notes.

——————. "Negro Characters in the Fiction of Doris Betts." *Critique: Studies in Modern Fiction* 17 (December, 1975): 59-76.
Review of Betts's portrayal of black characters in her short stories and novels. Evans finds the characters sensitively presented and well justified in their contexts, even when fulfilling more stereotypical roles such as servants. While Betts does not contend for social rights themes in her works, Evans suggests that "she does not choose to ignore the problems that surround daily living and social change."

Ferguson, Mary Anne. "Doris Betts." In *American Women Writers*, edited by Lina Mainiero. Vol. 1, pp. 151-152. New York: Frederick Ungar, 1980.
A short review of Betts's background and writings. Ferguson finds

the short stories superior to the novels "because it is in her short
stories that she succeeds in catching whole lives quickly." The essay
notes the recurring religious themes, animal imagery, and humor
throughout Betts's works.

Holman, David Marion. "Faith and the Unanswerable Questions: The
Fiction of Doris Betts." *The Southern Literary Journal* 15 (Fall,
1982): 15-22.
An extended discussion of Betts's choice of characters and the
challenges they face, with special reference to "The Ugliest Pilgrim,"
"The Astronomer," "The Mandarin," as well as her novels. Contends
that her characters are "grotesques" (either physical or spiritual)
"trying to solve mysteries of faith . . . seeking answers to unanswerable questions." The answers Betts hints at, according to Holman,
fully embrace the complex, paradox-ridden modern world, one in
which the underlying order is largely an article of faith.

Jones, A. Wesley. *"Beasts of the Southern Wild and Other Stories."* In
Survey of Contemporary Literature, edited by Frank N. Magill. Rev.
and enlarged ed. Vol. 1, pp. 579-583. Englewood Cliffs, N.J.: Salem
Press, 1977.
Review of Betts's story collection, with the longest discussion on
"The Ugliest Pilgrim." The other eight stories are considered on
more briefly. All are integrated into Jones's evaluation of Betts as
one who is attracted by the dehumanizing aspects of the most
vulnerable human relationships. "Betts' greatest gift to us consists of
tenacity and the courage to portray alienation in its most personal
and concrete forms."

Kimball, Sue Leslie, and Lynn Veach Sadler, eds. *Home Truths of
Doris Betts: Proceedings of the Eighth Annual Southern Writers'
Symposium.* Fayetteville, N.C.: Methodist College Press, 1992.
Extensive bibliography of primary and secondary sources, including
minor publications and local newspapers. Collects comments from
colleagues, former students, and admirers. Also contains a number
of academic essays from academicians and original comments from
Betts on her works and life. This is the only book-length work to
date that is focused solely on Betts.

Madden, David. *"The Astronomer and Other Stories."* In *Survey of
Contemporary Literature*, edited by Frank N. Magill. Rev. and

enlarged ed. Vol. 1, pp. 418-423. Englewood Cliffs, N.J.: Salem Press, 1977.
A somewhat theoretical reading of Betts's collection, noting that Betts's "rich technical imagination enables her to control a vitally alive raw material through her metaphorical means of discovering its possibilities and dimensions and interpreting them thematically." Madden sees great promise in Betts, particularly in her "brilliant" novella from the title of the collection.

Menshaw, Michael. "Surrealism and Fantasy: "Beasts of the Southern Wild." *The New York Times Book Review* (October 28, 1973): 40-41. High praise for Betts's style and imagery, strengths that "can undercut a story which isn't equal in substance or structure." Menshaw finds a few examples in the collection where style, structure, and theme mesh, as in "The Mother-in-Law." Menshaw believes Betts deserves close reading and critical attention.

Morrow, Mark. *Images of the Southern Writer*. Athens: University of Georgia Press, 1985.
A full-page photograph and brief informal interview, in which Betts reflects on her writing habits, life-style, and the vagaries of defining the Southern writer. According to Betts, "the stereotypes don't fit any more." Morrow's verbal portrait of Betts is as sensitive as his photographic study.

Peden, William. "Myth, Magic, and a Touch of Madness." *Saturday Review* 48 (February 6, 1965): 32.
Review of *The Scarlet Thread*. Peden enumerates the excesses of the novel, which follows the familiar pattern of stories about families of conflicting individuals. Particularly, Peden faults Betts's strained attempts at social significance, sensationalism, and predictable Southern gothic. He finds the biblical imagery too much and often too literal. The author praises Bett's short-story technique.

Prenshaw, Peggy Whitman. "A Conversation with Seven Fiction Writers." *Southern Quarterly* 29 (Winter, 1991): 69-93.
Familiar territory in the Betts contributions to this round-table discussion. Betts comments on how she began writing and offers definitions for "Southern writing" that have more to do with rural versus urban than with South versus North. According to Betts,

however, "southerners still tell stories" in a manner unique to that region.

Ragan, Sam. "Tribute to Doris Betts." *Pembroke Magazine* 18 (Winter, 1986): 275-284.
Speeches honoring Betts at a North Carolina Writers Conference. Comments are from a number of friends, including her former newspaper editor; Lee Smith; the former president of the University of North Carolina; and Betts herself.

Ray, William E. "Doris Betts on the Art and Teaching of Writing." In *Man in Seven Modes*, edited by William E. Ray, pp. 40-50. Winston-Salem, N.C.: Southern Humanities Conference, 1977.
A 1974 interview covering some familiar topics for Betts: defining the "Southern" writer; the shadow of Faulkner; views on other contemporary writers; teaching; and life as mother, wife, teacher, writer. Familiar questions yet with full, engaging answers from Betts. See also in this same volume Betts's "Prefatory to a Story" (pp. 32-34). She precedes a reading of her short story "This Is the Only Time I'll Tell It" with a lively, humorous version of her struggle to understand why she has to be a "woman" writer. Betts argues that her stories are often engendered by thoughts and events many times removed from "her X-chromosome alone."

Ross, Jean W. "Doris Betts." In *Dictionary of Literary Biography Yearbook: 1982*, edited by Richard Ziegfeld, pp. 219-227. Detroit: Gale Research, 1983.
A lengthy discussion of Betts's history as a woman and a writer, with references to critical reactions to her works. A short interview follows, covering *Heading West* predominantly, though also touching on her teaching and such ancillary work as being on the Literature Panel of the National Endowment for the Arts. Also includes comments on how "The Ugliest Pilgrim" struck her in film adaptation.

Scura, Dorothy. "Doris Betts." In *Fifty Southern Writers After 1900*, edited by Joseph M. Flora and Robert Bain, pp. 53-63. New York: Greenwood Press, 1987.
Research on Betts should probably begin here. Provides good, fundamental material on her life, writings, and critical assessment. The biographical information includes personal insights and revela-

tions about her work habits beyond what one might expect in such a general reference work. Scura points out the array of themes and characters (mostly lower and lower-middle class) to which Betts repeatedly returns. Useful review of critical literature and bibliography.

_____. "Doris Betts at Mid-Career: Her Voice and Her Art." In *Southern Women Writers: The New Generation*, edited by Tonette Bond Inge, pp. 161-179. Tuscaloosa: The University of Alabama Press, 1990.
An excellent short survey of who Betts is and what she writes about. Scura contends that Betts is deservedly on the verge of becoming more widely read, that her writing has continually improved, and that the themes of "time and mortality" have remained constant without becoming repetitive. The essay is more reportorial than critical, but valuable nevertheless.

_____. "Doris Betts's Nancy Finch: A Heroine for the 1980's." In *Women Writers of the Contemporary South*, edited by Peggy Whitman Prenshaw, pp. 135-145. Jackson: University Press of Mississippi, 1984.
This essay provides a brief review of Betts's heroes or narrators from previous novels, then argues for Nancy Finch from *Heading West* as the strongest and most satisfying of them all. That book also brings Betts "into her own" as a novelist and transports her beyond regional bounds. Scura praises Betts's portrayal of this "surprisingly literate woman" struggling to understand her family and herself.

Simpson, Lewis P. "Introduction." In *Three By Three: Masterworks of the Southern Gothic*, pp. vii-xiv. Atlanta: Peachtree, 1985.
The work collects three writers' stories, including Betts's *Beasts of the Southern Wild*. Simpson provides lucid notes on the tradition of the Southern Gothic and places Betts among its contemporary practitioners who blend "realism and grotesquery in a manner that we readily grasp as typical of the Southern literary imagination but find almost impossible to explicate critically."

Walsh, William J. "Doris Betts." In *Speak So I Shall Know Thee: Interviews with Southern Writers*, pp. 40-51. Jefferson, N.C.: McFarland, 1990.
The topics range from the definition of a "Southern" writer to the

difference between writing short stories and writing novels. Betts draws on her experience as a teacher of creative writing to discuss the changes in writing students from her day to the present, including the loss of the Bible as a literary reference and the dramatic increase in women students. Betts acknowledges the desire for more financial return from her work yet cherishes her private life too much to want fame. Of special note may be her explanation of the main character's name in *Heading West*.

Wolfe, George. "The Unique Voice: Doris Betts." In *Kite-Flying and Other Irrational Acts: Conversations with Twelve Southern Writers*, edited by John Carr, pp. 149-173. Baton Rouge: Louisiana State University Press, 1972.
This interview with a relatively young Doris Betts displays her early struggles with the novel form, something she claims to write only because it enables her to continue writing the short story. Betts grapples with her irritations at being categorized as "a Southern woman writer." She also describes her mode of work, cramming writing into any spare moment between teaching, housekeeping, and child-tending. Other familiar topics include the importance of the Bible, the influence of other writers (especially women writers), her views of her students' efforts, and her concerns with death.

Yardley, Jonathan. "The Librarian and the Highwayman." *The Washington Post Book World* 11 (November 29, 1981): 3.
Yardley, who calls Betts "one of the best writers of fiction in this country," is disappointed by *Heading West*. The first part of the novel is "quite brilliant," only to be betrayed by the second portion (Nancy Finch's recovery). The writing is stylistically beautiful, however, according to Yardley. The novel is not yet a form Betts can fully control, as she does her short fiction, the reviewer contends.

_____. "*The River to Pickle Beach.*" *The New York Times Book Review* (May 21, 1972): 12.
Yardley hopes the novel will help broaden Betts's audience with its "ingredients of good popular fiction" along with its merits as a serious novel. He finds fault with the novel's length and its attempts to make universal the struggles of the main characters. Yardley praises the prose style and contends that Betts "deserves to be read."

SALLIE BINGHAM

Bergonzi, Bernard. "Not Long Enough." *The New York Review of Books* (November 9, 1967): 33-35.

Bergonzi discusses the larger issues of the short-story form while reviewing four story collections, including Bingham's *The Touching Hand*. What little direct allusion there is to Bingham categorizes her as one "who is very competent but who relies heavily on the short story formula to compensate for the thinness of her material." Bergonzi believes the pathetic nature of its characters, the predictable ironies of its plots, and the self-consciousness of its authors leave the current short story in an unhealthy state.

Bingham, Sallie. *Passion and Prejudice: A Family Memoir*. New York: Alfred A. Knopf, 1989.

Bingham's autobiography of turmoil among her relatives. There is little mention of her published writings in the book (it has no index). "Interlude" (p. 328) discusses her first short- story publication and her dreams of being a novelist. Accounts of childhood and family tensions, however, provide insights into much of her fiction (which some critics have seen as thinly disguised grudges against her family). She makes numerous allusions to journals, such as her entry at age fifteen: "I have learned that to dream too much is suicide to hopes."

Brenner, Marie. *House of Dreams: The Bingham Family of Louisville*. New York: Random House, 1988.

This account of the Binghams includes numerous short references to Sallie Bingham's writing endeavors. Most revealing is Brenner's analysis of Bingham's sense of her own accomplishments: "Her sense of her place in the world was so warped that she had no idea that she was in fact thought of highly by her husband's colleagues, or that her short stories were admired, or that she was considered talented by almost everyone who met her." See the index for further allusions.

Chandler, David Leon, and Mary V. Chandler. *The Binghams of Louisville*. New York: Crown, 1987.
This study deals mostly with Sallie's forefathers. A short biographical sketch (pp. 226-227) mentions her novel, stories, and plays. The Chandlers allude to Bingham's claim that despite literary success "she never felt she had won the approval of her parents."

Degnan, James P. "Fiction Chronicle." *The Hudson Review* 25 (Summer, 1972): 330-337.
Review of a handful of fiction releases including *The Way It Is Now*. Degnan sees the main problem with the stories as "their thinness of experience—a thinness that makes her sound at times—e.g., in stories like The Facts of Life and Conversations—almost desperate to contrive something to say." Otherwise, Degnan detects narrative talent throughout the writing, especially in her attention to detail.

Dudar, Helen. "Southern Gothic." *The New York Times Book Review* (February 5, 1989): 13-14.
Review of *Passion and Prejudice*. Characterizes the book as "part memoir, part treatise and—why not, considering her view of the South's oppression of its women?—part vengeance." Dudar compares Bingham's life story to a multigenerational tale worthy of Faulkner. Bingham's writing gives the book a kind of "iron grace."

"Ellsworth, Sallie Bingham 1937-   ." In *Contemporary Authors*, New Revision Series, edited by Linda Metzger and Deborah A. Straub. Vol. 18, pp. 140-141. Detroit: Gale Research, 1986.
This entry provides personal and literary history. The discussion of her writings defines her themes as those that "hinge upon tensions within families and the isolation and loneliness of the wealthy." Short list of critical sources.

Frakes, James R. "Very Yin." *The New York Times Book Review* (June 18, 1967): 4-5.
Review of *The Touching Hand* collection of stories. Describes the title novella as "absolutely first-rate," comparing her writing to "a skillfully suggestive amalgam of Katherine Mansfield and Eudora Welty." Other stories are reviewed as powerful products of Bingham's "unblinking gaze." All in all, these are solidly feminine stories with no other particular theme to tie them together except "sheer talent."

Harris, Lis. "Passions, Prejudices." *The New Yorker* (September 11, 1989): 118-123.
Extended essay on Bingham's treatment of her family story in *Passion and Prejudice*. The book "has the feel of a novel, and although the author takes great pains to maintain a cool, even, elevated tone, the genre that most of her characters belong to is American gothic." Harris gives special attention to the contradictions Bingham points out in her family's liberal reputation in publishing but racist and sexist views at home. The end result was Bingham's "insistence that the term 'Southern liberal' is an oxymoron."

Hendin, Josephine. "Short Stories and Three Novels." *The New York Times Book Review* (April 2, 1972): 6.
The Way It Is Now is reviewed as "a finely written collection of stories about those narrow, unhappy women who connect with nothing but themselves." The pains of these "poor little rich girls" try Hendin's patience. The fact that Bingham writes so well only confounds the emptiness of the characters. All the main characters appear too much alike for Hendin, with problems that are engaging only to a select group.

Nash, Alanna. "Family Feud: The War Between the Binghams." *Working Woman* (September, 1985): 134-137, 170-173.
This article deals primarily with the newspaper stock Sallie proposed selling in 1984 and the uproar in her family that resulted. The few allusions to her creative writings define her central theme as "emotional pain"; Bingham says that "writing is the only way I can forget about everything else and lose myself." Of note may be Bingham's comments on her feminism: "I was really a feminist in the '50s when I wrote *After Such Knowledge*."

Sheppard, R. Z. "Sallie's Turn." *Time* (January 30, 1989): 73.
Review of *Passion and Prejudice: A Family Memoir*. Sheppard describes Bingham as "a millionaire Marxist-feminist" in her portrayal of the family politics and passions. Notes that her writing style is more appropriate to fiction than a memoir. Sheppard questions Bingham's descriptions of confrontations with her father but finds that her "relations with her mother ring truer."

Tifft, Susan E., and Alex S. Jones. *The Patriarch: The Rise and Fall of the Bingham Dynasty*. New York: Summit Books, 1991.

Tifft and Jones provide a heavily documented account of the family history. Sallie's writings are considered in the biographical context. "Increasingly, her writing seemed calculated to wound," the authors note, adding that Sallie's writing seemed to make her misery greater. Extensive chapter notes and index.

MARY WARD BROWN

Beidler, Philip D. "The Magical Realism of Mary Ward Brown."
Alabama English 1 (Spring, 1990): 59-67.
In this insightful essay, Beidler classifies Brown as a Magical
Realist, along with such other Alabama writers as William March
and Harper Lee. As she explores her major theme, that of change,
Brown is involved in the "creative juxtaposing of old and new."
While both her characters and her situations are familiar, there is a
subtle suggestion of magic or myth that transforms reality into
something mysterious and different.

Brown, Clarence. "Pen Pals." *The New Republic* (October 2, 1989): 40-
41.
A brief comment on the inclusion of Brown's short story "The Cure"
in a joint anthology of American and Soviet poetry and fiction. Calls
the story "a deftly nuanced miniature" that "hasn't a single false
note."

Brown, Jerry Elijah. Review of *Tongues of Flame. National Forum: Phi
Kappa Phi Journal* 67 (Summer, 1987): 46.
Admires the stories for their range and compassion. Brown's fiction
differs from that of others of her generation in that while, as a
Southern writer, she uses the materials that they have in common,
she progresses from the fact of change to the options available in
living with it. Her work "is the fruit of keen observation, a long
historical perspective, and considerable talent."

Brumas, Michael. "Alabama Writer in U.S.-Soviet Story Collection."
Birmingham News (May 7, 1989): pp. A21, A25.
Reports reactions to Brown's work at a symposium of Soviet and
American writers held in Washington, D.C. Soviet short-story writer
Boris Yekimov is quoted as praising her skill and commenting that
"The Cure," which is about poor blacks in Alabama, reflects
problems and feelings that are common to people throughout the
world. The article also includes an interview in which Brown speaks

of her late entry into professional writing and describes her approach and her routine. Although she calls herself a Southern writer, she feels that fiction with real depth has universal appeal.

LeVert, E. C. "Quiet, Craftsmanly Humor and Sly Sense of Ornament." *Birmingham News* (August 3, 1986): p. F6.
Review of *Tongues of Flame* that characterizes Brown's technique as "a quiet, craftsmanly attention to studied harmonies of scale, an art of understatement, enlivened by a sly sense of ornament," which makes her unique among contemporary writers. On the surface, she appears conventional, but in actuality, she is highly original. She emphasizes "human interdependence"; however, the very fact that her characters are presented as members of a community makes their isolation within personal tragedy more poignant.

Martin, Jean. "Tongues of Flame' Written on the Heart." *Selma Times-Journal* (July 9, 1986): p. B1.
A highly complimentary review of *Tongues of Flame* in a newspaper published near Brown's rural home. Notes that her stories are seen "through the eyes, and the heart, of a woman." The dialogue and the characters are realistic. While she has been compared to Eudora Welty and Peter Taylor, she is "uniquely herself and uniquely a product of the Black Belt," that is, the area of rich black cotton land that includes both Selma and nearby Browns, Alabama. Speaks of the "humor, wisdom, humanity, and above all, love" that are evident in the stories.

Morton, Kathryn. "Good Family Recipes." *The New York Times Book Review* (August 24, 1986): 6.
Appreciative review of *Tongues of Flame*. Points out that in each of the stories an individual must face the end of a way of life. The responses vary; some characters are stunned, while others adapt and even find new happiness. Morton sees Brown's South as neither Faulknerian nor Gothic; it is the South "where everyone is expected to behave himself, where people know who they are, and where good family recipes are handed down."

Stallworth, Clarke. "Working Hard at Words Is Her Life's Stimulation." *Birmingham News* (June 9, 1985): pp. E1-E2.
Essay-interview. Outlines Brown's early life and the events that led to her commitment to writing. Quotes at length her description of the

writing process, which she sees as the pursuit of truth, telling the whole story about both the sadness and the wonder of life.

Steinberg, Sybil. Review of *Tongues of Flame*. *Publishers Weekly* (May 23, 1986): 91.
Assesses Brown as "a writer of real potential," who shows both changing conditions specific to the South and universal emotions "with a light, sure hand." While she does not have the "emotional toughness" of Harper Lee and Eudora Welty, Brown does show "a powerful sense of place and mood."

Stephens, Elise Hopkins. "A Telephone Conversation with Mary Ward Brown." *Alabama Humanities* (Spring, 1989): 3.
A series of answers to questions that must be inferred. Brown's subject matter is not nature, but people; her interest is in the present, not the past. She writes about "race and religion" because "they are the overriding preoccupations of the South," along with family and place, which serve to establish the identity of Southerners. Brown believes it is theme that "makes the whole story work."

Walburn, Jackie. "Prize Time for Mary Ward Brown, from Perry Hamlet to Big Apple." *Birmingham News* (May 24, 1987): p. F6.
Written when Brown won the Hemingway Foundation award for her short stories. Includes biographical details and comments of the judges praising her steady, clear observation of life. Brown is still not interested in writing a novel; she says that her goal is still to write one truly superior short story.

VICKI COVINGTON

Avinger, Charles. "Vicki Covington's Vision of the New South." *Alabama English* 1 (Spring, 1990): 85-88.
A study of several of Covington's short stories and her novel *Gathering Home*. Focuses on the intertwining of past and present that the author sees as the dominant characteristic of the New South. Often Covington's characters, like her region itself, show surprising combinations of traditional and contemporary attitudes.

Covington, Vicki. "The Disappearing South." *Southpoint* (March, 1990): 90.
The writer comments on her sense of loss, which she attributes to the realization that the rural past and those who lived it will soon have vanished. She uses a story about an opal ring to suggest that it is actually the uneasy feeling that one has lost something that defines a present-day Southerner.

_____. "Southern Women Haven't Missed the Boat; They're Steering It." *Birmingham News* (April 28, 1991): p. C2.
Argues that Southern women have had both power and responsibility since the Civil War. Uses a personal anecdote to symbolize how women in the South are bound not by "feminist ideology" but by a tradition of nurturing and achieving.

_____. "Telling the Story." *Southern Living* (February, 1990): 84.
In this essay, Covington describes the efforts she and her husband have made to expose their children to the world of their grandparents, a world that includes a sense of history, "an ear for irony, and eye for detail, and a compulsion to talk in stories." In writing, she hopes to "have internalized the voices" of her kinfolk and her parents.

Kennedy, Veronica Pike. "Average People Are Special in Vicki Covington's Writing." *Birmingham News* (May 20, 1990): p. F5.

Review of *Bird of Paradise*, calling it "an exquisite work from a writer who has matured in her art." Has extensive quotations from a telephone interview with Covington on the subject of Southern women and on her own growing certainty that writing is her vocation.

_____. "Vicki Covington Makes Debut with a Nice Story Told Well." *Birmingham News* (September 4, 1988): p. F7.
Complimentary review of *Gathering Home*, which is not sensational but "a nice story told well." The characters are convincing and admirable.

Steinberg, Sybil. Review of *Bird of Paradise*. *Publishers Weekly* (March 2, 1990): 76.
Praises the novel as a "quiet, satisfying tale" about love's coming to a heroine who is past middle age. The narrator's voice is as authentic as her opinions and her religious faith.

_____. Review of *Gathering Home*. *Publishers Weekly* (July 29, 1988): 219.
Calls the book a "thoroughly credible, appealing story," in which likeable characters move toward reconciliation. It is both "subtle and affirming."

Whitehouse, Anne. Review of *Gathering Home*. *The New York Times Book Review* (January 1, 1989): 14.
Although the novelist follows a current fashion in attempting to "express the unsaid through the concrete," she fails because of "a paucity of telling details." Covington does, however, have "a bent for satire."

ELLEN DOUGLAS (JOSEPHINE HAXTON)

Bellows, Silence Buck. "One Step Toward Finding Answers." *The Christian Science Monitor* (October 31, 1963): 7.
A perceptive review arguing that the four works in *Black Cloud, White Cloud*, which appear to be "deceptively dispassionate behavior studies," actually deal with a profound issue, the theme of guilt and absolution. Although the works in this volume involve black-white relationships, they are not "stories of racial antagonism," but thoughtful stories that "set us to seeking reasons, which is one step toward finding answers."

Binding, Paul. "Tale of Two Women." *New Statesman and Society* (July 6, 1990): 44.
Praises Douglas' novels as "passionately intelligent and universalizing inquiries into southern experience" and often into American culture in general. She often writes about relationships between women and between blacks and whites. *Can't Quit You, Baby* is the story of a black woman and the white woman who employs her; it is also the story of the masks all human beings wear in order to "protect and condition" themselves against truths they prefer not to face.

Brandmark, Wendy. "Strange Fruit." *The Times Literary Supplement* (July 20, 1990): 782.
In *Can't Quit You, Baby*, Douglas explores a friendship that is haunted by habitual customs and attitudes. By the use of a narrator who is not involved in the action, Douglas frees herself to explore complex black-white relationships. Then she makes the story even more ambiguous by having the narrator remind her audience that as a white woman, she herself cannot be truly objective. Extols the craftsmanship and the "lucid, compassionate moral vision" of this novel.

Broughton, Panthea Reid, and Susan Millar Williams. "Ellen Douglas." In *Southern Women Writers: The New Generation*, edited by Tonette

Bond Inge, pp. 46-69. Tuscaloosa: University of Alabama Press, 1990.

Excellent essay tracing Douglas' steady development as a writer, from the early novels, in which she sometimes used stereotypical characters and often shrank from suggesting remedies for the social problems she dramatized, to more recent fiction, in which she strengthened characterization, broadened her themes, and experimented with new techniques. Includes a biographical sketch. Based on an unpublished interview as well as on two published ones.

Brown, Laurie L. "Interviews with Seven Contemporary Writers." In *Women Writers of the Contemporary South*, edited by Peggy Whitman Prenshaw, pp. 3-22. Jackson: University Press of Mississippi, 1984.

Douglas' answers to a series of questions proposed by the interviewer. Explains how her choice of a career was made easier by the fact that a number of women were already succeeding as writers. As to influences upon her, Douglas speaks of her Presbyterian upbringing and her consciousness of Southern racial problems. Asked about the problems peculiar to women writers, Douglas speaks feelingly of her own attempts to write when her children were young. In answer to a question about teaching writing, Douglas comments that as a teacher herself, she has discovered how difficult it is to teach anyone to write; most of one's skill is acquired through years of reading. Interesting, especially in conjunction with the responses of other writers.

Buckmaster, Henrietta. "Fiction: Families and Individuals." *The Christian Science Monitor* (June 14, 1962): 7.

Review of *A Family's Affairs*. Despite the Mississippi setting, the book is not regional. It shows how a close-knit family "absorbs the shocks for the three generations" and thus sustains its individual members, whether they are able to understand one another. Quotes a lengthy passage to indicate both the theme of the work and Douglas' "lucid, felicitous prose."

Dean, Michael P. "Ellen Douglas's Small Towns: Fictional Anchors." *Southern Quarterly: A Journal of the Arts in the South* 19 (Fall, 1980): 161-171.

Douglas chooses small town settings for many reasons, including the fact that they enable one to study diversity on a small scale. She usually concentrates on a few buildings in these towns, such as family homes and churches, showing how they both influence and symbolize the lives of the people who live and work within them. Moreover, in a small town setting she can illustrate the continuity that at best persists from generation to generation, carried on through language and through shared stories. Finally, the small towns themselves become images of a larger world.

Douglas, Ellen. *Walker Percy's "The Last Gentleman": Introduction and Commentary*, edited by Lee A. Belford. New York: Seabury Press, 1969.
Discussion of the philosophical issues raised in the novel, particularly humankind's alienation from the world in which he lives, while in the modern world it is also alienated from the God Who once enabled it to transcend this world. Also points out reflections of Kierkegaard in the novel. Douglas acknowledges Percy's assistance during her preparation of the monograph. Some relevance to Douglas' *Where the Dreams Cross*.

Grumbach, Doris. "*Apostles of Light.*" *America* (April 14, 1973): 338.
Sees *Apostles of Light* as a gothic novel based on the facts of life in a home for the elderly. Despite its wordiness, which may be attributed to the tradition in which it is written, the work is admirable as an expression of concern about a real social problem.

Isaacs, Susan. "Not Going Gentle at All." *The New York Times Book Review* (October 31, 1982): 11, 34.
While *A Lifetime Burning* is too dependent on clever technical devices, which draw the reader's attention away from the action, and although the motivation of the characters is sometimes farfetched, the book is successful in telling a tragic story about a woman who has everything but peace of mind. The novel displays Douglas' "depth, emotional range, wit, sensitivity, and . . . gift of language."

Jones, John Griffin. "Ellen Douglas." In *Mississippi Writers Talking*, edited by John Griffin Jones. Vol. 2, pp. 47-74. Jackson: University Press of Mississippi, 1983.
An important interview, conducted in 1980 at Douglas' home in Greenville, Mississippi. Douglas comments on the conventional values of her family, which precluded any early involvement in the flourishing Mississippi literary scene but did instill in her the

importance of hard work. In speaking of literary and environmental influences, she considers the significance of her Southern heritage, noting that there are great differences between Southern writers. Lengthy discussion of the sense of "gnawing guilt" for racial injustice that prompted the writing of *The Rock Cried Out.*

Lyell, Frank H. "Time Marches on in Homochitto." *The New York Times Book Review* (July 8, 1962): 18.
Rates *A Family's Affairs* as an uneven book, often wordy, often artificial. Attributes its overall dullness to the fact that Douglas is describing ordinary people leading ordinary lives. The final chapter, however, describing the heroine's illness and death, is moving and finely crafted. The emphasis on "domestic situations from the female point of view" indicates that the book will be read mostly by women. Nevertheless, the realistic description provides an "antidote to the run-of-the-mill Deep South novel."

Maloff, Saul. "To Be Southern Is to Be Obsessed." *The New York Times Book Review* (October 6, 1963): 5.
Contends that despite her use of predictable settings, situations, and themes, the pseudonymous Southern author of *Black Cloud, White Cloud* is a "fine and feeling writer." Finds "The House on the Bluff" and the novella *Jesse* disappointing, but praises the short story "I Just Love Carrie Lee" and the other novella *Hold On.*

Manning, Carol S. "Ellen Douglas: Moralist and Realist." In *Women Writers of the Contemporary South*, edited by Peggy Whitman Prenshaw, pp. 116-134. Jackson: University Press of Mississippi, 1984.
Maintains that while Douglas deals with such typical themes of Southern writers as race, family, and memory, her central preoccupation is responsibility. As a realist, Douglas recognizes the needs of individuals for independence and for reinterpretation of the past, as well as the problems inherent in human relationships; however, as a moralist, she emphasizes the need for individuals to subsume their selfish desires and to acknowledge their obligations toward others, particularly within the family. This essay is also available in *Southern Quarterly: A Journal of the Arts in the South* 21 (Summer, 1943): 116-134.

Morrow, Mark. "Ellen Douglas." In *Images of the Southern Writer*, pp. 18-19. Athens: University of Georgia Press, 1985.

In the brief interview that accompanies Morrow's photograph of her, Douglas describes the unusual beginning of her writing career, when she was working as a disk jockey and had spare time between records. She also speaks of her Mississippi heritage and of her friendship with writer Shelby Foote.

Prescott, Peter S. "Evil in the Golden Age." *Newsweek* (March 5, 1973): 84.
Review of *Apostles of Light* as a story of people who are not even sublimely evil, but merely self-centered and indifferent. The characters' behavior is consistent with their "disabling" philosophies of life. This "fine, strong novel" is complex and suspenseful enough to have a universal appeal.

Spearman, Walter. "Light on a Southern Exposure." *Saturday Review* (November 16, 1963): 42.
A review of *Black Cloud, White Cloud*, comparing the "exceptional" stories in Douglas' volume with early stories by Eudora Welty and Katherine Anne Porter. Racial stresses are shown as only one aspect of the Mississippi Delta environment that the author re-creates from her own observation, a society "woven from long, strong strands of plantation life and complex family relationships."

Stockwell, Joe. *Ellen Douglas*. Jackson: Mississippi Library Commission, 1977.
A perceptive and detailed chronological discussion of Douglas' works, concluding with *Apostles of Light*. Stockwell sees Douglas as an satirist and a moralist in the tradition of the eighteenth and nineteenth century English novel. Because she castigates vice, because she abhors betrayal in particular, she has often puzzled those contemporary critics who expect psychological analyses, not ethical judgments. In the Southern literary tradition, she is concerned with the effects of change, particularly when that change seems to be resulting in a denial of spiritual and ethical truths. Her work is characterized by the "good sense and moral indignation" of her literary forebears. Although this monograph does not deal with Douglas' later publications, it is more clearly relevant to them than many later, more superficial studies.

Uhry, Alfred. "Where There's Water There Are Snakes." *The New York Times Book Review* (July 10, 1988): 13.

Interprets *Can't Quit You, Baby* as an examination of the race issue set in a white kitchen. There Douglas exposes the white protagonist, Cornelia, who is "the essence of sheltered Southern womanhood," as the self-deceptive, self-centered person she is. Eventually, "Ms. Douglas lets Cornelia have it," and unlike the admirable black woman character, Cornelia breaks down under adversity. The reviewer extols the book as a "haunting examination of the lives of two memorable women."

Walters, Thomas N. *"The Rock Cried Out."* In *Magill's Literary Annual: Books of 1980*, edited by Frank N. Magill. Vol. 2, pp. 722-725. Englewood Cliffs, N.J.: Salem Press, 1991.
Both in plot and in theme, *The Rock Cried Out* is a coming-of-age novel, in which the white narrator discovers his own ignorance, both of his own nature and of the world around him. In this work, Douglas has drawn on familiar Southern materials to tell a new story, the story of the South in the process of change. Perhaps her greatest gift is in characterization; to an important degree, it is the characters speaking in their own voices who introduce her naïve protagonist to reality. At the end of the novel, he has discovered that salvation can come only through "reasoned exercise of will."

KAYE GIBBONS

Bell, Pearl K. "Southern Discomfort." *The New Republic* (February 29, 1988): 38-41.
This review of *Ellen Foster* is part of a larger essay on fellow contemporary writers McCorkle and Godwin and how they all fit into the Southern literary traditions. The one common denominator, according to Bell, is "that enduring concern with family." Gibbons' novel is credited as a "remarkable first novel." Bell is captivated by the narrative voice of Ellen, who "has a rare capacity for seeing through phonies and figuring things out."

D'Erasmo, Stacey. "*A Cure for Dreams.*" *The Village Voice Literary Supplement* (April, 1991): 5.
D'Erasmo considers Gibbons "at heart a 19th century novelist." *A Cure for Dreams*, like all of her novels, focuses on the woman's viewpoint. This time "it is on what women pass along to one another, through the ties of blood and friendship." The men of the book seem largely absent. D'Erasmo finds the stories linked smoothly from chapter to chapter.

Gibbons, Kaye. "My Mother, Literature, and a Life Split Neatly into Two Halves." In *The Writer on Her Work, Volume II: New Essays in New Territory*, edited by Janet Sternburg, pp. 52-60. New York: W. W. Norton, 1991.
Gibbons recounts the childhood world that seeded her writing. Her mother's strength and tenacity, not her mother's readings or artistic inclinations (of which there were little or none), began it all. From there, Gibbons added her own literary influences, from trite TV sitcoms to Poe and Shakespeare. Marriage and giving birth added their elements of pain, joy, and growth. Finally, Gibbons addresses her own supposed "Cinderella story" of seemingly "instant" success, contending that dues are paid in many ways for any writer.

Hoffman, Alice. "Shopping for a New Family." *The New York Times Book Review* (May 31, 1987): 13.

Review of *Ellen Foster*. "What might have been grim, melodramatic material in the hands of a less talented author is instead filled with lively humor . . . compassion and intimacy," Hoffman says. This reviewer believes in Ellen and her voice. Gibbons has chosen a traditional, rural setting brushing up against the modern world, according to Hoffman, who approves of the work's handling of race issues.

Kaveney, Roz. "As They Mean to Go On." *New Statesman* (May 13, 1988): 34.
Review of *Ellen Foster*. British magazine calls Gibbons' main character "one of those precocious *fausse naive* eleven-year-olds who may only exist in fiction." Kaveney seems satisfied by Ellen's telling of her tale, if still unimpressed by the literary achievement of the novel. Much of the tone and many of the elements of the book strike the reviewer as artificial.

_____. "Making Themselves Over." *The Times Literary Supplement* (September 15, 1989): 998.
According to this review, *A Virtuous Woman* "has the simplicity of a good Country-and-Western song." Kaveney finds biblical influences in the title and in the basic values of the characters. Ruby and Jack present a relationship rooted in "pride as well as love and sorrow." Overall, the review concludes, the novel dares "to transfigure the commonplace into a plain language that speaks with as much complexity as the rococo might, but with more appropriateness."

"Kaye Gibbons." In *Contemporary Literary Criticism: Yearbook 1987*, edited by Sharon K. Hull. Vol. 50, pp. 46-50. Detroit: Gale Research, 1988.
Worth looking up if for no other reason than the few sentences at the end of the entry quoting Gibbons on the inspiration for *Ellen Foster* and on the literary influence of Flannery O'Connor. There is a brief biographical sketch in the opening, followed by the usual excerpts from reviews of *Ellen Foster*.

Powell, Padgett. "*A Virtuous Woman*." *The New York Times Book Review* (April 30, 1989): 12-13.
A complex review of a complex novel. Powell draws parallels to Faulkner (*As I Lay Dying*, *The Wild Palms*), with two major differences: "First, the mythic is eschewed. . . . And, second, it is not

a multitude but merely two narrators who address us." While there is also not the verbal play of Faulkner, *A Virtuous Woman* manages well enough on its structural elements. According to Powell, "the architecture of this novel is remarkable."

Taylor, Linda. "A Kind of Primitive Charm." *Sunday* [London] *Times* (May 8, 1988): p. G6.
Review calls *Ellen Foster* "one of those novels that you feel compelled to read from cover to cover in one sitting. Gibbons' child narrator comes alive on every page with wit, pragmatism and revenge." The social issues of the novel—racism, sexism, and child abuse—"are dealt with through revelation rather than moral axe-grinding." The narrative voice strikes Taylor as being "wholly credible."

Wilcox, James. "Escape from Milk Road." *The New York Times Book Review* (May 12, 1991): 13-14.
Review of *A Cure for Dreams*. Whereas *A Virtuous Woman* has concentrated feelings somewhat dispersed in that expansive novel, Gibbons has in *Cure* "a maturity of vision that shows a distinct honing of [her] artistic sensibility." Wilcox praises the complexity of her characters, contrasting with some of the weaker ones in *Ellen Foster*. He also finds much more sociological detail in the more recent work.

ELLEN GILCHRIST

Allen, Bruce. "American Short Fiction Today." *New England Review* 4 (Spring, 1982): 478-488.
An overview of the genre. Commends Ellen Gilchrist as "a writer to watch," with a "vigorous style." Because of her detachment, her "oddly summary, noncommittal tone," Allen comments parenthetically that "she sounds, at times, like a foulmouthed Flannery O'Connor."

Bamber, Linda. *"Falling Through Space: The Journals of Ellen Gilchrist." The New York Times Book Review* (January 3, 1988): 19.
Expresses disappointment in this volume. The three-minute time limit on Gilchrist's monologues "trivializes all her subjects," and she has time to do no more than "flash her personality."

Bell, Carolyn Wilkerson. *"Victory over Japan."* In *Magill's Literary Annual: Books of 1984*, edited by Frank N. Magill. Vol. 2, pp. 973-977. Englewood Cliffs, N.J.: Salem Press, 1985.
As her gossipy, casual tone suggests, Gilchrist's primary purpose is to entertain her readers. Although her work reflects the feminist tradition, for example, by showing how marriage confines women, her women characters are not victims. Like the recurring character Nora Jane Whittington, they have a "heroic vitality." Bell is uneasy with Gilchrist's rendering of black speech; however, she admires her treatment of relationships between black and white women and of the theme of sisterhood in general.

Bolsterli, Margaret Jones. "Ellen Gilchrist's Characters and the Southern Woman's Experience: Rhoda Manning's Double Bind and Anna Hand's Creativity." *New Orleans Review* 15 (Spring, 1988): 7-9.
In characters such as Rhoda Manning and Anna Hand, Gilchrist reveals the attitudes that have prevented Southern women from finding their own identities. They are discouraged from creativity and encouraged to imitate role models. Those characters who do survive usually do so through turning their experiences into art.

Brown, Georgia. "Look at Me! The Writer as Flasher." *Mother Jones*
13 (December, 1988): 46-47.
An unfavorable review of *The Anna Papers*. Sees the protagonist,
Anna Hand, as a fictional representation of the author and the theme
of the novel as the superiority of Anna and the unimportance of
everyone else.

Brown, Rosellen. "Coming up Short." *Saturday Review* 9 (July/August,
1983): 53-54.
In *The Annunciation*, Gilchrist fails to sustain a single voice. The
first part of her first novel is a withering attack on New Orleans
society of the kind that is familiar from her earlier short stories. In
the second half, after the heroine moves to Arkansas, the tone
changes abruptly. Gilchrist jettisons her critical judgment and her
sense of irony, turning her heroine into a soft-headed, ordinary
woman in a predictable pattern of search for identity. Brown hopes
that in future work Gilchrist "will use her sharp intelligence to better
effect."

Cooke, Judy. "Intimate Voices." *Listener* 117 (March 19, 1987): 26-27.
A glowing review of *Drunk with Love*, as a collection of "exhilarat-
ing," highly dramatic stories. Points out "the sense of place, the
psychological subtleties, the vivid characterization" as the author's
special virtues.

Crace, Jim. "The Cold-eyed Terrors." *The Times Literary Supplement*
(October 15, 1982): 1142.
Review of *In the Land of Dreamy Dreams*. The Southern origin of
the title obscures the fact that Gilchrist's preoccupation in these
stories is not a particular place, but adolescence. The collection has
defects: Sometimes the narrators are unduly sophisticated, and
sometimes the conclusions of the stories are overwritten. The prose,
however, is generally "delicately and rhythmically modulated," and
the stories are "perceptive."

Fell, Allison. "Heaven and Hell." *New Statesman* 113 (April 3, 1987):
28-29.
A review of several short-story collections, including *Drunk with
Love*. Admires Gilchrist's "taut and spacious" prose, her persuasive
picture of a society filled with women who are drunk with consumer-
ism and desperate for love.

Garrett, George. "American Publishing Now." *The Sewanee Review* 96 (Summer, 1988): 516-525.
Within a general commentary on books dealing with publishing, Garrett compares Ellen Gilchrist's *Falling Through Space* and Rita Mae Brown's *Starting from Scratch*. Finds Gilchrist's book interesting and occasionally revealing. Gilchrist, however, presents herself as what publishers think writers are, "flaky and lucky" with occasional glimpses of the "ambitious, shrewd, strong-willed" person she really is. Brown's book, by contrast, is realistic, practical, and useful.

Gilchrist, Ellen. *Falling Through Space: The Journals of Ellen Gilchrist*. Boston: Little, Brown, 1987.
A collection of short essays, most of which were aired on National Public Radio in 1985 and 1986. The author has grouped them loosely, according to theme, as "Origins," "Influences," and "Work." While they are of interest, these random observations are of limited value because their brevity precludes any real development of ideas. Includes a number of photographs.

Hoffman, Roy. "Smart Enough for Their Own Good." *The New York Times Book Review* (October 22, 1989): 13.
A review of *Light Can Be Both Wave and Particle* as a collection that "bristles with new energy." New themes and new situations are introduced, and even the familiar characters who reappear in these stories take new directions. Suggests that "The Song of Songs" and "Life on the Earth," which otherwise are confusing, should be read as resolutions to *The Annunciation*.

Johnson, Greg. "Some Recent Herstories." *The Georgia Review* 44 (Spring/Summer, 1990): 278-288.
In an essay assessing recent publications by women, Johnson considers *Light Can Be Both Wave and Particle*, which he finds disappointing. While some of the stories are as well plotted, as vivid, and as insightful as those in earlier collections, in others the author seems to be substituting style for structure and real substance. Gilchrist resembles the four other writers considered in that she handles women's issues in a restrained and ironic fashion, rather than stridently and confrontationally.

Koenig, Rhoda. "Rosemary's Babies." *New York* (April 6, 1992): 92, 101.

A review of *Net of Jewels*. Finds the heroine's "intentionally funny jokes and unintentionally funny self-dramatization" amusing for a time, but as the book progresses, tires of the dramatics of "this road-company Tallulah."

Lesser, Wendy. "Home Movies." *The New York Times Book Review* (October 5, 1986): 18.
A review of *Drunk with Love* that focuses on characterization. While Gilchrist's habit of reintroducing the same characters in various works makes them appear to be well-rounded, actually she depends on a few stereotypes, which apply not only to unhappy women and cruel, insensitive men but also to Catholics, Jews, and Californians. Implies a real flaw in Gilchrist's powers of observation.

Lowry, Beverly. "Redheaded Hellions in the Crape Myrtle." *The New York Times Book Review* (September 23, 1984): 18.
Victory over Japan again illustrates Gilchrist's willingness to place her women characters in impossible situations, from which they must extricate themselves, revealing their zest for life in the process. While sometimes her handling of point of view or of a conclusion is less than perfect, Gilchrist compensates for such flaws by her skills in invention and in characterization.

McDowell, Margaret B. "Ellen Gilchrist." In *Contemporary Novelists*, edited by D. Kirkpatrick. 4th ed., pp. 338-339. New York: St. Martin's Press, 1986.
Biographical data and a critical essay. Describes Gilchrist's technique in detail. Points out that her setting is the Deep South, most often New Orleans, her style terse, her tone often satirical, and her subject matter timely, as when her episodes reflect the influence of drugs on contemporary society. Although her use of stereotypical characters is acceptable in the short stories, it mars her novel *The Annunciation*, a flawed work in other ways as well. Gilchrist must, however, be considered "one of America's best contemporary story writers."

Melly, George. "Southern Talent." *New Statesman and Society* (October 7, 1988): 38-39.
A negative review of *Falling Through Space*. Melly found the book "self-congratulatory," smug, and trite. Strangely, although she uses the same materials in her fiction, in the latter Gilchrist succeeds.

Morrow, Mark. "Ellen Gilchrist." In *Images of the Southern Writer*, 32-33. Athens: University of Georgia Press, 1985.
In a brief interview, Gilchrist laughs about New Orleans and makes superficial comments about her plans. Little substance, but a revealing glimpse of the writer behind the books.

Morton, Brian. "Southern Death." *The Times Literary Supplement* (April 6, 1984): 368.
A comparison of Ernest J. Gaines and Ellen Gilchrist. Unlike Gaines, Gilchrist does not write about a real South, but the South as it exists in the imaginations of her characters. *The Annunciation* is even more detached from real life than the short stories. The perceptions of the characters are "filtered through drink, dope and fantasy," and their actions are mere imitations of literature. Imprecision in style further contributes to the obscurity of this novel.

Paley, Maggie. "A Wake in Charlotte." *The New York Times Book Review* (January 15, 1989): 16.
Suggests that *The Anna Papers* suffered from a new attitude of the author, who seems to have abandoned her earlier ironic and often wickedly satirical stance for a new sentimentalism. Despite segments in which her "passionate, incantatory prose" brings a scene to life, the book is marred by overindulgence in introspection and by simplistic optimism.

Sexton, David. "The Wacky Woman's Whyyyyyy Not World." *The Times Literary Supplement* (May 24, 1985): 573.
A brief but interesting review, indicating that with *Victory over Japan* Gilchrist has moved from the theme of actual adolescence to that of prolonged innocence or deliberate childishness. By shifting point of view so that her speakers are no longer the characters under scrutiny, she has solved a problem with point of view that was troublesome in *The Annunciation*.

Smith, Wendy. "Ellen Gilchrist." *Publishers Weekly* (March 2, 1992): 46-47.
An essay-interview conducted at the writer's home in Fayetteville, Arkansas. The author speaks about her repeated use of the same characters, which enables her to chronicle their development. While she spent much of her youth in the Midwest, she credits her Southern background for her language. Traces the course of her writing career and plans for a book set in the 1990's.

Stubblefield, Charles. "A Triumph of the Human Will." *Prairie Schooner* 58 (Summer, 1984): 107-109.
Calls *The Annunciation* an "excellent first novel." If not feminist, it is certainly "pro-woman," emphasizing the protagonist's need to reject her region, her family, and Catholicism, in order to free her mind and her soul.

Taliaferro, Frances. *Harper's* (June, 1983): 76.
Review of *The Annunciation*, a "surprisingly likable" novel. It owes its appeal to the character of the heroine, an admitted romantic, who makes her way through periods reminiscent of William Faulkner, J. D. Salinger, and F. Scott Fitzgerald, before embarking on her search for self-fulfillment.

Thompson, Jeanie, and Anita Miller Garner. "The Miracle of Realism: The Bid for Self-Knowledge in the Fiction of Ellen Gilchrist." In *Women Writers of the Contemporary South*, edited by Peggy Whitman Prenshaw, pp. 233-247. Jackson: University Press of Mississippi, 1984.
Argues that although Gilchrist's fiction is realistic, it is not merely regional. While there are few fully-developed male characters in her work, her women are living human beings. In her attitude toward her gender, Gilchrist exhibits a "Romantic Calvinism," evidently persuaded of their innate depravity and at the same time sympathetic toward their dreams, which are destined to come to nothing. This thesis is illustrated in *The Land of Dreamy Dreams* and in *The Annunciation*. At the end of the second work, Gilchrist seems to suggest "a possibility of redemption" through self-knowledge. This essay is also available in *Southern Quarterly: A Journal of the Arts in the South* 22 (Fall, 1983).

Wells, Susan Spano. "A Maine Summer Night's Dream." *The New York Times Book Review* (November 4, 1990): 24.
A brief review of *I Cannot Get You Close Enough*. Like the Shakespearean play (*A Midsummer Night's Dream*) that inspired it, the book takes a group of characters to an unfamiliar environment, in this case, transporting a family from Charlotte, North Carolina, to New England. Gilchrist's strength is in her characterization. Instead of stereotypes, her characters prove to be individuals with "spontaneity and pathos."

GAIL GODWIN

Allen, John Alexander. "Researching Her Salvation: The Fiction of Gail Godwin." *The Hollins Critic* 25 (April, 1988): 1-9.

With *A Southern Family* as a point of reference, Allen surveys Godwin's earlier work in order to indicate not only characteristic themes and techniques but also the development of her art. The fact that the characters in *A Southern Family* are more complex than those in earlier works is important in terms of theme as well as of technique. A dominant theme in her fiction has been the importance of every individual; by presenting a "multi-faced view" of her major characters, Godwin stresses this theme, while also exhibiting an artistic maturity that promises well for the future. An essay that is admirable for its scope and its clarity.

Auerbach, Nina. "Women on Women's Destiny: Maturity as Penance." In *Romantic Imprisonment: Women and Other Glorified Outcasts*, pp. 83-91. New York: Columbia University Press, 1986.

When they assume that the life experiences of women cannot be described by male writers and that the writing of women cannot be understood by male critics and readers, feminists are not merely rejecting men, they are limiting themselves. In nineteenth century fiction, there are examples of women who rise above convention and find freedom and joy. It is significant that even the study of George Gissing's novel *The Odd Women*, in which a heroine triumphs, fails to inspire Jane Clifford, the protagonist of Gail Godwin's *The Odd Woman*. She can be seen as a symbol of feminist exclusion, "rejecting a literary endowment from men . . . in favor of the willed constriction of a very small room."

Brown, Laurie L. "Interviews with Seven Contemporary Writers." In *Women Writers of the Contemporary South*, edited by Peggy Whitman Prenshaw, pp. 3-22. Jackson: University Press of Mississippi, 1984.

Godwin's responses to various questions are quoted along with the responses of six other contemporary women writers. She denies that her writing is autobiographical; instead, each work originates in her imagination, and each work is conceived in a different way. As to the relationship between her life and her writing, Godwin finds that an alternation between social experience and solitary existence in the country works best for her. As to her audience, she can see from her mail that her fiction does not appeal only to women, but is read by intelligent, attentive people of all sorts whose concerns are the same as hers: "how to live life bravely and well and fully and curiously."

Brownstein, Rachel M. "Gail Godwin: *The Odd Woman* and Literary Feminism." In *American Women Writing Fiction: Memory, Identity, Family, Space*, edited by Mickey Pearlman, pp. 172-184. Lexington: University Press of Kentucky, 1989.

In its emphasis on the need for self-realization, *The Odd Woman* is typical of the feminism of the 1970's. Many of the thoughts and experiences of its protagonist reflect preoccupations and attitudes that became central during that period. In later years, Godwin's views have changed, even as feminism has changed. Moreover, she refuses to accept simplistic assumptions or to accede to any polarization of "life and art, feminist and literary values." Her finest characters continue to be women who, like herself, are "engaged in writing their lives," in a deliberate and rational approach to understanding.

Cheney, Anne. "Gail Godwin and Her Novels." In *Southern Women Writers: The New Generation*, edited by Tonette Bond Inge, pp. 204-235. Tuscaloosa: University of Alabama Press, 1990.

A valuable essay that includes ample biographical details, a thoughtful appraisal of Godwin's place in contemporary literature, and an analysis of each of seven novels, concluding with *A Southern Family*. However far she has ranged in geographical setting, to Godwin the American South represents stability, family, a religious tradition, moral values, and sometimes, unfortunately, lethargy. Her primary characters are intelligent women, who have more difficulty in finding appropriate men than in making progress in their quests for the meaning of life. While Godwin's most popular books are not necessarily her best, by any standard she is one of the United States' most important contemporary writers.

_____. "A Hut and Three Houses: Gail Godwin, Carl Jung, and *The Finishing School*." *The Southern Literary Journal* 21 (Spring, 1989): 64-71.

Argues that though *The Finishing School* is set in upstate New York, the protagonist, Justin Stokes, is redeemed by developing a peculiarly Southern sense of place. To be initiated, she must proceed through four stages, symbolized by places, that is, "a hut and three houses." In this pattern, Godwin's interest in Jungian psychology is evident. Praises the novel as "a study of the life of the imagination versus the mundane," whose protagonist is another of Godwin's unforgettable Southern women.

Civello, Catherine. "George Eliot: From Middlemarch to Manhattan." *George Eliot Fellowship Review* 20 (1989): 52-56.
Points out incorporation of George Eliot in works of three women novelists, including Gail Godwin. The protagonist of *The Odd Woman*, who wrote her doctoral dissertation on Eliot's work, is constantly looking for parallels between her life and that of Eliot. Thus, Godwin's response to Eliot has become embedded in her own fiction.

Dyer, Joyce Coyne. "Gail Godwin's *The Finishing School*: A Contemporary Link to the Classic and the Moral." *Iowa English Bulletin* 35 (1987): 57-59.
Suggests assignment of *The Finishing School* in classes to introduce students to good contemporary fiction. The writer has found students enthusiastic about the novel, which she uses to illustrate romanticism, tragedy, mystery, and the Gothic, as well as the handling of narrative, point of view, and allusion.

Frank, Katherine. "*Violet Clay*: Portrait of the Artist as a Woman." *Iowa Journal of Literary Studies* 3 (1981): 118-122.
Calls *Violet Clay* a "deeply moving, brilliant novel." Unlike contemporary feminist novels, in which "the path to salvation ends with getting a man or getting yours," the protagonist of Godwin's book finds her own identity when she learns to transcend the demands of the ego, through "patience, discipline, and even sacrifice," and to submit herself to her art.

Frye, Joanne S. "Beyond Teleology: *Violet Clay* and *The Stone Angel*." In *Living Stories, Telling Lives: Women and the Novel in Contemporary Experience*, pp. 109-142. Ann Arbor: University of Michigan Press, 1986.
A discussion of Godwin's novel *Violet Clay* as a work in which the

painter-protagonist herself uses first-person narration to arrive at full self-realization. Frye sees both Violet and the story she is telling as operating simultaneously on three time schemes (past, present, and future), all of which become both the pattern of the novel and the pattern of Violet Clay's development. This interpretation of one of Godwin's less-acclaimed novels may provide the basis of a critical reassessment.

_____. "Narrating the Self: The Autonomous Heroine in Gail Godwin's *Violet Clay.*" *Contemporary Literature* 24 (Spring, 1983): 66-85.
A study of *Violet Clay* as an example of "the dangers and values of narration itself." While the protagonist is a painter, not a writer, it is through telling her own story that she comes to understand her past and therefore to define herself. Godwin's heroine has used narrative properly, to liberate herself, rather than to "deny and confine" herself.

Gardiner, Judith K. "A Sorrowful Woman': Gail Godwin's Feminist Parable." *Studies in Short Fiction* 12 (Summer, 1975): 286-290.
Examines Godwin's uncommon treatment of a common situation in the feminist short story "A Sorrowful Woman." By dramatizing the withdrawal from life of a housewife who is neither abused nor oppressed, Godwin forces her readers to ask whether it is the traditional feminine role, not the cast of characters, which has led so many women to despair.

Gaston, Karen C. "Beauty and the Beast' in Gail Godwin's *Glass People.*" *Critique: Studies in Contemporary Fiction* 21 (Summer, 1980): 94-102.
Looks at *Glass People* as a re-creation of "Beauty and the Beast" in which the heroine has to deal with the fact that the Beast's adoration deprives her of her own humanity. Gaston lauds Gail Godwin for using myths, ordinarily the property of male writers, in order to state her own feminist position.

Godwin, Gail. "Becoming a Writer." In *The Writer on Her Work*, edited by Janet Sternberg, pp. 231-255. New York: W. W. Norton, 1980.
An interesting exploration of the interplay between fact and fiction in the lives and works of both Gail Godwin and her writer-mother. The unconventional household in which the author spent some of her

formative years, composed of her grandmother, her breadwinner-mother, and herself, is described as an example of role-change, as well as an illustration of the ways in which writers develop their materials into publishable (or rejectable) form.

_____. "A Diarist on Diarists." In *Writers on Writing: A Bread Loaf Anthology*, edited by Robert Pack and Jay Parini, pp. 68-73. Hanover, N.H.: Middlebury College Press, published by University Press of New England, 1991.
The fact that many writers have been diarists, while others have had no interest in keeping a diary, proves to Godwin that the motivations and the processes of writing are quite distinct from those of diary-keeping. Since she began keeping her diary at age thirteen, Godwin has seen her relationship with her "fellow-traveler" change, if not develop. She comments upon a diarist's possible audience but suggests that if the work is to remain honest, it should not be shared until after the writer's death, when it might provide "examples, warnings, courage, amusement even" for the reader and, like literary works, "another proof of our ongoing survival."

_____. "Keeping Track." In *Ariadne's Thread: A Collection of Contemporary Women's Journals*, edited by Lyn Lifshin, pp. 75-85. New York: Harper & Row, 1982.
Selections from Gail Godwin's journals, 1962-1981. In the introduction, Godwin says that in her personal writing, she is undoubtedly as conscious of form as in her work for publication, but less constrained. Sometimes she is pleased with "bursts of wild candor and arrogance" in her journals and uses them in her fiction. All the journal passages quoted touch on the writing process, for example, the need to summon up will power, the struggle with exhaustion, especially under the pressure of other jobs, and the bouts of discouragement, as well as preoccupation with works in progress, which involves constant rethinking of scenes and characters.

_____. "The Many Masks of Kathleen Godwin and Charlotte Ashe." In *Family Portraits: Remembrances by Twenty Distinguished Writers*, edited by Carolyn Anthony, pp. 93-111. New York: Doubleday, 1989.
An affectionate essay about Godwin's mother, Kathleen Godwin, who in her early life wore "the mask of submissive wife" but later divorced her father, entered the work force, and revealed herself as

a different person. The title refers to the names under which Kathleen Godwin published two short romantic stories, in which Gail Godwin finds evidence of her mother's inner conflicts.

_____. "One Woman Leads to Another." *The New York Times Book Review* (April 28, 1985): 13-14.
Godwin's controversial review of *The Norton Anthology of Literature by Women*, blasting the editors of the volume for including works not on the basis of literary merit, but because they contained materials that were thought essential for a full rendering of the feminine experience. Godwin believes that it is no service to women writers when they are separated from the mainstream of literature. Such treatment, such "leveling of artists and their art," is offensive to Godwin "as a lover and teacher and practitioner of literature. And as a woman."

_____. "The Southern Belle." *Ms.* (July, 1975): 45-52, 84-85.
Only in the South is a girl presented with a stereotypical system that will determine her conduct throughout her life. Her mother trains her to avoid unpleasantness and, if necessary, to sacrifice herself rather than to cause embarrassment to others. Unfortunately, Southern mothers may end up vaguely unhappy, while Southern daughters who insist on thinking for themselves often leave the South in search of freedom. They take with them, however, many of the values they were taught, some of which admittedly are the trappings of civilization. Godwin hopes that at some point human beings, including "Southern Belles," will be able to escape from the stereotypes that imprison them. One of her most important statements, which bears on all of her fiction.

Graff, Gerald. "Tradition Versus Theory." In *Professing Literature: An Institutional History*, pp. 247-262. Chicago: University of Chicago Press, 1987.
Explores the conflict between traditional humanism and contemporary literary theory, including feminist criticism, which has resulted in polarization rather than in compromise. Points out that in Godwin's review of *The Norton Anthology of Literature by Women*, she objected to the editors' choice of works based on the latter's ability to illustrate the female experience rather than on the basis of quality, which she believed would give students using the book a faulty standard of judgment. While sharing Godwin's concern, Graff

suggests ways in which teachers can use the controversy between tradition and contemporary theory openly, as a stimulus to classroom discussion.

Halisky, Linda H. "Redeeming the Irrational: The Inexplicable Heroines of "A Sorrowful Woman' and "To Room Nineteen.' *Studies in Short Fiction* 27 (Winter, 1990): 45-54.

A comparison of stories by Gail Godwin and Doris Lessing, in which the protagonists' motivations are not immediately obvious. Although there are many similarities between the stories, in form Godwin's is more like a parable, as Gardiner suggested, while Lessing's, which is far more detailed, resembles a case history. Both end in tragedy. If, however, they stimulate greater efforts to understand the seemingly inexplicable nature of women, they can be seen as essentially redemptive.

Henderson, Katherine Usher. "Gail Godwin." In *Inter/View: Talks with America's Writing Women*, edited by Mickey Pearlman and Katherine Usher Henderson, pp. 30-39. Lexington: University Press of Kentucky, 1990.

An essay based on an interview. Of special interest are Godwin's remarks about *A Southern Family*, which is "based in part on a private family tragedy." In this book, the memories and dreams that influence the action must be related by women, since they are more open and less threatened than men. Women are capable of great depth of character; the young, modern heroine of *Father Melancholy's Daughter*, which is "a redemptory book" is an example. As writers, however, women must avoid their tendency to "qualify"; Godwin makes a conscious effort to be precise and direct. It is notable that she lists Mary Lee Settle among the contemporary writers who have influenced her work.

Lay, Mary M. "Gail (Kathleen) Godwin." In *Contemporary Novelists*, edited by D. Kirkpatrick, pp. 348-350. 4th ed. New York: St. Martin's Press, 1986.

Biographical data and critical essay. A central theme in Godwin's fiction is that women are forced to make choices that are only partially satisfactory and that later, at a time of crisis, can only be endured through the production of art or at least an artistic creation of a new identity. An excellent overview.

Lorsch, Susan E. "Gail Godwin's *The Odd Woman*: Literature and the Retreat from Life." *Critique: Studies in Contemporary Fiction* 20 (Winter, 1978): 21-32.
The author of this lucid and insightful essay sees the central theme of *The Odd Woman* as the relationship between literature and life. The effects of equating the two are particularly harmful for women, who then exercise poor judgment and set themselves up for disappointment. Even when she recognizes the fact that literature and life are not the same, a literary woman has difficulty fitting into the world and may eventually simply retreat into her imagination. Even though she recognizes the dangers of art, however, Godwin concludes her novel with an affirmation of its value.

Mickelson, Anne Z. "Gail Godwin: Order and Accommodation." In *Reaching Out: Sensitivity and Order in Recent American Fiction by Women*, pp. 68-86. Metuchen, N.J.: Scarecrow Press, 1979.
While many other contemporary women writers stress sexual freedom and outside activity as crucial goals for women, Godwin concentrates on the inner life, the need to preserve the self, despite the demands of relationships with others, and to "impose one's own order on life" so as to satisfy personal needs. This major theme is traced through the novels. Mickelson begins her essay by comparing Godwin's technique to that of George Eliot; she concludes with an analysis of *The Odd Woman* in which she says that "the spirit of George Eliot hovers over the book," and presumably over all of Godwin's fiction.

Miller, Nancy K. "Introduction." In *Subject to Change: Reading Feminist Writing*, pp. 1-21. New York: Columbia University Press, 1988.
After an overview of the growth of feminist criticism, Miller proceeds to a rebuttal of Godwin's review of the *Norton Anthology of Literature by Women*. Contends that Godwin's argument must be negated in that she based it on a passage from Virginia Woolf, which she misinterpreted. Explains Woolf's position in the context of feminist criticism.

Morrow, Mark. "Gail Godwin." In *Images of the Southern Writer*, pp. 34-35. Athens: University of Georgia Press, 1985.
In a brief and superficial interview conducted at a photo session, Godwin speaks of her years in journalism, her "education" through

novel-reading while she lived in London, and her association with other writers while she studied for her Ph.D. at the University of Iowa.

Naff, Beatrice. "A Mentor-Protégé Relationship: A Look at Gail Godwin's *The Finishing School.*" *Virginia English Bulletin* 36 (Winter, 1986): 126-130.
Explains how Godwin dramatizes the importance of a relationship between a teacher and a student, who absorbs her mentor's perceptions, even her "images, allusions and symbols," as well as her attitudes. The novel suggests how teachers in the liberal arts can help students develop their creative and critical abilities.

Nance, Guin A. "Gail Godwin." In *American Women Writers: A Critical Reference Guide from Colonial Times to the Present*, edited by Lina Mainiero. Vol. 2, pp. 148-150. New York: Frederick Ungar, 1979.
Biographical sketch and a discussion of Godwin's earlier fiction. A continuing preoccupation of the author is the difficulty of achieving a happy marriage. Too often wives are mere objects, powerless and without direction for their lives. Only in the final novel discussed, *Violet Clay*, does the woman protagonist manage to find self-fulfillment.

Reisman, Rosemary M. Canfield. "*Father Melancholy's Daughter.*" In *Magill's Literary Annual: Books of 1991*, edited by Frank N. Magill. Vol. 1, pp. 201-204. Englewood Cliffs, N.J.: Salem Press, 1992.
Examines the novel as a quest for truth conducted by the protagonist and narrator, Margaret Gower. Since the factual truth Margaret seeks is why her mother had long ago deserted her husband and her child, clearly the novel involves Godwin's major theme, the conflict between the demands of the self and the demands of others. In *Father Melancholy's Daughter*, however, Godwin has made an important change in the definition of self-fulfillment. Unlike her mother, Margaret attains a "spiritually significant life" through "selfless devotion to a higher good."

Renwick, Joyce. "An Interview with Gail Godwin." *Writer* (October, 1983): 15-17.
Interesting comments on technique: what Godwin does when a novel in progress falters, how she handles description, how she develops

plot and dialogue. She has changed her approach in that she depends
more on observation, less on abstract ideas. She also has become
confident about writing from a man's viewpoint.

Rhodes, Carolyn. "Gail Godwin and the Ideal of Southern Womanhood." In *Women Writers of the Contemporary South*, edited by
Peggy Whitman Prenshaw, pp. 54-66. Jackson: University Press of
Mississippi, 1984.
In her criticism and in her journalism, Godwin has outlined the ideal
of Southern womanhood, a system of behavior that has been
transmitted from mother to daughter for generations. The persistence
of this code can be seen in Godwin's women characters. Most of
them are complex, feeling at home with the graceful traditions of the
South, but experiencing frustration when they try to harmonize the
demands of the self with the rules of the code. Until *A Mother and
Two Daughters*, Godwin seemed to believe that the only way for a
Southern "lady" or "belle" to find her own identity is to leave the
South. In this comic novel, she shows three women remaining within
Southern society and managing to retain the "graces of Southern
ladies" while rejecting "hypocrisy and shallowness." For the first
time, in this novel Godwin suggests solutions for the problem that
has forced so many young Southern women to leave home.

Rogers, Kim Lacy. "A Mother's Story in a Daughter's Life: Gail
Godwin's *A Southern Family*." In *Mother Puzzles: Daughters and
Mothers in Contemporary American Literature*, edited by Mickey
Pearlman, pp. 59-66. Westport, Conn.: Greenwood Press, 1989.
Analysis of the novel on the basis of the study of family systems, as
the story of a family whose impetus to upward mobility is based on
self-deception and a misreading of the past. The daughter in the
story, Clare Quick, a writer, is hampered both in her life and in her
writing by her need to retell her mother's romantic version of family
history. With this novel, Godwin, too, has broken from her previous
insistence on happy endings and may herself move on "to a woman's
story, free of a mother's powerful charm and feminine delusions."

Smith, Marilynn J. "The Role of the South in the Novels of Gail
Godwin." *Critique: Studies in Contemporary Fiction* 21 (Summer,
1980): 103-110.
Contends that Godwin's Southern women are ambivalent about the
South and therefore unable to resolve their problems. On the one

hand, they see the South as a tempting retreat from life; on the other hand, they rebel against its traditional atmosphere, which they blame for their own inactivity and their inability to attain perfect happiness, which, unfortunately, they have been led to believe is attainable.

Smith, Virginia. "Gail Godwin's Paralyzing Plots and the Woman Professor." *West Virginia University Philological Papers* 36 (1990): 82-89.
A close analysis of *The Odd Woman*, illustrating Godwin's habit of echoing other texts and using references to earlier literary traditions, especially works reflecting the repressive, patriarchal attitudes of the nineteenth century. Godwin's references are particularly appropriate when, as in *The Odd Woman*, her heroine is a professor teaching fiction and, at the same time, reacting to it. The book ends on a note of hope, as the heroine begins to control her own imagination and to create her own life.

Taylor, Louise Todd. "Gail Godwin's *Odd Woman*: Not So Odd After All." *Mount Olive Review* 1 (Spring, 1987): 29-37.
Argues that the novel usually considered in terms of feminism is also profoundly Southern, not only in setting and in the theme of change and loss but also in the sense of place, emphasis on the family, and "the power of story-telling and myth." It is also, however, universal, reflecting the reactions of people in general, not only women, to a world that, in changing, seems to be stripping them of their identities.

Welch, Kathleen. "An Interview with Gail Godwin." *Iowa Journal of Literary Studies* 3 (1981): 77-86.
Focuses on the feminist tradition and Godwin's fiction, especially *The Odd Woman* and *Violet Clay*. Godwin objects to being limited in any way, such as being classified as "feminist" or "Southern." She is also concerned about readers who assume that her novels are feminist handbooks and change their own lives accordingly. Believes that American fiction is "fermenting," as seen, for example, in the new emphasis on women characters by men writers such as John Irving.

Wimsatt, Mary Ann. "Gail Godwin's Evolving Heroine: The Search for Self." *Mississippi Quarterly: The Journal of Southern Culture* 42 (Winter, 1988-1989): 27-45.

Pursuant to Godwin's own frequently expressed interest in the relationship between art and life, this essay points out the autobiographical basis for Godwin's novels. In the early books, her heroines were searching for their identity. With *A Southern Family*, Godwin seems to have moved on to protagonists whose self-sufficiency enables them, like Godwin herself, to focus on the outside world.

SHIRLEY ANN GRAU

Berland, Alwyn. "The Fiction of Shirley Ann Grau." *Critique* 6 (Spring, 1963): 78-84.
A review of Grau's "opus" after her third book, *The House on Coliseum Street*, was published. The reviewer is frustrated by the great promise of Grau's prose in the context of plots that seem to withdraw before their emotional or intellectual climax is achieved. In reference to *The Hard Blue Sky*, Berland finds Grau without "the firm center, the center of a vision, and hence the conviction of why her characters behave as they do."

"*The Black Prince and Other Stories*." In *Survey of Contemporary Literature*, edited by Frank N. Magill. Rev. and enlarged ed. Vol. 2, pp. 761-763. Englewood Cliffs, N.J.: Salem Press, 1977.
The reviewer finds Grau's presentation of the South "welcome, and seemingly more accurate" in her collection of stories. Particularly, Grau's control of detail and characterization is praised, with special attention to "White Girl, Fine Girl" and "The Black Prince." The reviewer is also impressed by Grau's portrayal of "the Negro side of Southern life."

Bukoski, Anthony. "The Burden of Home: Shirley Ann Grau's Fiction." *Critique* 28 (Summer, 1987): 181-194.
Takes on the many critics who fail to find a unifying principle behind Grau's works. For Bukoski, Grau's "characters fight the constricting regimen of domestic life and the houses which project it." This use of the house provides, in part, a unification of purpose in Grau, according to Bukoski. Notes and short bibliography.

Canfield, John. "A Conversation with Shirley Ann Grau." *Southern Quarterly* 25 (Winter, 1987): 39-52.
An interesting and probing interview covering a wide range of topics. Grau confirms the power of nature and place over her characters, as well as her concern for racial issues, especially her use of blacks as "mythical characters" at times as opposed to "primitives." Grau also

discusses what "Southern" writing means to her and the conscious
decision occasionally to depart from the South as her setting.

_____. "Women Alone." *The Southern Review* 22 (October,
1986): 904-906.
A favorable review of *Nine Women*, Grau's collection of short
stories. Points out the broadening theme of retrospection in her
stories (ironic given Grau's personal claims of always looking ahead,
not back). Credits her control of language as integral to the success
of the pieces in the collection.

Coles, Robert. "Mood and Revelation in the South." *The New Republic*
150 (April 18, 1964): 17-19.
Coles finds *The Keepers of the House* a pointed and eloquent
portrayal of class and race relations in the South. Grau's knowing
depiction of the "outside agitator" receives special praise. Coles
relates the novel to racial clashes being faced at the time of the
review and contends that Grau "does not shirk the complicated
nature of the problem."

DeBellis, Jack. "Two Southern Novels and a Diversion." *The Sewanee
Review* 70 (October-December, 1962): 691-694.
Charges Grau with forcing the characters of *The House on Coliseum
Street* into clichés. DeBellis believes that with such characters there
is little chance of success in treating Grau's main theme—"a sterile
society's self-conviction that evil can be negated by not acknowledging it." Praises her descriptive skills but finds the sum of the work
unrealized.

Donoghue, Denis. "Life Sentence." *The New York Review of Books* 17
(December 2, 1971): 28-30.
A clear reading of *The Condor Passes* with praise for Grau's
discipline against narrative effusions. Still, the reviewer longs for a
little more warmth and clutter. "Every episode is vividly illuminated,
but there is very little sense of a world and a time between the
lights," Donaghue states.

Eisinger, Chester E. "Grau, Shirley Ann." In *Contemporary Novelists*,
edited by James Vinson, pp. 514-516. New York: St. Martin's Press,
1972.
Categorizes Grau as a "local colorist" lacking true originality and

vision. Particularly faults Grau for being a white author attempting to depict black characters. Eisinger believes *The Keepers of the House* to be her best work to date, dealing with a broad range of issues from sense of place to interracial love. Still, he finds that "in depicting the defeat of the racist, Grau seems to depart from her characteristically objective stance."

Going, William T. "Alabama Geography in Shirley Ann Grau's *The Keepers of the House.*" In *Essays on Alabama Literature*, pp. 32-38. Tuscaloosa: The University of Alabama Press, 1975.
Intricately analyzes the geographic allusions of the novel and concludes that the setting is most likely Alabama. Going sees hints in everything from place names to jacket notes about Grau's upbringing in Alabama. The investigation seems circular, however, when the author himself posits that it is the mental state that is more important to the setting than the geographic state.

Gossett, Louise Y. "VIII. Primitives and Violence: Shirley Ann Grau." In *Violence in Recent Southern Fiction*, pp. 177-195. Durham, N.C.: Duke University Press, 1965.
Speaks of the inevitability of violent characters in Grau's fiction as a result of her selection of themes and places. Environment (be it climatic or social) seems more influential than inherent human flaws in outbreaks of violence. Grau, according to Gossett, "denies the romantic thesis that the elemental man is a free agent protected by his environment, for she stresses the violence of nature which assails him."

Grau, Joseph A., and Paul Schlueter. *Shirley Ann Grau: An Annotated Bibliography.* New York: Garland, 1981.
Expands on the bibliography at the end of Schlueter's book-length study (below). Valuable for more limited references to Grau in other works.

"Grau, Shirley Ann." In *World Authors, 1950-1970*, edited by John Wakeman, pp. 590-592. New York: H. W. Wilson, 1975.
Contains an amusing note by Grau in which she describes herself as "a happy and contented woman, and that's rather dull, I'm afraid—at least for other people, not for me." Also reviews the critical response to works published through 1973 as well as giving a short biographical sketch.

Grissom, Margaret S. "Shirley Ann Grau: A Checklist." *Bulletin of Bibliography* 28 (July-September, 1971): 76-78.
A useful compilation of sources for finding Grau's writings, including those not collected in book form. The bibliography does not contain critical sources. There is, however, a short introduction with biographical notes on Grau. Of special note may be the section listing "Articles" written by Grau on a range of topics from James Joyce to a New Orleans restaurant.

"*The Hard Blue Sky.*" In *Survey of Contemporary Literature*, edited by Frank N. Magill, Rev. and enlarged ed. Vol. 5, pp. 3253-3256. Englewood Cliffs, N.J.: Salem Press, 1977.
A review of Grau's second book (and first published novel). Notes her strong sense of place and avoidance of sentimentality. Characterizes Grau as a regional writer whose "effects are not those of style, symbol, or legend joined to moral intention, but of values close to . . . her chosen locale." Contains a bibliography pointing to further reviews of the novel.

Hoffman, Frederick J. *The Art of Southern Fiction: A Study of Some Modern Novelists*, pp. 106-109. Carbondale: Southern Illinois University Press, 1967.
A very brief review of Grau's works, with special emphasis on *The Keepers of the House*. Finds Grau's works full of great ambition and evident skill, but unfortunately occasionally diminished by rambling and repetitive narrative. Hoffman contends that Grau is overly concerned by "the genuinely native particulars of a scene" at the expense of larger themes.

Husband, John D. *New Mexico Quarterly* 28 (Spring, 1958): 61-65.
Husband is Grau's former writing teacher. He praises *The Hard Blue Sky* as a first novel promising a great deal. He does hope for a less removed tone in future writing but finds the design of her work full of merit. Interesting notes on Husband's view of what constitutes creative writing "training" are interspersed with his review of the novel.

Johnson, Richard A. "*The Keepers of the House.*" In *Survey of Contemporary Literature*, edited by Frank N. Magill, Rev. and enlarged ed. Vol. 6, pp. 3981-3983. Englewood Cliffs, N.J.: Salem Press, 1977.

Review of Grau's novel, noting the role of the natural world in
defining character, particularly in the "frontier society" of the South.
According to Johnson, Grau pilots her narrative directly between
segregationist and antisegregationist views because "both ignore . . .
the importance both of building civilization and of doing so with full
awareness of the harsh realities of the natural world."

Luedtke, Luther S. "The Condor Passes." In *Survey of Contemporary
Literature*, edited by Frank N. Magill, Rev. and enlarged ed., Vol. 3,
pp. 1513-1516. Englewood Cliffs, N.J.: Salem Press, 1977.
A worthwhile summary of the novel with special note of its
antecedents in other literature. Luedtke finds the tale engaging in
concept but unfulfilling in execution, lacking either passionate
subjectivity or telling objectivity. *"The Condor Passes* is a strangely
mute, hollow, and dispersive work, its rapacities and adulteries
notwithstanding," the reviewer posits. Overall, he believes Grau has
yet to establish a clear, definitive voice throughout her works.

Pearlman, Mickey. "Shirley Ann Grau." In *Inter/View: Talks with
America's Writing Women*, by Mickey Pearlman and Katherine
Usher Henderson, pp. 132-135. Lexington: University Press of
Kentucky, 1990.
In a piece that is more essay than interview, Pearlman relates the
biographical background of Grau and charts her publishing history
(up through *Nine Women*). One of the topics here is Grau's views on
children (her own) and mother-daughter relationships. Grau appears
to favor genetic over environmental influences for the end products.
She also finds "that some people are just so hooked into eternal self-
analysis." Grau is reluctant to analyze her own writings. Pearlman
comments on *Nine Women* as being about women "caught in that
amorphous middle place between the initiation of events and their
resolution."

Pearson, Ann. "Shirley Ann Grau: Nature Is the Vision." *Critique* 17
(December, 1975): 47-58.
A study of Grau's recurring use of the natural setting as a primary
force in her fiction. Concludes that Grau frustrates her own intent by
the impersonality of her portrayal of nature. Even those drawn to
Grau's fine details will be let down by the lack of thematic force,
Pearson contends.

Rohrberger, Mary. "Conversation with Shirley Ann Grau and James K. Feibleman." *Cimarron Review* 43 (April, 1978): 35-45.
A noteworthy encounter between Grau and her husband (Feibleman). Feibleman is a poet and philosopher whose "theoretical" approaches to art contrast greatly with his wife's. Grau comments on her identification as a "Southern" writer, finding it limiting, adding, "I don't think there is any 'Southern' literature now at all." Short biographies of each at the end.

_____. "Shirley Ann Grau and the Short Story." In *Women Writers of the Contemporary South*, edited by Peggy Whitman Prenshaw, pp. 83-102. Jackson: University Press of Mississippi, 1984.
Survey of Grau's developing short story technique, beginning with her early undergraduate days at Tulane. Rohrberger places special emphasis on the thread of themes running throughout, especially as they contradict the "regionalist" label often applied to Grau's work. Worthwhile for summaries of early stories not otherwise collected. Also of note, see Laurie L. Brown's "Interview with Seven Contemporary Writers" (pp. 3-22) in this same volume. Grau responds (as do the other six authors) to an array of questions concerning why she writes, for whom she writes, and how she deals with being a "woman" writer.

_____. "So Distinct a Shade': Shirley Ann Grau's *Evidence of Love*." *The Southern Review* 14 (January, 1978): 195-198.
More analysis than review of the novel, with close examination of narrative structures and the theme of the love quest. The search is "for order and understanding that can only come through an apprehension of shadows," Rohrberger posits. Ends with an appeal for Grau to receive better attention than has been given her, countering the regionalist tag.

Ross, Jean W. "Shirley Ann Grau." In *Dictionary of Literary Biography: American Novelists Since World War II*, edited by Jeffrey Helterman and Richard Layman. Vol. 2, pp. 208-215. Detroit: Gale Research, 1978.
A general review of her writings. Posits an early focus on the primitives of the Southern Gothic tradition that was expanded in later, more complex works. Finds her recurring weaknesses to be "a lack of dramatic force and depth of characterization." Suggests that,

in trying to avoid the "Southern" label, Grau may be turning her back on what is one of her greatest strengths.

Saunders, John K. "Shirley Ann Grau." In *Critical Survey of Long Fiction*, edited by Frank N. Magill. Vol. 3, pp. 1182-1190. Englewood Cliffs, N.J.: Salem Press, 1983.
Consideration of Grau's achievements in works through *Evidence of Love* (1977). Saunders believes that Grau "has shifted her emphasis away from the engaging plot to the creation of a cool, ironic vision of psychological intensity." Notes her battle against labels of "local colorist" or "one-novel writer." Covers biographical background, critical reception, and analysis of her works. Limited bibliography.

Schlueter, Paul. *Shirley Ann Grau*. Boston: Twayne, 1981.
The starting point for any investigation, since this is the only comprehensive study of Grau and her work (as of 1992). The author is reluctant to label Grau "a major southern writer" yet finds that "many of her characters are among the most memorable in recent American fiction." Also contains helpful notes, bibliography, and index. See the entry under Joseph Grau and Paul Schlueter, above, for an annotated bibliography of this volume.

_____. "Shirley Ann Grau." In *Fifty Southern Writers After 1900*, edited by Joseph M. Flora and Robert Bain, pp. 225-234. New York: Greenwood Press, 1987.
An excellent summary of Grau's biography, major themes, and critical response. In this essay, Schlueter condenses many of his opinions from his book, including his disappointment at the lack of substantial study of her works. Schlueter contends that Grau has grown past her regional limitations. Includes bibliography.

Shinn, Thelma J. "Shirley Ann Grau." In *American Women Writers*, edited by Lina Mainiero. Vol. 2, pp. 171-174. New York: Frederick Ungar, 1980.
Quick outline of Grau's works. Praises her stylistic mastery, descriptive power, and feminine imagery. Shinn defines Grau's compelling elements as her fascination with primitives, "her interest in family and social heritage," and "her consummate skill at manipulating point of view." She further praises Grau's ability "to empathize with each character." Brief bibliography.

Simpson, Lewis P. "Introduction." In *Three By Three: Masterworks of the Southern Gothic*, pp. vii-xiv. Atlanta: Peachtree, 1985.
The work collects three writers' stories, including Grau's *The Black Prince*. Simpson provides lucid notes on the tradition of the Southern gothic and places Grau among its contemporary practitioners who blend "realism and grotesquery in a manner that we readily grasp as typical of the Southern literary imagination but find almost impossible to explicate critically."

Wagner-Martin, Linda. "Shirley Ann Grau's Wise Fictions." In *Southern Women Writers: The New Generation*, edited by Tonette Bond Inge, pp. 143-160. Tuscaloosa: The University of Alabama Press, 1990.
Despite Grau's personal objection to the labels "Southern" and "woman" writer, Wagner-Martin places her in both categories and finds Grau's work significant in both contexts. The author argues that much of Grau has been misread partially because of Grau's "distance" from her characters in her narrative style. Further, Wagner-Martin contends that what makes Grau most memorable is "her consistent concern for non-white culture . . . and the way that culture impinges on the patriarchal matrix that seems to dominate Southern life."

Walsh, William J. "Shirley Ann Grau." In *Speak So I Shall Know Thee: Interviews with Southern Writers*, pp. 135-145. Jefferson, N.C.: McFarland, 1990.
Grau speaks in her characteristic straightforward manner about her life as a writer. She finds no great reward in being a Pulitzer Prize winner or in looking back at her early works. The interview contains interesting references to a "very comfortable" childhood that provided the environment more than the material for her later writing. Grau reemphasizes her dislike for the labels "Southern" or "woman" writer.

Williams, Thomas. "Ducks, Ships, Custard, and a King." *The Kenyon Review* 24 (Winter, 1962): 184-188.
Williams feels confounded by limitations of *The House on Coliseum Street*'s main characters, especially as they reflect Grau's self-imposed stylistic limitations. He finds the protagonist's world dull and dulling to the reader. Grau's faithfulness to Joan's limited perceptions makes Williams "uncomfortably aware of style."

SHELBY HEARON

Ames, Katrine. "*Hug Dancing*." *Newsweek* (November 18, 1991): 81.
This review calls the novel a "tangy Texas fairy tale." Ames notes
a favorite theme of Hearon's—"freewill versus determinism"—at
work in *Hug Dancing*. Hearon's particular attention to language,
most notably in Cile Tait's words, is praised: "Cile is word perfect,
a woman who knows the real meaning of practically everything."

"*Armadillo in the Grass.*" *The New York Times Book Review* (September 22, 1968): 37.
A short note on the novel. Sees the work as presenting a choice for
Clara Blue between two men: her sculpture teacher on the one hand,
and her husband ("a cloddish academician") on the other. "Unfortunately, her resources in this novel are too limited to make either
contender very interesting," concludes the review.

Bennett, Patrick. "Shelby Hearon: Time, Sex, and God." In *Talking with
Texas Writers: Twelve Interviews*, pp. 111-134. College Station:
Texas A&M Press, 1980.
This interview took place in 1978. Hearon discusses in some
theoretical detail the movements in her writing—from determinism
to the structural elements of her books (theater as a strong structural
element). Also provides colorful autobiographical notes. Hearon
claims she has no understanding of the short story. She details her
work habits. As far as her characters, Hearon concludes: "I have to
know where everybody stands on God and sex and time."

Brans, Jo. "She Liked Whate'er She Looked On." *Southwest Review* 69
(Autumn, 1984): 470-472.
Brans is drawn to Lutie in *Group Therapy* in much the same way
that "Lutie moves toward pleasure as a sunflower turns toward
light." Brans's essay draws on her own life as a Texan transplanted
to New York: "I find nuggets of sociological insight that I am
validating with my own experience." The vivid characterizations are
a special delight to the essayist.

Cunningham, Laura. "Lovers and Movies." *The New York Times Book Review* (August 2, 1981): 15.
Review of *Painted Dresses* as "a very lacy Valentine." Cunningham is sympathetic to a reader's confusion early on but finds Hearon's design unfolded by the end. "Every scene is painted in color, and the outlines are drawn with equal care," the reviewer says. Cunningham admires the depiction of the minor characters as well.

Flynt, Candace. "Generational Gaps and Gripes." *The Washington Post Book World* (April 10, 1983): 8.
Afternoon of a Faun reviewed as a promising failure. Flynt blames the failure not on the writing and characterizations but on the resolution of the book. The characters appear to learn nothing, and Flynt poses that "perhaps Hearon thought it would be too easy a resolution to let the children learn something from each other."

Geeslin, Campbell. "*A Small Town*." *People* (October 28, 1985): 16.
Geeslin calls this novel "funny, paranoid, prickly, loving and true." Wonders how Alma misses the clues to her mother's alcoholism given how bright she seems to be otherwise. Still, the book "delivers a whole town full of complex, eccentric and intense characters."

Guy, David. "Meetings at Midlife." *The Washington Post Book World* (June 14, 1981): 8, 13.
Guy finds *Painted Dresses* slow to start but worth the wait. Hearon "writes with the buoyant precise prose of a veteran novelist." The most important theme of the book, Guy posits, is that love comes to the characters "after years of sorting through things they don't really want."

Jefferson, Margo. "*A Prince of a Fellow*." *Newsweek* (July 3, 1978): 80.
"Hearon writes with quick intelligence and a humor that is both tender and ironic," according to Jefferson's review. *A Prince of a Fellow* is a fairy tale but one with a difference. The happy ending is postponed until the main character comes to terms with the concrete truths of her choice. As Jefferson puts it, Hearon "understands that the nicest fantasies sometimes have a firm grounding in reality."

Levin, Beth. "PW Interviews Shelby Hearon." *Publishers Weekly* (April 3, 1987): 56-57.
An essay based on an interview. Promotes *Five Hundred Scorpions*

but also covers most of her other novels. Hearon speaks of her continual play with the idea of determinism. She concedes that she considers place first in her works. "I always want to walk the ground and get a feel for its power, its limitations. From that I find out who would live there and what could happen there." Hearon details the extensive research that goes into her works.

Levin, Martin. *"Hannah's House."* *The New York Times Book Review* (June 15, 1975): 26.
Review of *Hannah's House.* Notes the family satire implicit in this novel. "Shelby Hearon works up an interesting set of tensions among her characters: mothers, daughters, sisters, fathers, ex-spouses." Levin believes the novel "is constructed of quiet familial paradoxes."

_____. "New and Novel." *The New York Times Book Review* (October 7, 1973): 47.
Short review of *The Second Dune.* The book, in Levin's succinct summation, proves "being married isn't easy." In the Texas world of Ellen Marshall, Hearon "says interesting things about a contretemps that usually generates more heat than light."

Marshall, Carol. "The Fairy Tale and the Frontier: Images of Women in Texas Fiction." In *The Texas Literary Tradition: Fiction, Folklore, History*, edited by Don Graham, James W. Lee, and William T. Pilkington, pp. 195-206. Austin: University of Texas Press, 1983.
Among the works considered here is Hearon's *Hannah's House.* Marshall explores the portrayals of Texas women facing conflicts between traditional expectations of the "fairy tale" and their needs for self-definition. Hannah is driven to realize her dream version of life. "Hannah arranges her house and herself with great care to be sure that the wind [of chaos] does no damage."

Pei, Lowry. "He Should Have Stayed in Charlottesville." *The New York Times Book Review* (May 10, 1987): 7.
"Five Hundred Scorpions is witty, fast-paced and oddly (given everything else) benign," Pei contends in this review. The odd combination comes from the challenge Hearon has given herself in depicting both "the demonic and the domestic" wherein the ambiguous can be as compelling as the definitive. Hearon is praised for avoiding the easy ideologies her narrative might have allowed.

"*A Prince of a Fellow.*" *The New Yorker* (June 5, 1978): 116-117.
Short review. Suggests "the book is less important for its plot than for the thorough portrait of a woman that rises out of Mrs. Hearon's short and sweet account of most particular people living and working in a most particular place."

Rimland, Ingrid. "A Pleasure of Craft Sails Below a Story." *Los Angeles Times Book Review* (April 3, 1983): 9.
Rimland considers the material thin but the execution masterly in *Afternoon of a Faun*. Hearon's plot makes liberal use of fate, but her characters are full and understandable, Rimland suggests. Overall, however, it is Hearon's writing that carries the work. "There are still writers who write so well they manage to be published for no other reason. That is a pleasure in itself."

Sandlin, Tim. "A Normal Life, with Oven Mitts." *The New York Times Book Review* (January 22, 1989): 10-11.
Sandlin reviews *Owning Jolene* as one that amazingly holds together given the twists of plot and character, especially for the main character, Jolene. "A lot is made of normal in *Owning Jolene,* maybe because no one in the book has a whiff of what the concept means." The ending tends to pull events together too quickly to be believable, but Sandlin is still charmed, mostly by Jolene. "Somehow, out of the strangeness of her childhood, she has developed that mixture of toughness and vulnerability most of us strive for, both in fiction and in life."

Tallent, Elizabeth. "Venice Observed." *The New York Times Book Review* (October 20, 1985): 22.
Review of *A Small Town*. Tallent sees Alma as growing "from an abused child with a Huckleberry Finn spunkiness into a high-school Lolita, from a principal's dutiful wife into a trailer-park adulteress." The links between those transitions are not always clear to the reader, however, and details of plot and character sometimes get misplaced, according to Tallent. The flow of the writing soothes some of those cracks.

Tyler, Anne. "Lady of the Lone Star State." *The Washington Post Book World* (April 2, 1978): E4.
Tyler reviews *A Prince of a Fellow* in light of Hearon's prior works. When Avery Krause is compared to "the complex and original

women" of those works, Avery falls short. Tyler praises the landscape of the fiction, the unexpected relationships Hearon creates, yet concludes that Hearon falls short with the main character. Tyler offers an axiom for the work: "A book can have just about anyone for a heroine—even an outright villainess—as long as she assigns herself some worth that makes us want to identify with her."

Willison, Marilyn Murray. "A Novel Exercise to Emotional Catharsis." *Los Angeles Times Book Review* (May 27, 1984): 14.
Review of *Group Therapy*. Willison compares Hearon to "a female Larry McMurtry with humor, pain, surprise and resolution in a single entertaining package." Willison is most compelled by the main character, Lutie, who "combines straightforwardness with a touching no-nonsense brand of vulnerability." Predicts greater popularity for Hearon.

JILL McCORKLE

Bell, Pearl K. "Southern Discomfort." *The New Republic* (February 29, 1988): 38-41.

Reviews *Tending to Virginia* in the larger context of other contemporary writers such as Gail Godwin and Kaye Gibbons and the history of Southern literature. Bell finds much of the literary landscape altered since the time of Faulkner and Welty but with the common link to the past authors being "that enduring concern with family." Unlike her earlier *The Cheer Leader*, McCorkle's *Tending* is intimately connected to its Southern locale. Unfortunately for Bell, it is too full of details causing "a coma of boredom." She believes the novel to be "stillborn."

Chappell, Fred. "Powder Puffs and Loose Peanuts." *Chronicles of Culture* 9 (July, 1985): 6-7.

This essay discusses McCorkle in the context of similar writers— such as Lee Smith, Bobbie Ann Mason, Anne Tyler—with a penchant for detailed portrayals of "lower-middle-class" characters. Chappell believes "*The Cheer Leader* and *July 7th* well deserve their success and celebrity." Notes the cynicism about the world depicted and the almost valueless tone of the authors toward their characters.

"*Crash Diet: Stories.*" *Publishers Weekly* (February 3, 1992): 61.

Short review denotes *Crash Diet* as a book of special merit, calling it a "peppery, potent collection" of short stories about women. The eleven stories portray women characters of "extraordinary depth and dimension." The reviewer finds no weak stories in the group, which range from optimistic to sorrowful in tone.

"*Ferris Beach.*" *The Virginia Quarterly Review* 67 (Spring, 1991): 57.

This brief note applauds the "poetic clarity" of McCorkle's narrative. Recommends the book as one that "invites both tears and laughter" in the portrayal of "funny, real characters who show us that ultimately people are good."

Gottlieb, Annie. "Manic Jo and Romantic Sam." *The New York Times Book Review* (October 7, 1984): 9.

This review of *The Cheer Leader* and *July 7th* helped bring McCorkle national regard. Gottlieb makes special note of the growth apparent from the "first" novel to the "second." "The leap from "The Cheer Leader,' a good but familiar first novel showing glimmers of wicked talent, to "July 7th,' a book bighearted enough to embrace a whole small town, is startling."

Harris, Michael. *"Ferris Beach."* *Los Angeles Times Book Review* (October 14, 1990): 6.

This review pinpoints the issue of class above race as central to Kate's struggle. Harris finds the level of detail and empathy in the account engaging. McCorkle is credited with avoiding obvious morals. Harris concludes that McCorkle's "skill with character, in particular, adds an adult dimension to a novel that will also appeal to readers Kate's age."

Hegi, Ursula. "A Couple of Novels from the Same Southern Milieu." *Los Angeles Times* (November 15, 1984): p. 34.

Review of *The Cheer Leader* and *July 7th*. In the first, Hegi sees McCorkle taking "a startling and unsentimental look at popularity and its price, at the rituals that hold people together." In *July 7th*, "McCorkle's attempt at multiple point of view is ambitious but lends a fragmented quality to the first part of the novel," according to the review.

Hooper, Brad. "Adult Fiction." *Booklist* 88 (January 15, 1992): 883.

Reviews *Crash Diet*, a collection of stories "on women who, when pushed, show untapped reservoir of moxie." Hooper notes the "purposely flat style" of McCorkle's narratives as a way to portray the characters' ordinariness, yet without passing up the chance for "droll humor."

Leider, Emily. "Brer Rabbit's Gone, but Burger King's Doing Fine." *San Francisco Chronicle Review* (November 22, 1987): 1, 10.

Tending to Virginia is described as "an abundant, lyrical and great-hearted third novel." Young and old characters shine, in Leider's estimation, although the men are dim creations next to the women of the novel. Leider believes Ginny Sue comes off at times as "a bit of a sap" but finds her well-balanced by the other characters in this "novel to be remembered and celebrated."

Levering, Frank. "New South Humor." *Los Angeles Times Book Review* (November 29, 1987): 15.

Review of *Tending to Virginia* that at first labels the book as "static," then calls it "nonetheless, the work of a prodigious young talent." Levering finds the characters of working-class women exceptional portrayals, especially with regard to the on-target dialogue. He wishes, however, that their thoughts were less revealing and their actions more so. The same review appears again on January 10, 1988.

Loewinsohn, Ron. "The World Across the Street." *The New York Times Book Review* (October 7, 1990): 10.

A review of *Ferris Beach*, "her most satisfying performance to date, again allowing us to laugh at her characters' follies and illusions while empathizing with their pain." Loewinsohn finds her women complex and engaging (while her men remain somewhat less developed). The reviewer also differentiates McCorkle's approach from stories about "the emotionally anesthetized New South of broken families and fast-food chains that we find in Frederick Barthelme's books."

McDermott, Alice. *"Tending to Virginia."* *The New York Times Book Review* (October 11, 1987): 1, 26.

McDermott admires the use of voice in the novel. "It is this talking—the perfect dialogue, the vivid recollections, the memories and emotions that in the end will not fit neatly into the shape of its plot—that make "Tending to Virginia' so rewarding." The end of the review has a brief biographical note based on a phone interview by Deborah Stead.

Manuel, Diane. "Southern Eccentrics Worthy of Off-Broadway." *The Christian Science Monitor* (January 5, 1988): 18.

Reviews *Tending to Virginia* as "a distinctly regional work that brims over with the cadence of small-town conversations and events." Manuel is enthusiastic about the colorful characters and the frank exchanges to which the reader is privy. The dramatic devices employed are effective in the reviewer's eye, causing her to conclude that "McCorkle has a heart wise beyond her years."

Max, Daniel. *"Tending to Virginia."* *Boston Review* 13 (February, 1988): 27.

Max believes McCorkle is the finest new writer of the Algonquin Press and that *Tending to Virginia* presents "greater complexity" than her previous accomplished works. "McCorkle simply has a gift for rendering voices," Max posits. He wishfully looks forward to a movie version of the book.

Moss, Ann DeWitt. "Jill McCorkle." In *Dictionary of Literary Biography Yearbook: 1987*, edited by J. M. Brook, pp. 366-370. Detroit: Gale Research, 1988.
Moss works for the publishing house that released McCorkle's first two novels (simultaneously). Thus, the entry contains authoritative insights into McCorkle's young but notable career, especially her indebtedness to North Carolina writers and teachers such as Lee Smith and Louis Rubin. Summarizes the novels (up through *Tending*) and critical responses to them. No bibliography but internal allusions to some secondary works.

Muchnick, Laurie. "Southern Discomfort." *The Village Voice* 35 (November 20, 1990): 82.
Review of *Ferris Beach*. Initially put off by the "coming-of-age" theme, the reviewer is pleasantly surprised by McCorkle's feat. "Kate's voice is the book's greatest pleasure. From the opening lines, I was hooked by her vulnerability and wit," Muchnick writes. She acknowledges the sometimes random nature of the plot but finds the growth of Kate compelling enough "to follow wherever the novel may take her."

"*Tending to Virginia*." *The Virginia Quarterly Review* 64 (Spring, 1988): 58.
High praise for this book, as well as McCorkle's two prior ones. The reviewer believes that the author has become one of the most talented writers of her region. "McCorkle digs ever deeper into the psyches of these ordinary women whose lives have ranged from constructive to blighted," the reviewer notes, adding that "they become extraordinary, fascinating, and, one predicts, unforgettable."

BOBBIE ANN MASON

Anderson, Nancy G. "Bobbie Ann Mason." In *Dictionary of Literary Biography Yearbook: 1987*, edited by J. M. Brook, pp. 351-359. Detroit: Gale Research, 1988.

A fine summary of Mason's career and writings. Includes discussion of her nonfiction works as well as her short stories and her novel *In Country*. Notes that "rural Kentucky and the changes caused by urban development have provided Bobbie Ann Mason with many of her subjects, characters, and themes." Helpful bibliographies of works by and about Mason.

Arnold, Edwin T. "Falling Apart and Staying Together: Bobbie Ann Mason and Leon Driskell Explore the State of the Modern Family." *Appalachian Journal* 12 (Winter, 1985): 135-141.

A general discussion of Mason's contribution to the voice of Kentucky storytelling. Arnold makes a few pointed observations. For example, he posits the "central irony" of Mason's stories: "[T]he young look to the traditions, the histories, they had once scorned or been ashamed of, while the old tend to cut themselves off from the same traditions and histories in order to face the world as they find it."

Barnes, Linda Adams. "The Freak Endures: The Southern Grotesque from Flannery O'Connor to Bobbie Ann Mason." In *Since Flannery O'Connor: Essays on the Contemporary American Short Story*, edited by Loren Logsdon and Charles W. Mayer, pp. 133-141. Macomb: Western Illinois University, 1987.

Barnes believes "the grotesque of Bobbie Ann Mason is firmly rooted in the tradition of Flannery O'Connor." This essay traces a path from O'Connor to Mason, noting a shift from the redemptive aspects of these characters in O'Connor to the more matter-of-fact tone in Mason. Still, Barnes concludes, both share an eye for the comic and instructional uses of the grotesque.

Blais, Ellen A. "Gender Issues in Bobbie Ann Mason's *In Country*." *South Atlantic Review* 56 (May, 1991): 107-118.

Examines *In Country* as being about changing roles for men and women. Blais believes both Sam and Emmett challenge traditional versions of their genders. Mason connects these gender issues to questions about the Vietnam War. According to Blais, for Sam "to understand her father is, in a sense, to understand the masculine part of herself." Notes, bibliography.

Bloom, Alice. Review of *In Country*. *New England Review and Bread Loaf Quarterly* 8 (Summer, 1986): 513-525.
Along with Tyler's *The Accidental Tourist* and George Dennison's *Luisa Domic*, Mason's novel is a hard examination of the United States. "I have no heart left for life in America at all, and no hope for any of her characters, or real-life people like them, when Mason is finished with them," Bloom proclaims. Bloom finds the very limited vocabulary of Sam and the people around her part of the limitations of the novel.

Brinkmeyer, Robert H., Jr. "Finding One's History: Bobbie Ann Mason and Contemporary Southern Literature." *The Southern Literary Journal* 19 (Spring, 1987): 20-33.
Mason is seen as standing apart from the portion of Southern literature so concerned with historical perspective. Mason's scenes "illustrate the undermining, if not the utter collapse, of the family unit," according to Brinkmeyer. *In Country* is populated by people for whom history "is merely a saccharine nostalgia." This fading of lines between what is Southern and what is American indicates, to Brinkmeyer, a growing new approach to the region's literature.

_____. "Never Stop Rocking: Bobbie Ann Mason and Rock-and-Roll." *Mississippi Quarterly* 42 (Winter, 1988-1989): 5-17.
Brinkmeyer traces rock images and influences through Mason's fiction. "Mason's fascination with rock music clearly transcends merely musical enjoyment . . . and might be best understood as a crucial element in her larger interest in and sympathy for popular culture." The essay concludes by suggesting that the music is a metaphor for the tensions of the characters' lives, "the dream of a better life, the displacement in crossing cultures."

DeVries, Hilary. "Mining the Vagaries of Rural America." *The Christian Science Monitor* (November 20, 1985): 28.
An essay based on an interview. Mason questions all the acclaim she

has received so quickly: "[N]o human ought to have that much attention." She also claims a close attachment to the struggles and escapes of her rural characters yet does not believe that "they're going to find answers in a K mart."

Durham, Sandra Bonilla. "Women and War: Bobbie Ann Mason's *In Country.*" *The Southern Literary Journal* 22 (Spring, 1990): 45-52. Largely a review of the novel and its major themes. Durham notes the range of effects examined by *In Country*, beyond Sam's quest for her father's history to the very nature of family and American culture. "*In Country* shows how the conscious and subconscious minds of three generations of men and women have been affected by the Vietnam War."

Gholson, Craig. "Bobbie Ann Mason." *Bomb* 28 (Summer, 1989): 40-43.
An interview with Mason as *In Country* is preparing for release and *Spence + Lila* is being adapted for Public Broadcasting Service. Usual range of topics from her Kentucky upbringing to the strivings of her characters. Includes notable answers on the importance of the language for Mason. "I feel that my style derives from the language of farm life which is very practical and not decorative," she observes.

Gilman, Owen W., Jr., and Lorrie Smith, eds. *America Rediscovered: Critical Essays on Literature and Film of the Vietnam War.* New York: Garland, 1990.
Two essays in this collection refer to Mason's *In Country.* Milton J. Bates's "Men, Women, and Vietnam" (pp. 27-63) examines the roles of the sexes as seen through a number of works, particularly citing Mason's as one that does "not use war to challenge conventional notions of manhood and womanhood." Marilyn Durham's "Narrative Strategies in Recent Vietnam War Fiction" looks at how point of view strengthens or weakens a Vietnam tale. Sam's perspective as a nonsoldier helps the reader (as a nonsoldier) become more involved and "deepens our emotional response."

Havens, Lila. "Residents and Transients: An Interview with Bobbie Ann Mason." *Crazy Horse* 29 (Fall, 1985): 87-104.
This interview contains a good number of pithy observations by Mason on her writing. She calls her genre "Southern Gothic Goes to

the Supermarket" and proclaims, "I learned more from the Bobbsey Twins than I did from creative writing workshops." Wide array of other topics included.

Henning, Barbara. "Minimalism and the American Dream: "Shiloh' by Bobbie Ann Mason and "Preservation' by Raymond Carver." *Modern Fiction Studies* 35 (Winter, 1989): 689-698.
A response to critics of Mason and Carver who are "suspicious of their stories because of the lack of metaphoric depth and because of the flat and robotic lives the characters lead." Henning attempts to show how Mason is a minimalist in the best sense, inviting the reader "to do her part, to make connections, . . . simply to care about the characters and their predicaments."

Hulbert, Ann. "Rural Chic." *The New Republic* (September 2, 1985): 25-30.
Comments on *In Country* in the context of other books and films exploring the "pastoral myth" of the rural United States. Hulbert questions the motives of the writers and filmmakers. The populist ideal seems to betray itself in close examination, she seems to say, even more so in the fiction than in the films.

Mason, Bobbie Ann. "Reaching the Stars: My Life as a Fifties Groupie." In *A World Unsuspected: Portraits of Southern Childhood*, edited by Alex Harris, pp. 53-77. Chapel Hill: University of North Carolina Press, 1987.
This essay originally appeared in *The New Yorker* (May 26, 1985). Recounts Mason's early obsession with music and film stars, especially the Hilltoppers, for whose fan club she was national president during her mid-teens. Mason quotes from the newsletter she wrote and relates her reluctant retirement from the post in college. Useful as a source for her literary obsessions with pop culture.

Morphew, G. O. "Downhome Feminists in *Shiloh and Other Stories*." *The Southern Literary Journal* 21 (Spring, 1989): 41-49.
Mason presents the rural version of women's rights, according to Morphew. "Mason's women simply want breathing space in their relationships with their men." Instead of reaching for the city version of equal pay, political rights, and so forth, Mason's female characters choose divorce or casual adultery to break free, Morphew explains.

Myers, Thomas. "Dispatches from Ghost Country: The Vietnam Veteran in Recent American Fiction." *Genre* 21 (Winter, 1988): 409-428.
Places *In Country* in the context of other fiction and film on the Vietnam experience. Myers concludes that, while not being an innovative masterpiece, the novel "succeeds as a healing ritual because of its specific dramatic elements"—that is, because its realistic portrayal allows the reader to enter the world of Emmett and Sam and accept the reality of their experiences.

Pierce, Constance. "Contemporary Fiction and Popular Culture." *Michigan Quarterly Review* 26 (Fall, 1987): 663-672.
According to Pierce, "Mason's work . . . resonates with the implications of popular artifacts and entertainments." Pierce also finds *In Country* telling as to the readers' own "dumping ground" minds, filled as they are with pop icons. Also considers "Shiloh" in the context of the discussion.

Rothstein, Mervyn. "Homegrown Fiction." *The New York Times Magazine* (May 15, 1988): 50- .
From an interview. Mason explains how she has attempted to violate the literary tradition of the "alienated hero." "I think where I wind up now is writing about people who are trying to get into the mainstream, or they're in the mainstream, just trying to live their lives." Mason also recounts her biographical history and responds to critical judgments on the limitations of her characters.

Ryan, Barbara T. "Decentered Authority in Bobbie Ann Mason's *In Country*." *Critique* 31 (Spring, 1990): 199-212.
Views the novel as a realistic work on one level, yet with "poststructuralist" elements in its view of authority and coherence. "Sam Hughes' search for her father is a symbolic representation of modern man's desire for the Logos-origin of meaning and authoritative discourse." That search is frustrated and leads to Sam's realization that she is her own authority and contributor to meaning, Ryan argues.

Ryan, Maureen. "Stopping Places: Bobbie Ann Mason's Short Stories." In *Women Writers of the Contemporary South*, edited by Peggy Whitman Prenshaw, pp. 283-294. Jackson: University Press of Mississippi, 1984.
Ryan considers Mason's stories as "stopping places" for character in

the otherwise constantly moving and changing realities of their lives. The chaos spares neither man nor woman, according to the essay. "If many of Mason's female characters are stronger, more in control than their husbands and lovers, their assertiveness is as new and tentative as their men's awareness."

Shomer, Enid. "An Interview with Bobbie Ann Mason." *Black Warrior Review* 12 (Spring, 1986): 87-102.
Mason denies having much background in "the Southern literary tradition" yet considers herself a Southerner. Also explores Mason's working habits, her consciously limited writing vocabulary, and the research behind *In Country*.

Smith, Wendy. "PW Interviews Bobbie Ann Mason." *Publishers Weekly* (August 30, 1985): 424-425.
Interview covers *In Country* primarily but weaves in pertinent biographical information and allusions to other writers. Mason remarks on her lack of Southern concern for history: "I don't think the people I write about are obsessed with the past. I don't think they know anything about the Civil War, and I don't think they care." Contains other pointed comments on her motivation for writing and connections to Southern culture.

Tyler, Anne. "Kentucky Cameos." *The New Republic* 187 (November 1, 1982): 36, 38.
Review of *Shiloh and Other Stories*. Tyler is more than enthusiastic. She has special praise for the sympathetic portrayal of male characters and the everyday-life details. Concludes with admonition to "go buy this book. Don't borrow it, don't look for it in the library, but buy it, as a way of casting your vote for real literature."

Underwood, Karen. "Mason's 'Drawing Names." *Explicator* 48 (Spring, 1990): 231-232.
Essay on Mason's short story read as "a modern-day version of the journey of the Wise Men." Underwood sees each of the sisters' men as analogous to one of the Wise Men: Cecil as Melchior, Ray as Gaspar, Jim as Balthazar, and the absent Kent as Artaban.

Ward, William S. "Bobbie Ann Mason." In *A Literary History of Kentucky*, pp. 426-428. Knoxville: University of Tennessee Press, 1988.

Characterizes Mason as "a slow starter but a sudden achiever." Reviews her biographical and publishing history along with the critical reception of her work. Ward believes Mason "has succeeded well in catching the laconic manner and limited emotional range of her young people while at the same time reflecting the ambivalence of their lives."

White, Leslie. "The Function of Popular Culture in Bobbie Ann Mason's *Shiloh and Other Stories* and *In Country*." *Southern Quarterly* 26 (Summer, 1988): 69-79.
Questions images of popular culture in Mason and their importance to the works. White contends that they are more than set dressing. Rather, "no matter how banal, demeaning or forgettable, popular culture is formative, and in Mason's fiction it appears as the foreground on which her characters move."

Wilhelm, Albert E. "An Interview with Bobbie Ann Mason." *Southern Quarterly* 26 (Winter, 1988): 27-38.
Mason talks about writers she admires (E. B. White, Tom Wolfe, John Updike, Nabokov—"those that have a unique style"), the everyday culture used throughout her writing (music, TV, shopping centers), and her philosophy as projected in her works ("my attitude toward life is not negative. I'm very hopeful about people like Norma Jean"). Other topics include her writing methods and recurring themes.

_____. "Making over or Making off: The Problem of Identity in Bobbie Ann Mason's Short Fiction." *The Southern Literary Journal* 18 (Spring, 1986): 76-82.
Identifies "culture shock and its jarring effects on an individual's sense of identity" as the dominant theme for *Shiloh and Other Stories*. Wilhelm shows an array of characters out "to construct a new identity," from Norma Jean in "Shiloh" to Mack Skaggs in "The Rookers." Unfortunately, according to Wilhelm, too many of the characters end up right where they started, struggling and frustrated.

_____. "Private Rituals: Coping with Change in the Fiction of Bobbie Ann Mason." *Midwest Quarterly* 28 (Winter, 1987): 271-282.
Notes "the effects on ordinary people of rapid social change" as a major theme. Wilhelm proposes one category of change, the "poverty of ritual," as endemic to much of Mason's writings. "Painful

transitions have become more frequent and more intense, but the adaptive and adjusting response previously offered by ritual is frequently lacking."

HELEN NORRIS

Drinkard, Tom. "Despite Gothic Elements, Norris Avoids the Trite." *Birmingham News* (January 21, 1990): p. F5.
A review of *Walk with the Sickle Moon*. Mentions such characteristics of Norris' fiction as her effective description of setting and character. Although like many of her short stories this novel deals with love, it differs in tone. Its "romantic coloration" may be justified as an expression of the heroine's viewpoint.

Kuznets, Miriam. "A Consistency of Fictions." *North American Review* 274 (June, 1989): 69-72.
A review of four books published in the 1988 Illinois Short Fiction series and including *Water into Wine*, which the reviewer calls "an intoxicating collection of stories overflowing with beauty and conflict." Admires Norris' use of imagery in the physical world to express the feelings of her characters, who resemble one another only in their isolation. Is also impressed by her detachment, her subtlety, and her careful, traditional handling of structure.

Leonard, John. Review of television production of *The Christmas Wife*. *New York* 21 (December 12, 1988): 109.
Praises the Hallmark Hall of Fame production of Norris' story, with Jason Robards and Julie Harris as "two strangers who try to bring their separate solitudes" into a fantasy of a happy Christmas. The play has "an O. Henry twist," and then an effective "twist-within-a-twist."

Norris, Emma Coburn. "The Courage to Read': An Interview with Helen Norris." *Alabama Literary Review* 2 (Spring, 1988): 49-59.
A 1987 interview. Includes the customary description of an author's system of work, as well as more unusual comments, such as the value of writers' colonies and the effect on one's writing of living in the academic world. Of particular significance are Norris' statements about the problems peculiar to women writers, ranging from domestic responsibilities to critical prejudices, and of the difficulties involved in publishing a work perceived as religious.

Norris, Helen. "The Self and the Matrix of Fiction." *The Sewanee Review* 99 (Spring, 1991): 259.

A profound and original psychological exploration of the writing process. Norris classifies writers into those who write from their memories and from self-exploration and those who write by drawing the outside world into themselves and then imaginatively identifying with the characters they have observed.

Olmstead, Robert. "Actors and Miracles." *The New York Times Book Review* (October 16, 1988): 18.

A review that finds *Water into Wine* disappointing. Unlike the fiction in her fine first collection, these stories have defects in plot, characterization, and style. The characters do not reveal either past events in their lives or present feelings; instead, they make stylized and static speeches. The style is convoluted. In the best stories of the book, the "gestures" of the characters become symbolic and moving. In too many of the stories, they remain merely gestures.

Steinberg, Sybil. *Walk with the Fickle Moon. Publishers Weekly* (September 1, 1989): 75.

A review, erroneously titled, of *More than Seven Watchmen*. Describes that novel as an imitation of Henry James. Like James, Norris uses minor characters simply as confidants for her hypersensitive major characters. Unlike James, she has "a facile happy ending." The work is ineffective.

_____. Review of *Water into Wine. Publishers Weekly* (July 1, 1988): 65-66.

Praises "Norris's enchanting narrative voice," which finds the magical dimension in ordinary lives of ordinary people. Her "mellifluous" and "lyrical" style is appropriate for characters who, artistlike, are struggling to make their own lives beautiful. Like her characters, Norris achieves "a higher conception of stylistic excellence" than can be found in most other contemporary fiction.

Tager, Marcia. "Short Stories Map Secret Territories." *New Directions for Women* (November/December, 1985): 14.

A brief, perceptive review of *The Christmas Wife*, calling the stories "mythic in their simplicity and eerieness." Norris' "impeccable art" is evident in her "seamless blending of story and style." In her stories, as in the three other collections in the annual Illinois Short

Fiction series, setting is subordinated to the real dramas, which take place within the hearts of the characters.

Walton, Edith H. "A Provocative Tale." *The New York Times Book Review* (October 6, 1940): 7-8.
A review of *Something More than Earth*, noting Norris' "fastidious" style and the "dreamlike quality" of her fiction. Despite the "sensitiveness" and "frequent beauty" of the novel, her characters are not believable. The book "is finely fashioned, but it lacks the pulse of life."

JAYNE ANNE PHILLIPS

Adams, Carolyn Hazlett. *"Machine Dreams." Appalachian Journal* 12 (Summer, 1985): 367-371.

A lively review of Phillips' novel and career. Adams calls *Machine Dreams* "one of those novels fashionable now in which nothing much ever happens but in which everyone is thinking real hard—the Bobbie Ann Mason quiet school." She finds good writing in the novel, yet without much attention to a sense of place, especially the West Virginia mountain world that the characters are supposed to inhabit.

Adams, Michael. "Jayne Anne Phillips." In *Dictionary of Literary Biography Yearbook: 1980*, edited by Karen L. Rood, Jean W. Ross, and Richard Ziegfeld, pp. 297-300. Detroit: Gale Research, 1981.

This entry appeared after the publication of *Black Tickets*. Recounts Phillips' biography and critical response, especially to her most recent short-story collection. Describes Phillips as a writer with more promise than proof, concluding from the 1980 vantage point that "Phillips's biggest problem may be learning to cope with the high expectations so many have for her."

_____. "Jayne Anne Phillips." In *Postmodern Fiction: A Bio-Bibliographical Guide*, edited by Larry McCaffery, pp. 481-483. New York: Greenwood Press, 1986.

This short essay discusses *Black Tickets*, along with Phillips' biographical background and the familiar list of her literary anteced-ents. Adams ventures that "it is also clear that she is a highly original stylist in her own right who may influence those writers who come after her." The attached bibliography provides little, if any, additional information.

Baker, James N. "Being Led by a Whisper." *Newsweek* (October 22, 1979): 116, 118.

Early interview-based essay, soon after the publication of *Black Tickets* (see the review preceding this article). Talks about the early days from West Virginia to hitchhiking to California. Phillips states her main interest to be "what home consists of" in such a mobile society.

Cushman, Keith. "*Black Tickets.*" *Studies in Short Fiction* 18 (Winter, 1981): 92-94.
Review. Makes comparisons to Flannery O'Connor and Eudora Welty in terms of "invalids and grotesques." Cushman finds the poet's ear for condensed language much in evidence in these stories. The shorter ones "tend to be splashy and self-indulgent" while the longer stories show a depth to her imagination that prompts Cushman to eagerly await her novel.

Edelstein, David. "The Short Story of Jayne Anne Phillips." *Esquire* (December, 1985): 108-112.
Based on a visit and an interview. Interweaves the history of Phillips' life with comments on her writings. Edelstein notes the private and distant nature of Phillips, noting how she did not like teaching because, in part, she "wasn't interested in helping anyone else—she was fiercely independent and loyal to her driven vision." Substantial insights here.

Eder, Richard. "*Fast Lanes.*" *Los Angeles Times Book Review* (April 19, 1987): 3, 11.
Review praises the balance Phillips finds in letting her characters speak for themselves without letting them rule the content of the stories. Mickey, of "How Mickey Made It," is compared to characters of Jay McInerney except that Mickey "seeks a way out; instead of hugging his pain, he delivers it to the silent woman he is with." In general, Phillips is seen as very sympathetic to her characters while maintaining a cool precision in her style. In a later interview, Phillips mentions the insights of this particular review as being useful to her.

Garrett, George. "Arts and Letters: Technics and Pyrotechnics." *The Sewanee Review* 88 (Summer, 1980): 414-416.
Part of a discussion of what new voices in short fiction have to offer. Considerably more here about how Phillips' *Black Tickets* is launched by the publishing company than about the book itself. Still, Garrett finds Phillips a competent writer with an established and distinctive voice, if somewhat limited.

Gilbert, Celia. "PW Interviews Jayne Anne Phillips." *Publishers Weekly* (June 8, 1984): 65-66.
Phillips talks a great deal about *Machine Dreams* and what went into the novel. She also relates significant details of her upbringing and the influences that it has provided for her writing, explaining that "the writer in the family structure is the one who has been entrusted with the psyche of the family." Phillips talks about her writing patterns as well.

Hulbert, Ann. "Rural Chic." *The New Republic* (September 2, 1985): 25-30.
Passing references to and analysis of *Machine Dreams* in the context of other books and films exploring the "pastoral myth" of the rural United States. Hulbert questions the motives of the writers and filmmakers. The populist ideal seems to betray itself in close examination, she seems to say, even more so in the fiction than in the films.

Irving, John. "Stories with Voiceprints." *The New York Times Book Review* (September 30, 1979): 13, 28.
Novelist Irving reviews *Black Tickets* as representing someone making the transition from creative writing classwork to professional work. In the collection he finds both levels of writing. The "little oddities too precious to the author" are forgiven in light of the stories in which "her characters and their stories matter most to us." Predicts Phillips might shine best in a novel.

Lassner, Phyllis. "Women's Narrative and the Recreation of History." In *American Women Writing Fiction: Memory, Identity, Family, Space*, edited by Mickey Pearlman, pp. 193-210. Lexington: University Press of Kentucky, 1989.
Focusing on *Machine Dreams*, the essay explains how, in "Phillips's creative imagination, there are compelling differences between how we participate in events and how and why we write stories about them." According to Lassner, the special gift for understanding the power of "the figurative language of narrative is given to the women in Phillips's fiction." Contains a useful bibliography of works by and about Phillips.

McGowan, William. "*Machine Dreams*: Retooling Fiction." *Washington Monthly* (March, 1985): 42-46.

Compares Phillips' novel to Steinbeck's *The Grapes of Wrath* in that it "is important not for the facts it provides about a particular era in history but for its empathy for people who lived through those times and its understanding of how their lives connected to other lives." Goes on to consider other aspects of the decline of "social realism" in literature and how works such as Phillips' can help.

McInerney, Jay. "Lost on the Open Road." *The New York Times Book Review* (May 3, 1987): 7.
Review of *Fast Lanes* with references to her other works. McInerney is most pleased with the poetic language of stories such as "Blue-gill." He also prefers those of history and family to those more contemporary pieces. Overall, McInerney sees Phillips as "evolving into a regional writer and family chronicler, a cousin of Reynolds Price and Eudora Welty." It is meant as a compliment.

Nichols, Capper. "Jayne Anne Phillips (1952-   ): An Annotated Primary and Secondary Bibliography, 1976-1989." *Bulletin of Bibliography* 47 (September, 1990): 177-185.
Excellent source of information on writings by and about Phillips. A biographical introduction is followed by annotated entries divided into categories such as "Uncollected Works" and "Interviews." Perhaps most useful for more comprehensive lists of reviews listed according to individual works by Phillips.

Pierce, Constance. "Contemporary Fiction and Popular Culture." *Michigan Quarterly Review* 26 (Fall, 1987): 663-672.
Briefly considers Phillips' short story "Home" as indicative of the way authors use references to popular culture for more than setting and time clues. The mother's reference to network anchormen "says worlds about the woman's insularity, and it locates a revealing habit shared by many Americans."

Ross, Jean W. "CA Interview." In *Contemporary Authors*, New Revision Series, edited by Deborah A. Straub. Vol. 24, pp. 365-367. Detroit: Gale Research, 1988.
Interview at end of brief biographical/critical entry. Phillips speaks of her transition from poetry into fiction and her approaches to finding the voice for her work. Phillips rejects the label "regional writer." When asked about the political intentions of *Machine*

Dreams, she responds, "I think good writing is intrinsically political."
List of sources at end.

Simpson, Mona. "An American Beauty." *Vogue* (July, 1984): 117-118.
A short review of *Machine Dreams* followed by an interview.
Simpson finds the switch from the extreme narrative experiments in
the short stories to the "single, colloquial" voices of the novel
successful. In the interview portion, Phillips talks about the meaning
of her title wherein "machine represents myth" and "dreams come
out of the characters."

Tyler, Anne. "The Wounds of War." *The New York Times Book Review*
(July 1, 1984): 3.
Review of *Machine Dreams*. Tyler credits Phillips for choosing the
family theme for the novel over her more shocking, stylistic
character studies. In this novel, the "shocks arise from small,
ordinary moments, patiently developed" by "an assured and gifted
writer." Tyler summarizes the movements of the book and the
changes in voice—"a patchwork quilt of American voices."

Yardley, Jonathan. "Jayne Anne Phillips: West Virginia Breakdown."
The Washington Post Book World (June 24, 1984): 3.
Yardley calls *Machine Dreams* "an elegiac, wistful, rueful book
under which runs a vein of political commentary." The political
commentary aspect troubles the reviewer, while the attention to
nuance and the well-chosen voices of the characters please him.
Claims Phillips to be "a literary writer who does not write about
literary people or settings."

VALERIE SAYERS

Benson, Sonia. "Sayers, Valerie, 1952-   ." In *Contemporary Authors*, edited by Susan M. Trosky. Vol. 134, pp. 421-422. Detroit: Gale Research, 1992.

Profile of Sayers with personal data, career history, list of writings, and short bibliography. Includes quote from Sayers about her childhood in Beaufort, South Carolina: "I moved to New York at seventeen, but evidently have a compunction to return to that particular southern landscape." Benson notes the critical reception her three novels have to date received.

Butler, Jack. "Mary Faith Pleads Virginity." *The New York Times Book Review* (March 8, 1987): 9.

Review of *Due East*. What "begins like a domestic comedy of errors" is seen to be upon ending "a hard-eyed if not hardhearted tale, and gives nothing up to sentimentality." Butler's review finds few faults except perhaps the extreme dichotomy of Mary's attributes versus the small-mindedness of those who frustrate her. At that point the story momentarily threatens to become "the familiar tale of the good and sensitive teenager against the cruel and insensitive world."

Corn, Alfred. "Trouble in the Form of a Redhead." *The New York Times Book Review* (January 29, 1989): 7.

Review of *How I Got Him Back*. "Ms. Sayers has a gift for voice and the honest, gritty commentary about human behavior in stressful circumstances," says Corn. He takes exception to some of the plot, the "melodramatic flourishes" of the novel, and the conclusion. Review notes the religious symbolic structure. Corn places Sayers and *Due East* in the New South.

Dirlam, Sharon. "*Who Do You Love?*" *Los Angeles Times Book Review* (March 10, 1991): 6.

Very brief review of the novel. *Who Do You Love?* "is a heavy little slice of life, narrow and rich," according to Dirlam. The review summarizes the political and social changes infringing on the Rooney world. Symbolically, the "handsome stranger" with whom Kate observes her mother "momentarily lifts the veil of illusion from their eyes . . . and they don't like what they see."

Harvey, Bret. "Faith, Hope, and Clarity." *The Village Voice* (May 19, 1987): 52.
Review of *Due East*. Harvey admires the delicate touch Sayers uses in exploring the relationships of the book. "The heart of this book is the relationship between father and daughter, which is clogged with unspoken tenderness and disappointment. Sayers knows just to let their relationship play itself out in her characters' actions." The end of the book, Harvey concludes, does more to frame events and character than to resolve them artificially.

Kendall, Elaine. "Start at Mid-Confusion in a Parochial Catholic South." *Los Angeles Times* (January 27, 1989): p. V8.
Kendall faults Sayers for assuming from readers so much prior knowledge of her characters in *How I Got Him Back*. Those who had not read the first novel are likely to be lost for sometime, Kendall says. Otherwise, "Sayers is a gentle and affectionate satirist of Southern Catholic folkways."

McDaniel, Maude. "Feeling the Hurt of Sadness and Madness." *Chicago Tribune* (February 19, 1989): sec. 14, p. 4.
McDaniel describes *How I Got Him Back* as "an excellent book that is difficult to like" in this review. The reviewer is impressed with the writing, the characterization, the ambition of Sayers in touching "on almost every reigning theme of contemporary writing," yet is disappointed in the end. McDaniel concedes a personal aversion to what's-wrong-with-the-world books. She also complains of the "clutter" of the book—"too much undigested symbolism, too many possible connections."

Mitcham, Carl. "Footsteps That Did Not Follow." *Commonweal* 114 (May 22, 1987): 329-331.
A review of *Due East* with particular focus on its religious elements. Mitcham sees the novel as much more than popular fiction: "[I]t is a fictive study of our rejection of God, the motherhood of faith, and how both depend on and transcend our relationships with others." The Southern gothic aspects of her narrative leave plenty of room for resonating words and images with deep significance.

Mosher, Howard Frank. "Twenty-four Hours in Due East, S.C." *The New York Times Book Review* (April 7, 1991): 3, 29.
Reviews *Who Do You Love?* as part of the "new regionalism" tradition. While the town of Due East may be solidly in its geography, the writing provides meaning beyond the region, Mosher believes. Delores "manages to achieve at last, in a single crowded day, a remarkably wise insight into herself and her relationship with her big, squabbling, funny, smart, problem-ridden and immensely likable family." Only the lengthy personal histories check Mosher's enthusiasm for the novel.

Petroski, Catherine. "Three Debuts Prove the Vitality of the Novel." *Chicago Tribune—The Arts* (March 8, 1987): 7.
Due East reviewed as "one of those beautifully realized novels that takes over the reader's life." Petroski summarizes the theme as being "about substitutes and the diversionary tactics through which we fool ourselves about ourselves." The complicated narrative approach taken in the novel succeeds, according to the review.

MARY LEE SETTLE

Bach, Peggy. "The Searching Voice and Vision of Mary Lee Settle."
The Southern Review 20 (Autumn, 1984): 842-850.
Accounts for the widely differing critical evaluations of Settle by
pointing out the fact that she cannot easily be labeled. Although
traces of Settle's own experience can be seen in her novels, no single
character speaks for the author; instead, there is a distinct authorial
voice. Although she bases her works on scrupulous historical
research, Settle's focus is not on figures from history, but on the
lives of ordinary people created in her imagination. If her work is
difficult, it is also profound. She is the kind of artist who "expands
the mind."

Betts, Doris. Review of *Celebration*. *America* 156 (October 18, 1986):
211-212.
Settle's novel is reviewed by another distinguished fiction writer,
who lauds Settle for eschewing the obsession with self that is
symptomatic of contemporary literature and, similarly, for moving
beyond the boundaries of her geographical area "to encompass the
human spirit." The work illustrates Settle's "recognition of death and
her celebration of life."

Boyd, William. "Teresa Cerrutti Can Take It." *The New York Times
Book Review* (October 26, 1986): 14.
Finds *Celebration* "rambling" and "dull," in part because of the use
of lengthy first-person monologues along with narration by an
omniscient author. The tone comes "perilously close to the precious
and coy," suggesting that Settle's attempt at optimism "fogged [her]
normally clear vision."

Brown, Laurie L. "Interviews with Seven Contemporary Writers." In
Women Writers of the Contemporary South, edited by Peggy
Whitman Prenshaw, pp. 3-22. Jackson: University Press of Missis-
sippi, 1984.
In a lengthy telephone interview, Settle answered set questions on

various subjects. She comments on the parallel between herself and Hannah McKarkle, who is the fictional author of Settle's own *The Beulah Quintet*. Her other responses have to do with her writing routine, with the imagined audience, and with criticism.

Brown, Rosellen. "Trapped in the Mines." *The New Republic* 183 (December 27, 1980): 37-39.
This reviewer finds *The Scapegoat* more enlightening than passionate. Admires Settle's technical skill; her use of multiple voices is so effective that it seems the ideal way to re-create social history. This "absorbing and ambitious" novel suggests that most people are doomed to remain in the prisons of their inherited opinions and of their positions in society as the powerful or the powerless.

Canfield, Rosemary M. "*The Beulah Quintet.*" In *Masterplots II: American Fiction Series*, edited by Frank N. Magill, pp. 151-160. Englewood Cliffs, N.J.: Salem Press, 1986.
A critical essay that traces characters, patterns, and themes throughout the series. Argues that all the novels deal with rebellion against some kind of enslavement. Although from book to book the source of enslavement varies, in every case the protagonists rebel against it, fighting a battle within themselves, as well as the obvious battle against outside oppressors.

_____. "Mary Lee Settle." In *Critical Survey of Long Fiction: Supplement*, edited by Frank N. Magill, pp. 342-350. Englewood Cliffs, N.J.: Salem Press, 1987.
An overview of Settle's novels, pointing out similarities between those in *The Beulah Quintet* and the others, which are classified as "Southern" and "European" novels. The later books evidence increasing mastery of her medium, as well as a growing tolerance for human imperfections, which permits "the possibility of redemption" for more of her characters.

Doctorow, E. L. "Mother Jones Had Some Advice." *The New York Times Book Review* (October 26, 1980): 1, 40-42.
Review of *The Scapegoat*, arguing that although Settle describes dramatic events in the novel, her real emphasis is on the inner lives of her characters, who "suffer their fate in the act of meditation." Praises Settle's vivid, historically accurate description and her panoramic vision.

Dyer, Joyce Coyne. *"The Clam Shell*: Mary Lee Settle on East Coast Gentility." *Appalachian Journal* 13 (Winter, 1986): 171-183.
Sees *The Clam Shell* as autobiographical, an account of Settle's girlhood and her college experience at Sweet Briar. During the same period in her life, the protagonist in the novel becomes aware of class conflicts, even as Settle seems to have done. In order to be accepted in genteel society, someone on the fringe of it is tempted to close her shell and her mind, to deny her past and her family history. Like Settle, however, the narrator decides that only by discovering the truth can she have any hope of improving this society or any other. A well-reasoned and fully supported analysis, with useful notes.

_____. "Embracing the Common: Mary Lee Settle in World War II." *Appalachian Journal* 12 (Winter, 1985): 127-134.
Because Settle's autobiographical book *All the Brave Promises* was inadequately promoted upon its publication, it failed to achieve the notice it deserves. Settle's dedication of the book "To the wartime other ranks of the Women's Auxilary Air Force, (RAF)—below the rank of sergeant," shows her sympathies with the powerless, not the powerful. The existence of oppressive class distinctions is a major theme not only in this book but also in all Settle's fiction.

_____. "Mary Lee Settle's *Prisons*: Taproots History." *The Southern Literary Journal* 17 (Fall, 1984): 26-39.
In *Prisons*, when the protagonist, Johnny Church, muses that the rebellions in history actually arise not from public actions but from an accumulation of private grievances, he is expressing Settle's own "taproots" theory of history. This theory is illustrated throughout *Prisons*. A close analysis of the book points out the patterns and themes that are basic to *The Beulah Quintet*.

Garrett, George. "An Invitation to the Dance: A Few Words on the Art of Mary Lee Settle." *Blue Ridge Review* 1 (1978): 18-24.
A "critical appreciation" of Settle, whose works, as well as her disciplined professional life, should serve as models for contemporary writers. Points out that all of her work, including the *Quintet*, is part of a single whole. Although her characters are complex, her style is "transparent, accessible, unselfconscious," and always brilliantly adapted to the situation. Admires her dedication to her craft, her unwillingness to compromise.

_____. "Mary Lee Settle's Beulah Land Trilogy." In *Rediscoveries*, edited by David Madden, pp. 171-178. New York: Crown, 1971.

Even though her publishers brought out *O Beulah Land*, *Know Nothing*, and *Fight Night on a Sweet Saturday* as separate works, they should be considered as the trilogy that they were intended to be. They are linked by the family ties of the characters and by the place where all the novels are set. Although these works demand some effort from the reader, they are brilliant in concept and in execution. Written before the trilogy became a quintet and at a time when Settle's works were little known, this essay reflects Garrett's sound judgment as to her proper place in contemporary fiction, as an artist who is "one of the few and finest of our times."

_____. *Understanding Mary Lee Settle*. Columbia: University of South Carolina Press, 1988.

A perceptive and highly readable book-length study by a distinguished critic and writer and an early admirer of Settle. After a biographical sketch, a useful discussion of her publishing history, and some generalizations about her strengths and weaknesses, Garrett discusses Settle's work in detail. He devotes a chapter to *The Beulah Quintet*, which he considers her major achievement, one chapter to three novels related to the *Quintet*, and another chapter to *Blood Tie* and *Celebration*. A final chapter discusses other works, including *All the Brave Promises*, a memoir of her experiences during World War II; her short stories; and various essays and reviews. Carefully indexed, with a bibliography that is helpfully divided by categories.

Godwin, Gail. "An Epic of West Virginia." *The New Republic* (June 16, 1982): 30-32.

Perceives a paradoxical pattern in Settle's works: Over and over again, those very people who fight against political and economic oppression, once they have won, themselves turn into oppressors. Because of this pessimistic theme and because of Hannah McKarkle's own unattractive personality, *The Killing Ground*, impressive though it is, lacks hope, joy, and compassion.

Houston, Robert. "Blood Sacrifice." *The Nation* 231 (November 8, 1980): 469-471.

Enthusiastic and perceptive review of *The Scapegoat*. Sees the major themes of the novel as violence and change, its greatest strengths as a superb style, which is original rather than Faulknerian, and vivid characterization, achieved by the use of varying voices. Reminds critics who are concerned about Settle's use of the historical figure Mother Jones that this is a novel, not history; therefore her appearance as a "catalyst" or "vice figure," in the medieval sense, is appropriate.

Joyner, Nancy Carol. "Mary Lee Settle's Connections: Class and Clothes in *The Beulah Quintet.*" *Southern Quarterly: A Journal of the Arts in the South* 22 (Fall, 1983): 32-45. Also in *Women Writers of the Contemporary South*, edited by Peggy Whitman Prenshaw, pp. 166-178. Jackson: University Press of Mississippi, 1984.
Throughout *The Beulah Quintet*, Settle uses descriptions of the characters' clothing and the decoration of their houses in order to illustrate the themes of class consciousness, of family pride, and of obsession with money. Her skillful handling of this motif is merely one evidence of the vision and artisanship that make *The Beulah Quintet* a "major contribution to American fiction."

Latham, Aaron. "The End of *The Beulah Quintet.*" *The New York Times Book Review* (July 11, 1982): 1, 20-21.
In the final book of her series, Settle focuses on Hannah McKarkle's motivation for writing, the need to work through the death of her brother. Like other artists, she builds her work on "the killing ground," in this case, protesting the death of her brother in jail and "resurrecting in writing" the lives and deaths of his ancestors, back to the original Johnny Church, who was also imprisoned and destroyed. The series is brilliant at times, but uneven. Suggests that it would be better if it were reduced to a single volume.

Leavitt, David. "A Man Too Attractive to Marry." *The New York Times Book Review* (October 22, 1989): 12.
A review of *Charley Bland*, a book reflecting Settle's "consciousness of herself as a Southern writer." Sees the theme of the book as the heroine's desperate attempt to win the approval of her society. Admire's Settle's evocation of place, her "exalted, oratorical prose," when it is not overdone, and her "emotional power."

McPherson, Myra. "Mary Lee Settle, Forthrightly." *The Washington Post* (January 15, 1987): pp. C1, C8-C9.
Lengthy essay-interview with Mary Lee Settle. Even though Settle

denies writing autobiographical novels, the biographical details in this article, some of which are lacking in other interviews, help to explain the development of her thought and her fiction. Even after ten books, she intends to continue writing, which enables her to be a complete person in a world of her own creation.

Neal, G. Dale. "Filling an Empty Room—The Art of Mary Lee Settle." *Wake Forest University Student* (Spring, 1980): 18-22.
An unusual interview with Mary Lee Settle conducted in her home in Norfolk and filled with revealing details. Includes outspoken statements about revolution and democracy, as well as comments about the genesis of her novels and descriptions of her work methods. She speaks of her surprise at winning the National Book Award for Fiction in 1978, particularly since only four out of thirty-two winners have been women. Also includes an excerpt from Settle's acceptance speech.

O'Hara, J. D. "What Rogue Elephants Know." *The Nation* 226 (May, 1978): 605-606.
Defends *Blood Tie* against charges that it did not deserve the National Book Award. Suggests that the attacks on the judges' decision arise from the fact that the novelist is too conscious of specific details, too much interested in the results of political and economic factors on relationships, to be in fashion. Notes that Settle's characters are in one way or another dissociated from their environment. Their alienation from one another is not merely chance, however, but a universal human problem. While there are occasional lapses in Settle's style, and although the book may have been too ambitious, it evidences "a dazzling perceptivity, a sharp intelligence, and wide-ranging knowledge."

Peden, William. "Back to Beulah Land." *Saturday Review* (November 5, 1960): 33.
An early review of *Know Nothing* that finds Settle's characterization vague and her "floating point of view" perplexing. Praises, however, her knowledge of the area and its people, her "literary integrity" and her "seriousness of purpose."

Rosenberg, Brian. "Mary Lee Settle and the Critics." *The Virginia Quarterly Review* 65 (Summer, 1989): 401.
Prompted by the publication of George Garrett's *Understanding*

Mary Lee Settle (above), this essay focuses on the disappointing critical response to Settle's work, which was expressed after the publication of her third book. Attributes much of the mixed reaction to her being categorized not as a realist but as a historical novelist. This genre is not in vogue with academicians, partly because it insists on objective, rather than on subjective, truth. Furthermore, Settle's strong interest in "family and politics" and her moral earnestness do not appeal to "structurally and linguistically oriented critics." The shapers of the literary canon should have enough aesthetic integrity to include not only current fads but also writers of Settle's stature. Thoughtful and convincing.

_____. "Mary Lee Settle and the Tradition of Historical Fiction." *The South Atlantic Quarterly* 86 (Summer, 1987): 229-243. Lauds *The Beulah Quintet* as historical fiction of lasting significance, primarily because of Settle's success in showing the connections that exist between the past and the present. Although the other four books in the series are clearly in the American tradition, Rosenberg argues that *Prisons* grafts the American theme of freedom onto the pattern of historical fiction that is familiar in such nineteenth century English writers as Scott, Dickens, and Thackeray.

_____. *Mary Lee Settle's "Beulah Quintet": The Price of Freedom.* Baton Rouge: Louisiana State University Press, 1991. A comprehensive study of the *Quintet* that places it within the context of the tradition of the historical novel and attempts to account for its relative obscurity, despite the obvious merit of the novels. Each of the works in the *Quintet* is discussed in terms of a dominant theme. Appended are a useful genealogy of the characters in the series and a revised version of Rosenberg's 1987 interview with Mary Lee Settle, which appeared in *The Southern Review* (immediately above). Selected bibliography.

_____. "The Price of Freedom: An Interview with Mary Lee Settle." *The Southern Review* 25 (Spring, 1989): 351-365. A important interview, in which Settle explains specifically how other writers have influenced her own work and comments at length on the relationship between real life, whether autobiography or history, and fiction. Describes Joseph Conrad as her "grandfather," in style and intention. Interestingly, defines history as the story of people, often unknown, who have changed the world. Each book of

The Beulah Quintet shows that "the price of freedom" for these people is alienation and rejection. Significantly, Settle believes *Prisons* is the central novel of the series. It is also this novel that most closely resembles those of Conrad in depth and in vision.

Rosenfelt, Deborah S. "Getting into the Game: American Women Writers and the Radical Tradition." *Women's Studies International Forum* 9 (1986): 363-372.
An analysis of *The Killing Ground* as a work that evidences both socialist and feminist viewpoints, which the author sees as necessarily united. In this novel, as in others in the tradition, the central action is "the growth of social consciousness as an essential part of the quest for individual identity." Even though Settle does not expect basic social change, except insofar as change is a normal part of life, her work is connected to the socialist feminist tradition. In *The Scapegoat*, the female protagonist is called upon to make a choice that denies both her class and her gender. In *The Killing Ground*, Hannah McKarkle goes a step further, seeking to understand such choices and to find the language in which to express them.

Sanoff, Alvin P. "Life Is Really a Dance." *U.S. News & World Report* (December 22, 1986): 64.
An informal conversation with Settle after the publication of *Celebration*, in which she emphasizes her new awareness of the value of life that has resulted from her own bout with cancer. Cites specific examples of how her works evolve out of a combination of visual images, memory, reading, and research.

Schafer, William J. "Mary Lee Settle's *Beulah Quintet*: History Darkly, Through a Single-Lens Reflex." *Appalachian Journal* 10 (Autumn, 1982): 77-86.
A comprehensive and original study of Settle's approach to history, using analogies from cinematography. There are problems in what is unarguably an impressive work, including narrative fragmentation and historical inaccuracy. Although Settle repeats images, patterns, and themes from book to book, the final effect is like that in some movies, of memorable scenes but not of a single panoramic vision.

Settle, Mary Lee. "Facts of Censorship." *TriQuarterly* 65 (1986): 260-273.
Talk given by Settle at a symposium on "The Writer in Our World."

Points out that even in a free society, three forms of censorship affect the writer. In response to questions from panelists and from the audience, Settle comments on the overall issue of the symposium, explaining at length why she believes that merely putting more power in the hands of women will not ensure peace in the world.

_____. "Hard Road to a Boxed Edition." *Publishers Weekly* (February 12, 1988): 65.
An outspoken and detailed description of Settle's problems with publishers and reviewers over the last thirty-four years, prompted by the scheduled publication of the definitive *The Beulah Quintet*. Revealing and useful.

_____. "How Pleasant to Meet Mr. Eliot." *The New York Times Book Review* (December 16, 1984): 10-11.
Settle's moving account of her meeting with T. S. Eliot in 1946, when she and other young writers were exhausted from the strain of war and uncertain about the future. She expresses her gratitude for his instinctive understanding and kindly reassurance.

_____. "London—1944." *The Virginia Quarterly Review* 63 (Autumn, 1987): 565-586.
An account of Settle's life in wartime London. She observes the gap between the deprivations of ordinary people and the luxurious life-styles of the privileged, but she also dramatizes the fear felt by everyone during buzz-bomb and V-2 attacks. She concludes with the belief that although evil will still exist, since World War II "decent people" in democracies will no longer accept it.

_____. "Mary Lee Settle." In *Contemporary Authors Autobiography Series*, edited by Dedria Bryfonski. Vol. 1, pp. 307-323. Detroit: Gale Research, 1984.
The author's life story, with emphasis on incidents that influenced or hindered her writing, such as her early problems with eyesight and her later injury in a fire, both of which isolated her, causing her to take refuge in her imagination. Also points to various mentors and friends who aided her. Particularly interesting are Settle's comments on Southern society, in the context of her attempt to reenter her parents' world, which nearly destroyed her. Essential.

_____. "Recapturing the Past in Fiction." *The New York Times Book Review* (February 12, 1984): 1, 36-37.

A justification for historical fiction, in that unlike history, it can recapture "the rhythms, the images, the sensuousness of a lost time" and show readers the ever-present patterns of power. Uses detailed examples from her own work.

_____. "The Search for Beulah Land." *The Southern Review* 24 (1988): 13-26.

Describes the development of *The Beulah Quintet*, from the initial drunk-tank image to the troubling "search for the American metaphor," which involved discovering through research the profound implications of the hymn "O Beulah Land." At the end of the essay, Settle denies that her books are in any way autobiographical and then points out that descriptions of artistic method such as are found in this essay cannot and should not substitute for the works themselves. Given the truth of this comment, Settle's essay should still be considered essential reading as one of the best critical analyses of her work.

Shattuck, Roger. "A Talk with Mary Lee Settle." *The New York Times Book Review* (October 26, 1980): 43-46.

A vivid portrait of Settle as a person and as a writer. Although her recollections of research can be found in other interviews, her responses to questions about feminism are new, perhaps because she herself did not recognize a feminist theme in the Beulah series until after she had finished it. Interestingly, she suggests that since the Civil War, Southern men have been "dominated" by women. Other comments have to do with her publishing history and the reception of her works by critics.

Smith, Wendy. "Mary Lee Settle." *Publishers Weekly* (October 10, 1986): 73-75.

An interview conducted at Settle's new home in Charlottesville, Virginia, after the publication of *Celebration*. Settle calls Johnny Church the character closest to herself, "a Puritan in a Cavalier world." She herself has evolved from a rebel "who violently rejected the Southern myths about the past" to an artist who returned to those myths to discover the truth. As for her mission as a writer, she quotes Joseph Conrad: "to make you see."

Steel, Edward M., Jr. "Review Essay: Fact or Fiction." *West Virginia History* 42 (Spring/Summer, 1981): 314-315.
Categorizes *The Scapegoat* as the best kind of historical novel, in which historical events and private lives are masterfully intertwined. The author has been scrupulously accurate in her details, and she has a clear understanding of the forces at work during the period.

Swain, Kathleen M. "A Fictional Gloss on the History of the 1640's." *Milton Quarterly* 15 (1981): 97-98.
A brief review of *Prisons*, indicating a scholar's approval of Settle's work. Her picture of Oliver Cromwell is "more balanced" than Milton's. Despite the limited perspective of the protagonist, in this novel "historical events and issues emerge with some clarity."

Taormina, C. A. "On Time with Mary Lee Settle." *Blue Ridge Review* 1 (1978): 8-17.
A 1977 interview with Mary Lee Settle, in which she denies that there has been a real change in viewpoint or in style during her writing of the Beulah series. The language and the voice used in each book in the series were appropriate for that book. Interesting statements about the work in progress, *The Scapegoat*, and, more generally, about the writer's use of reality.

Tyler, Anne. "Mary Lee Settle: Mining a Rich Vein." *The Washington Post Book World* (September 28, 1980): 1, 13.
Focuses on the women in *The Scapegoat*, observing that it is the rebellious Lily, playing her little games with real people's lives, whose presence makes this novel more than a "period piece." The book is riveting and realistic, "a quiet masterpiece."

Vance, Jane Gentry. "Historical Voices in Mary Lee Settle's *Prisons*: "Too Far in Freedom." *Mississippi Quarterly: The Journal of Southern Culture* 38 (Fall, 1985): 391-413.
A detailed recapitulation of the historical events that are the background of Settle's novel. Explains the significance of the New Model Army discussed extensively in contemporary accounts and exemplified by Johnny Church. At his death, Church freely gives his life for liberty. Although his dream is carried to the New World, the male descendants of the New Model soldiers lose it and their integrity. In *The Killing Ground*, "the choice of freedom devolves to women," especially to Hannah McKarkle.

——————. "Mary Lee Settle: "Ambiguity of Steel."" In *American Women Writing Fiction: Memory, Identity, Family, Space*, edited by Mickey Pearlman, pp. 212-229. Lexington: University Press of Kentucky, 1989.

Although her other novels are well-crafted, it is Settle's *The Beulah Quintet* that places her among "major" contemporary novelists. Suggests that the quintet can best be understood when it is read in reverse chronological order, ending with *Prisons*, which is set during the English Civil War, the period in which Settle sees the beginnings of "American ideas of liberty." All Settle's works emphasize the ambiguity inherent in human life, the need for an understanding of history and of others, and "the necessity for freedom to become oneself within the limits of the ambiguities." An important essay. Bibliography by Vance and Pearlman is appended.

——————. "Mary Lee Settle's *The Beulah Quintet*: History Inherited, History Created." *The Southern Literary Journal* 17 (Fall, 1984): 40-53.

An overview of the series. Stresses Settle's emphasis on the contemporary perception of events, not on later interpretations. Thus, through her characters she creates an authentic version of history. Also looks at the importance of women characters in the series, explaining how Hannah McKarkle is the spiritual heir of both Mother Jones and the well-meaning Lily of *The Scapegoat*. While Johnny McKarkle has lost his history, his identity, and his reason for living or for dying, at the end of *The Killing Ground* Hannah has won her freedom, "the emotionally and intellectually liberating knowledge of the self and its history."

ANNE RIVERS SIDDONS

Bromley, Robin. Review of *Homeplace*. *The New York Times Book Review* (August 30, 1987): 20.
The novel presents a convincing picture of the New South, seen through the eyes of a heroine who has returned to the home and the family that she had despised and left. Siddons follows her change of mind and heart toward an eventual reconciliation. An excellent, if brief, summary.

Butler, Wanda. Review of *King's Oak*. *Southern Living* (March, 1991): 118.
Calls the novel "a riveting tale of struggle" that pits those who love the natural beauty of a small Georgia town against those who would endanger it. It is interesting that a heroic environmentalist "breaks the rules" of a "clannish community" and succeeds in making changes.

Childress, Mark. "Novelist Proves You Can Go Home Again." *Atlanta Journal-Constitution* (June 14, 1987): p. J10.
A review of *Homeplace* as a contemporary novel about the traditional subjects of home and family. One cannot fault Siddons for writing an undramatic story; in real life, too, families are broken up by "small injustices" and petty hatreds. The novel is, however, flawed by its predictable ending. Siddons' most admirable quality is her descriptive style, the "luminous language" that enables her to capture a mood and an atmosphere.

Ferguson, Sarah. Review of *Peachtree Road*. *The New York Times Book Review* (January 1, 1989): 14.
A typical "Southern saga," the novel is filled with violence and melodrama. Siddons' description is well written and her two main characters are interesting. The book is cluttered with peripheral characters and incidents, however, and it fails to fulfill the author's epic intentions.

Lyons, Gene. "She Didn't Hate Herself in the Morning." *The New York Times Book Review* (November 4, 1990): 33.
Contemptuously places *King's Oak* with *Peachtree Road* as a "grandiloquent saga" of the Southern aristocracy, designed to appeal to the readers of "gamey" paperback romances. Characterizes Siddons' style as "lots and lots of adjectives and adverbs," her plot as "repetitious folderol," but admits that she does know how to tell a story.

Naipaul, V. S. "Tuning In." In *A Turn in the South*, pp. 19-76. New York: Alfred A. Knopf, 1989.
Recounts an interview with Siddons on "growing up in the South." She speaks of racial repression, which she believes has forced many Southern intellectuals to leave the South, and of the similar repression of talented women, who take refuge in alcohol or in madness. She also voices regret that protest about such injustices eventually loses its original passion and becomes perfunctory. Naipaul's questions are to the point; Siddons' responses reveal much about her thinking and about Southern culture.

Pollitt, Katha. "*Heartbreak Hotel*." *The New York Times Book Review* (September 12, 1976): 43.
A complimentary review, praising Siddons for her accurate depiction of a Southern campus during the 1950's. Even though she presents in simplistic terms the heroine's choice between two men and what they represent, the tone of the book is "good-natured," perhaps because of the wealth of detail so lovingly recorded.

Siddons, Anne Rivers. "Introduction by the Author." *Publishers Weekly* (March 30, 1992): 26.
Asked to "think aloud" about her novel *Colony*, Siddons points out that, in this book, she takes a Southern heroine north to record her impressions of the "lovely but austere lifestyle" in coastal Maine, where, like Siddons herself, she spends her summers. Interestingly, Siddons describes this little world as traditional, sometimes "stifling," but worth preserving.

Summer, Bob. "Anne Rivers Siddons: A Woman of Outspoken Opinions, Her Novels Chronicle 'the Truth' About the South Today." *Publishers Weekly* (November 18, 1988): 55.
Account of an interview with Siddons after the publication of

Peachtree Road. Siddons traces the development of her writing career, explaining how her involvement in the Civil Rights movement and her interest in women's history have been influential in the creation of her novels. Comments on her annoyance when she is compared to Margaret Mitchell; her own aim is not to reaffirm "some pretty dangerous myths" but to tell the truth about the evolution of the South into the Sunbelt.

_____. "Peachtree Road' Is Journey Through Modern Atlanta." *Atlanta Journal-Constitution* (October 16, 1988): p. M10.
A review that argues that *Peachtree Road* is "the Atlanta novel for our time." Despite occasional "overwrought prose," Siddons is to be commended for her subtle characterizations, her humor, and her control over a complex plot. Her accuracy of observation makes her worthy to be called "the Jane Austen of modern Atlanta."

Walsh, William J. "Anne Rivers Siddons." In *Speak So I Shall Know Thee: Interviews with Southern Writers*, pp. 242-252. Jefferson, N.C.: McFarland, 1990.
In this informative interview, Siddons spends considerable time defining the Southern writer and differentiating between writers of the Old South and those, such as herself and her friend Pat Conroy, of the New. She also discusses at length her experiences in writing and promoting her books. Interviews such as this one are useful correctives to the more superficial reviews of Siddons' books.

York, Lamar. "From Hebe to Hippolyta: Anne Rivers Siddons' Novels." *The Southern Literary Journal* 17 (Spring, 1985): 91-99.
Analyzes the first three novels of Siddons as stories of young women who reject the "rigid code of conduct" that was formulated to ensure their docility and choose instead to become strong and independent. The names "Hebe" and "Hippolyta" used in *Fox's Earth* thus typify two directions in which Southern women can go. Although other characters approach Siddons' ideal, it is Nell, Hebe's daughter in *Fox's Earth*, who is "the complete protagonist," the woman most capable of attaining freedom from the code and therefore freedom to love.

LEE SMITH

Arnold, Edwin T. "An Interview with Lee Smith." *Appalachian Journal* 11 (Spring, 1984): 240-254.
A lively exchange covering an array of topics. Main emphasis is on *Oral History*, its characters, and the critical reception. Also discusses the writing process (especially the detailed research Smith undertakes before actual writing). A useful introduction by Arnold outlines Smith's biography and works to date of interview.

Bradley, David. "Lee Smith's Home Truths." *The Village Voice* (August 2, 1983): 39.
A highly complimentary review of *Oral History*. Bradley sees in Smith comparisons to Faulkner and Carson McCullers. The novel is "deserving of unique praise" as a testament to Smith's superior handiwork. Bradley finds every different voice perfectly conceived and executed. This review is indicative of the praise for *Oral History* that brought Smith more national exposure.

Broughton, Irv. "Lee Smith." In *The Writer's Mind: Interviews with American Authors*, edited by Irv Broughton. Vol. 3, pp. 277-297. Fayetteville: University of Arkansas Press, 1990.
A short biographical sketch leads into this lengthy interview. Smith speaks of her writing as a compulsion that makes the act seem effortless. She also discusses her upbringing and the images of childhood that reappear in much of her work. Includes comments on *Fair and Tender Ladies* as a book "about writing in a sense. It's about writing as a way to make it through the night—or save your life, whatever."

Buchanan, Harriette C. "Lee Smith: The Storyteller's Voice." In *Southern Women Writers: The New Generation*, edited by Tonette Bond Inge, pp. 324-345. Tuscaloosa: The University of Alabama Press, 1990.
Considers narrative devices, especially tone and voice, as they enhance the worlds of Smith's characters. Buchanan covers a broad

spectrum of Smith's writings, noting how "attention to detail and to point of view are conscious devices that Smith deliberately manipulates in her work." Despite Smith's comments to the contrary, Buchanan believes the techniques do aim toward an overarching "Deep Hidden Meaning" in the writings. Short bibliography attached.

Canin, Ethan. "The Courage of Their Foolishness." *The New York Times Book Review* (February 11, 1990): 11.
Canin extols the sincerity of Smith's stories in *Me and My Baby View the Eclipse*. "It seems to me that nearly every one of the stories . . . could move a reader to tears," the reviewer admits. Where the stories may ramble, or have loose joints, Canin forgives. Finds "Tongues of Fire" the strongest in the collection.

Coggeshall, Rosanne. *"Black Mountain Breakdown." The Hollins Critic* 18 (April, 1981): 15.
A brief review of the novel, praising the development of Smith as a writer. The book, according to Coggeshall, "signals in her work new dimensions in vision as well as new stylistic and technical mastery." Yet the reviewer finds something missing, something about the main character, Crystal, that is never explained. Coggeshall concludes that ambiguity may be the very point of Crystal's life.

_____. *"Cakewalk." The Hollins Critic* 18 (December, 1981): 17.
A glowing review of the short-story collection. "Smith's *Cakewalk* commands first our attention, then our affection, and then our awe-filled delight," Coggeshall concludes. Though often starting in the concrete world of discount stores and television shows, Smith deftly transports "us to existential borders we've never before imagined."

Dale, Corinne. "The Power of Language in Lee Smith's *Oral History*." *Southern Quarterly* 28 (Winter, 1990): 21-34.
Dale explores the thesis that "all of Smith's novels are about language." Employing feminist critical theories, Dale concludes that "Smith demonstrates the alienating nature of patriarchal language, probing both its anatomical and its cultural roots."

"The Devil's Dream." Publishers Weekly (May 4, 1992): 39-40.
Review of the to-be-published novel *The Devil's Dream*. "Smith's strong, believable characters, their gossipy, matter-of-fact voices and

their affection for their rustic mountain home makes this a rich, inviting multi-generational tale." The humor subsides enough to reveal the poignancy of Katie's lost love and found religion. Notes the empathy for character that marks all of her fiction.

Ehle, John. "Home-Style Mayhem." *The New York Times Book Review* (October 6, 1985): 15.
This reviewer calls *Family Linen* "a friendly book, easily read." He finds it somewhat disorderly at times but as such in keeping with its themes. Ehle notes that Smith is a master of encounters between women while being less distinctive in scenes where men are involved. Finds the characters full and distinct if not exactly inspiring.

Evans, Nancy H., Jean W. Ross, and Katherine Kearns. "Smith, Lee." In *Contemporary Authors*, edited by Hal May. Vol. 119, pp. 344-348. Detroit: Gale Research, 1987.
A full-length biographical/critical citation with interview (conducted in June, 1985). The interview includes familiar discussion of Smith's writing technique and extensive research. She also remarks on the value of teaching to her work and the community of writers in North Carolina. Short bibliography appended.

Gottlieb, Annie. "Three Hapless Heroines." *The New York Times Book Review* (March 29, 1981): 14-15, 22.
Gottlieb understands Crystal as "not a failure but simply a stranger, one who, passing through life at a different angle, found it luminous." The turns of Crystal's life are not fatalistic but surprising and deftly handled by Smith, according to the review. Smith paints a world where "ordinary life has its own comforting poetry."

Hill, Dorothy Combs. "An Interview with Lee Smith." *Southern Quarterly* 28 (Winter, 1990): 5-19.
Taken during the Lee Smith Festival, October, 1985. Smith comments in a straightforward manner on her identity as a writer ("it is fine with me to be called all those things—woman writer, southern writer, Appalachian writer"); her creation of *Oral History* ("I never felt like I wrote that anyway. . . . I had never used research in anything I had written before"); and, in an attached introduction to a reading from *Family Linen*, how each point of view in a story is different ("you can never finally know the truth, if it exists at all").

_____. *Lee Smith*. New York: Twayne, 1992.
Essential. Combining biography with literary analysis, Hill brings together the first book-length study of Smith's life and works. "The wound that the whole important body of Lee Smith's works redresses is the terrible cultural wound inflicted on creative women that keeps them from understanding themselves and even denies them any access to themselves," Hill theorizes in her "Introduction." Covers works through *Fair and Tender Ladies* and *Me and My Baby View the Eclipse*. Notes, selected annotated bibliography, and index.

Jones, Anne Goodwyn. "The World of Lee Smith." In *Women Writers of the Contemporary South*, edited by Peggy Whitman Prenshaw, pp. 249-272. Jackson: University Press of Mississippi, 1984.
A meandering essay covering everything from Smith's personal history to her satirizing of intellectuals. Eventually, Jones considers all Smith's writings in some light or another. Whatever the work, Jones asserts that "technical virtuosities . . . serve her human meaning; vision always takes priority over technique." A good, general review of Smith's themes.

Jones, Suzanne W. "City Folks in Hoot Owl Holler: Narrative Strategy in Lee Smith's *Oral History*." *The Southern Literary Journal* 20 (Fall, 1987): 101-112.
Jones examines ways in which Smith's novel presents widely differing (and often equally prejudiced) perspectives on Appalachian people. Lee Smith, according to Jones, "gives her readers an encounter with Appalachia that forces us to acknowledge our preconception, that shows us how storytelling functions in a community, and that makes us understand how a different place may tempt us with the empty promise of fulfillment." The focus is on the characters of Richard Burlage and Jennifer Bingham.

Kalb, John D. "The Second 'Rape' of Crystal Spangler." *The Southern Literary Journal* 21 (Fall, 1988): 23-30.
Short examination of Crystal's response to rape and misfortune in *Black Mountain Breakdown*. "Crystal's passivity paradoxically becomes an active force, a determined and purposeful surrender that saves her from accepting her role as helpless victim," Kalb claims. For Crystal, paralysis is her only way out of her realities, according to the essay.

Kearns, Katherine. "Lee Smith." In *Dictionary of Literary Biography Yearbook: 1983*, edited by Mary Bruccoli and Jean W. Ross, pp. 314-324. Detroit: Gale Research, 1984.

An extended discussion of Smith's biography and writings. Kearns finds that "Smith's changing attitude toward herself as a writer is the clue to her fiction, which has explored all the ways that women search for identity." Kearns also notes that the characters seem possessed by passivity, though she does not mark this as fatal to the works they populate. Contains references to reviews and a very short bibliography.

Kinsella, W. P. "Left Behind on Blue Star Mountain." *The New York Times Book Review* (September 18, 1988): 9.

Kinsella believes *Fair and Tender Ladies* to be Smith's "most ambitious and most fully realized novel to date." Finds her voice confident and revealing of Ivy's growth. Also praises the portrayal of pop culture's infiltration of Southern life. "Readers will be sorry when this literate, intelligent, insightful and entertaining novel draws to a close," Kinsella concludes.

Lodge, Michelle. "Lee Smith." *Publishers Weekly* (September 20, 1985): 110-111.

A conversational essay based on an interview with Smith in New York. Most of the information concerns *Family Linen*, but Lodge covers a range of other aspects of Smith's writings and life. A minor but interesting note concerns Smith's need to differentiate her fiction from her nonfiction. One she composes in longhand, the other on the typewriter. The essay is useful but not particularly insightful.

MacKethan, Lucinda H. "Artists and Beauticians: Balance in Lee Smith's Fiction." *The Southern Literary Journal* 15 (Fall, 1982): 3-14.

Authoritative study of Smith's fiction. MacKethan very meticulously addresses her balancing act between "art," with its array of high techniques and ideas, and the "rumpled realities" that more often concern Smith and her characters. According to MacKethan, Smith finds that balance most completely in *Black Mountain Breakdown* and *Cakewalk*, "particularly in their choices of tone, point of view, and texture."

_____. *Daughters of Time: Creating Woman's Voice in Southern Story*, pp. 102-111. Athens: University of Georgia Press, 1990.

A brief examination of Smith's *Fair and Tender Ladies*. The author explores ways in which Ivy Rowe struggles to integrate her ordained roles of daughter and mother. Like Celie in Alice Walker's *The Color Purple*, Ivy longs to escape societal boundaries. MacKethan compares and contrasts the means that the characters employ to create a new life and the letters, filled with pain, that they write.

Manuel, Diane. "Voices from Virginia's Heartland." *The Christian Science Monitor* (November 25, 1988): 26.

Review of *Fair and Tender Ladies*. Places Smith among the new Southern women writers—such as Godwin, Tyler, Mason—"staking out . . . provocative settings and themes." The current novel continues Smith's move toward the top of that list. The letters, according to Manuel, are rich and moving. "Ivy's voice is the heart of her work, and it shimmers with the surprise of a Mason jar filled with July's brightest lightning bugs."

Morrow, Mark. *Images of the Southern Writer*. Athens: University of Georgia Press, 1985.

A full-page photograph and brief informal interview, in which Smith reflects on her writing habits, life-style, and the driving force behind much of her writing. According to Smith, "Southern women are always trying to fit themselves into an image and trying to find the proper way to act. I mean, *Black Mountain Breakdown* is all about the dangers of this passivity." Morrow's verbal portrait of Smith is as sensitive as his photographic study.

Pollitt, Katha. "Southern Stories." *The New York Times Book Review* (November 22, 1981): 14, 24.

A review of *Cakewalk*. Pollitt proclaims that Smith "is to Southern writing what the New South is to the South." That is, Smith populates her South with the mundane realities of tract housing, television, and strip malls, not so much with the gothic relics of forgotten history. What Smith lacks in ambition for the stories, according to Pollitt, she makes up for in clarity of voice and compassion.

Reilly, Rosalind B. "*Oral History*: The Enchanted Circle of Narrative and Dream." *The Southern Literary Journal* 23 (Fall, 1990): 79-92.
Reilly traces images of circularity in the novel, relating them to the characters' dreams and to the narrative structure of the work as a whole. "For both men and women in Hoot Owl Holler, dreams of perfection tend to be embodied by someone of the opposite sex so that the magic circle of the imagination is also a magic circle of union with another person," this essay theorizes. Highly suggestive if not thoroughly convincing.

Seay, Marshall. "*Fancy Strut*." In *Survey of Contemporary Literature*, edited by Frank N. Magill. Rev. and enlarged ed., Vol. 4, pp. 2446-2448. Englewood Cliffs, N.J.: Salem Press, 1977.
A largely uncritical review of Smith's "lusty and often humorous" novel. Seay does present the major themes at work, including the idea of changing times and of a changing persona for the town and characters. This is a novel about "a new South and a new town," according to the reviewer.

Skow, John. "This Old House." *Time* 126 (November 18, 1985): 104.
Review of *Family Linen*. Skow notes the pressures on Smith after the "bell ringer" success of *Oral History*. This novel, he seems to conclude, does not disappoint. Smith once again, according to Skow, "is interested in her plot, but she is fascinated by her people." The murder mystery of the book is more an "undercurrent" to the main purpose of exposing character vulnerabilities and family tensions.

Smith, Lee. "In the Beginning . . ." *Writer* 96 (December, 1983): 9-11, 43.
A succinct, simply worded essay on how to begin a story. Smith believes "a story happens at the point at which plot and character intersect." She warns against long introductory descriptions, preferring to place the reader in the action as soon as possible, especially in the short story. This article may provide useful clues in analyzing Smith's own fiction.

_____. "A Stubborn Sense of Place." *Harper's* 273 (August, 1986): 38.
Smith is one of nine Southern authors asked by *Harper's* to respond to questions about "the place of the writer in the new American South." This brief entry is witty and demonstrates Smith's toying

with the narrative voice. The most succinct summation of Smith's "answer" may be: The more things change, the more they stay the same.

_____. "The Voice Behind the Story." In *Voicelust: Eight Contemporary Fiction Writers on Style*, edited by Allen Wier and Don Hendrie, Jr., pp. 93-100. Lincoln: University of Nebraska Press, 1985.
An essay on Smith's process for finding her voice as an author. She discusses her early difficulties in choosing subjects and appropriate narrative point of view for writing. For Smith those elements are crucial to defining voice, and voice is crucial to defining literature, especially "Southern" literature, which has largely been "done." Smith argues that "the best we can hope for . . . is to make it new through language—through point of view, through tone, through style."

Taylor, Henry. "The Last Day the Dogbushes Bloomed." In *Survey of Contemporary Literature*, edited by Frank N. Magill. Rev. and enlarged ed. Vol. 6, pp. 4105-4108. Englewood Cliffs, N.J.: Salem Press, 1977.
Reading of Smith's first novel, noting her as "a promising new talent." Taylor focuses much of his discussion on the fine line Smith must walk between being true to the narrator's nine-year-old voice and projecting the truths of the mature author. For the most part, the reviewer believes Smith keeps her balance, though he points out "minor" flaws throughout the story.

Thompson, Caroline. "The Particulars of Crystal Gazing." *Los Angeles Times* (February 16, 1981): sec. 4, p. 6.
Review of *Black Mountain Breakdown*, noting the strength of descriptions, yet bemoaning the contrivances of plot. Thompson believes the events in Crystal's life "reek of phoniness, losing all meaning and whatever power they might otherwise have."

Walsh, William J. "Lee Smith." In *Speak So I Shall Know Thee: Interviews with Southern Writers*, pp. 256-262. Jefferson, N.C.: McFarland, 1990.
An extensive, engaging interview with a special discussion of Smith's publishing history and of how difficult the commercial aspects of writing can be. Smith also confesses to difficulties with

Crystal as a main character in *Black Mountain Breakdown* as well as what her intentions for the book were. Other topics include the writer as teacher, the importance of a writer's community, and the motivations for writing either short stories or novels.

Yardley, Jonathan. "Bewitched Voices." *The Washington Post* (June 15, 1983): pp. B1, B8.
Review of *Oral History*. Yardley considers the novel Smith's best to date. He finds the creation of the varied voices and the tensions among them to be one of the book's strengths, along with "its utterly unsympathetic view of the mountain people and its vivid description of the physical world they inhabit."

ELIZABETH SPENCER

Anderson, Hilton. *Elizabeth Spencer*. Jackson: Mississippi Library Commission, 1976.
A short monograph that emphasizes the influence of Spencer's Mississippi background on her fiction. In a chronological discussion of individual works, Anderson demonstrates the importance of Spencer's historical consciousness, as well as her sense of place, in the formulation of her plots and the creation of her characters. Summarizes and comments upon reactions of critics to various works. Includes an excellent, though dated, bibliography.

_____. "Elizabeth Spencer's Two Italian Novellas." *Notes on Mississippi Writers* 13 (1981): 18-35.
Although Spencer's novellas about Americans in Italy invite comparison with the works of Henry James, she describes not an external conflict between duplicitous Italians and innocent, culture-seeking Americans but an internal one, which takes place within the minds of the heroines. Critics have erred in stressing superficial similarities to James; in fact, there are far more differences than likenesses. Spencer has been inspired by her own observations of Americans in Italy, not by the literary heritage. Well reasoned.

_____. "Fleur du mal: Elizabeth Spencer's Portrait of New Orleans." *Xavier Review* 8 (1988): 47-52.
In Spencer's fiction, New Orleans represents a contrast to the stability and conservativism of Mississippi. It is also the place where Mississippians go to indulge in evil. In *The Snare*, set in New Orleans, Julia Garrett chooses to live an evil life rather than one that is empty and dull, thus symbolizing her wicked but fascinating city, a place where everything is permitted.

Bell, Madison Smartt. "A Bond of Braided Histories." *The New York Times Book Review* (September 4, 1988): 6.
Points out the importance of setting in *Jack of Diamond and Other Stories*. Spencer sees it as more than mere landscape, but as a

complex of customs, traditions, and historical consciousness that influence attitudes and behavior. As a result, her short stories have more depth than those of most other contemporary writers.

Bradbury, John M. "The Later Traditionalists." In *Renaissance in the South: A Critical History of Literature, 1920-1960*, pp. 107-139. Chapel Hill: University of North Carolina Press, 1963.
Classifies Elizabeth Spencer as one of the New Traditionalists, following the generation of New Critics in technical virtuosity and in her "concern with the problems of innocence and guilt, with family and heritage." It is perhaps not surprising that this former student at Vanderbilt, home of the Nashville Agrarians of the previous generation, is herself an agrarian. Her first four novels place her "in the direct line of descent from Faulkner, Warren, and Eudora Welty." Along with Peter Taylor, Spencer ranks at the top of her generation of writers. *The Light in the Piazza*, set in Italy, indicates that she is reaching beyond the South for themes and settings.

Brinnin, John Malcolm. "Black and White in Redneck Country." *The Washington Post* (May 15, 1983): p. 10.
A reconsideration of *The Voice at the Back Door* twenty-seven years after its publication, arguing that it dramatized a shift in values that was already taking place before desegregation. While many characters in the novel are selfish and ambitious, more significant is the "decency" shown by both blacks and whites, responding to each other with "natural charity." Although Spencer considered updating her book before it was published, fortunately she did not do so but published the novel as she had written it, realistically reflecting "a way of life obscured by outrage and oversimplified by headlines."

Broadwell, Elizabeth Pell, and Ronald Wesley Hoag. "A Conversation with Elizabeth Spencer." *The Southern Review* 18 (Winter, 1982): 111-130. Also in *Conversations with Elizabeth Spencer*, edited by Peggy Whitman Prenshaw, pp. 56-76. Jackson: University Press of Mississippi, 1991.
A wide-ranging "conversation" that elicits information and opinions from Spencer not found in other sources, for example, a clear statement of the dominant theme in her stories: "liberation and the regret you have when you liberate yourself." As for style, Spencer aims at a middle ground between Ernest Hemingway, who "hobbled" language, and William Faulkner, who "inflated" it. Style must also

be flexible; a work set outside the South must not be written in the "rhythms, cadences, and expressions" that constitute the "idiomatic language of the South." The characters in a number of short stories and novels are considered. The interview ends with Spencer's statement that male characters are easier for her to create than female characters because as a woman, she has difficulty eliminating her own characteristics from a woman character.

Broughton, Irv. "Elizabeth Spencer." In *The Writer's Mind: Interviews with American Authors.* Vol. 2, pp. 97-126. Fayetteville: University of Arkansas Press, 1990. Also in *Conversations with Elizabeth Spencer*, edited by Peggy Whitman Prenshaw, pp. 148-169. Jackson: University Press of Mississippi, 1991.
Spencer's interest in writing, which began during her childhood, was a response to the delight in reading and in storytelling that she saw in family members. Southern traditions are important to her. Spencer needed to live outside the South for a time, however, in order to see it more clearly. In Italy, she found much that reminded her of the South, particularly the class structure and the emphasis on a code of behavior. Eventually, she felt a need to return to the South that was as compelling as her earlier need to leave it. As for the purpose of her fiction, she wishes it to become so much a part of the readers' experience that it will influence their lives.

Brown, Laurie L. "Interviews with Seven Contemporary Writers." In *Women Writers of the Contemporary South*, edited by Peggy Whitman Prenshaw, pp. 3-22. Jackson: University Press of Mississippi, 1984.
Based on the answers seven writers gave to specific questions about their experience with writing as a vocation. Because it is organized question by question, the essay can show similarities and contrasts between the writers. In her case, Spencer does not think that being a woman hampered her becoming a writer; in fact, since she was not expected to support a family, the idea probably met less opposition than if she had been a man. Several other responses by Spencer have to do with the writer's need for balance; for example, between solitude and companionship, particularly friendships with other writers, and between intellectual independence and the need to communicate with the public and to win critical approval.

Bunting, Charles T. "In That Time and at That Place': The Literary World of Elizabeth Spencer." *Mississippi Quarterly: The Journal of Southern Culture* 28 (Fall, 1975): 435-460. Also in *Conversations with Elizabeth Spencer*, edited by Peggy Whitman Prenshaw, pp. 17-40. Jackson: University of Mississippi Press.

An interview that focuses on the importance of Spencer's Southern heritage in her fiction. She characterizes the South as tending to the "mythical" and the "primitive," perhaps because of fundamentalist religion, which emphasizes an instinctive, not a rational, response. She also describes the surprisingly sympathetic reaction of some of her hometown neighbors to *The Voice at the Back Door*. In her later work, there is a preoccupation with good and evil, fantasy and madness. For Spencer, the impulse to write comes from the imagination, however, not from a philosophical position, and thus it is only after the writing that she can perceive the patterns in her work.

Burger, Nash K. "Elizabeth Spencer's Three Mississippi Novels." *The South Atlantic Quarterly* 63 (Summer, 1964): 351-362.

A critique and an appreciation of three early novels, all set in Mississippi: *Fire in the Morning, This Crooked Way*, and *The Voice at the Back Door*. Like Faulkner in her sense of place and in the scope of her narratives, Spencer has her own "feminine sensibility," as well as a "sharp, discerning eye and ear" and a "fondness for neat and intricate plotting." As a knowledgeable Southerner, Spencer insists on writing realistically about a complex society, showing, for example, that there are great differences in opinion and in motivation within both the black and the white communities, as well as long-standing personal ties that cross the racial boundary.

Cole, Hunter McKelva. "Elizabeth Spencer at Sycamore Fair." *Notes on Mississippi Writers* 6 (Winter, 1974): 81-86.

A 1973 interview, which includes comments on various subjects. Spencer speaks of the "woman writer" category, which she finds useful if it merely implies a different sensibility. She also muses on Faulkner's well-known reclusiveness, having found him pleasant when she saw him in Italy. Spencer voices her admiration for Ellen Douglas and Eudora Welty, as well as for Walker Percy.

_____. "Windsor in Spencer and Welty: A Real and an Imaginary Landscape." *Notes on Mississippi Writers* 7 (Spring, 1974): 2-11.

The ruins of Windsor, a plantation house near Port Gibson, Mississippi, have fascinated both Eudora Welty and Elizabeth Spencer. In Spencer's short story "A Southern Landscape," a young, rascally aristocrat, Foster Hamilton, chooses Windsor for his attempt to seduce Marilee Summerall, a girl whose family background is more modest than his. Although his scheme does not succeed, in later years both the decadent Foster Hamilton and Windsor itself become "monuments" that represent permanence in Marilee's imagination.

Evoy, Karen. *"Marilee*: "A Permanent Landscape of the Heart." *Mississippi Quarterly: The Journal of Southern Culture* 36 (Fall, 1983): 569-578.
The three stories in which Marilee Summerall appears are united not only by common characters, a single setting, and persistent themes but also by the voice of Marilee herself. Although this voice might seem to be Spencer's, who shares many qualities with Marilee, the author maintains an ironic distance from her heroine. A thoughtful, detailed analysis of stories that are of major importance in the totality of Spencer's work.

French, Warren. "Elizabeth Spencer." In *Contemporary Novelists*, edited by D. L. Kirkpatrick. 4th ed., pp. 775-776. New York: St. Martin's Press, 1986.
Biographical and bibliographical information, comments by Spencer, and a critical essay. Spencer's impulse to write developed out of her early perception of the world as composed of "stories," whose source might be local anecdote, the Bible, classics, myths, or history. In his essay, French suggests that though Spencer's characters may survive, they rarely triumph. Thus, in *The Salt Line*, where love seems to promise redemption, it actually "helps people endure, but not prevail."

Gill, Brendan. "All Praise." *The New Yorker* (December 15, 1956): 180-181.
A review calling *The Voice at the Back Door* "a practically perfect novel" that combines "charm and humor" with moral seriousness. The work is optimistic, rather than tragic, in tone, as seen in the fact that even the antihero finally chooses good and rejects evil. While Spencer uses the materials of Faulkner, she lacks his baroque quality and is more comparable to James Gould Cozzens.

Haley, Josephine. "An Interview with Elizabeth Spencer." *Notes on Mississippi Writers* 1 (Fall, 1968): 42-55.
An early interview. Deals with Spencer's use of her Southern material. Also involves a lengthy discussion of her approach to her craft. Her motivation is "to clarify the world for myself." She is happy when her stories are published but surprised when occasionally, as with *The Light in the Piazza*, she actually makes money from them.

Herz, Judith Scherer, and Robert K. Martin, eds. "Writers' Panel." In *E. M. Forster: Centenary Revaluations*, pp. 285-307. Toronto: University of Toronto Press, 1982.
At a conference in Montreal, Canada, held in May, 1979, five writers, including Elizabeth Spencer and Eudora Welty, were asked to comment on the influence of E. M. Forster on their work. In her initial statement, Spencer describes her first encounter with Forster's writing and then suggests that her own style was influenced by his "modestly woven manner of expression," with "its own rhythms." She illustrates that by reading a passage from Forster's *Where Angels Fear to Tread* and then one from her book *The Light on the Piazza*, which, like Forster's, is set in Italy. Spencer replies briefly to questions from the audience as to the keeping or disposal of manuscripts and as to the exact nature of inspiration.

Hoffman, Frederick J. "The Mark of Time: Society and History in Southern Fiction." In *The Art of Southern Fiction: A Study of Some Modern Novelists*, pp. 96-114. Carbondale: Southern Illinois University Press, 1967.
Southern writers have always been "interested in and puzzled by history." The nostalgia for the old order that dominated Southern literature as late as the 1930's was followed by a more complex perception of what Southern society had been and still continued to be. Writers recognized that the most difficult issue Southerners had to face was that of black-white relationships. In *The Voice at the Back Door*, Elizabeth Spencer makes it clear that the attitude of whites toward blacks is both a moral and a political problem, and that when, as in this story, the liberal protagonist's clear moral stance appears to threaten the safety of his community, violence and death may result. Spencer's recognition of this problem is admirable, even though as a whole the book is "bloated" with unconvincing love affairs and with complications that are inadequately developed.

Jones, John Griffin. "Elizabeth Spencer." In *Mississippi Writers Talking*, edited by John Griffin Jones. Vol. 1, pp. 94-129. Jackson: University Press of Mississippi, 1982. Also in *Conversations with Elizabeth Spencer*, edited by Peggy Whitman Prenshaw, pp. 113-133. Jackson: University Press of Mississippi, 1991.

Spencer describes her family history at length, explaining in detail the way in which geography shaped the lives of family members, as it also affects characters in her works. She speculates on the complex process that culminates in one's becoming a writer, with references to her own experiences in childhood and in college. She also comments on the degree to which she feels her fiction was influenced by that of William Faulkner and Eudora Welty. While admitting the importance of her Southern background and of her gender to her writing, Spencer feels that she should not be limited by being categorized either as a Southern writer or as a woman writer.

Meeker, Richard K. "The Youngest Generation of Southern Fiction Writers." In *Southern Writers: Appraisals in Our Time*, edited by R. C. Simonini, Jr., pp. 162-191. Charlottesville: University Press of Virginia, 1964.

Includes Elizabeth Spencer, along with Peter Taylor, Madison Jones, and Walter Sullivan, as writers of the "second-generation Vanderbilt school," influenced by the Nashville Agrarians. They are analytical, polished, proficient in their craft. In both *This Crooked Way* and *The Voice at the Back Door*, Spencer concentrates on the contrast between the old, traditional society, which is decaying, and the new, which at its best may outlaw oppressive customs, and at its worst, may replace a graceful kind of order with brutal materialism.

Morrow, Mark. "Elizabeth Spencer." In *Images of the Southern Writer*, pp. 72-73. Athens: University of Georgia Press, 1985.

A full-page photograph and a brief interview, which was conducted in Atlanta before Spencer came back to the South to live. She comments on her residence in Canada and in Europe but claims "her heart" is "still in the South." Despite frequent visits to the South, she "regrets she has had to catch the changing South "on the run." Also speaks about the effects of her contacts with Eudora Welty and Donald Davidson on the progress of her career and credits her brief job as a journalist with improving her style.

Nance, Guin A. "Elizabeth Spencer." In *American Women Writers: A Critical Reference Guide from Colonial Times to the Present*, edited by Lina Mainiero. Vol. 4, pp. 139-141. New York: Frederick Ungar, 1982.
Brief biographical sketch and critical commentary on her works, emphasizing Spencer's expanded scope as she ventured beyond settings in her native South. Indicates that the dominant theme in Spencer's work is the alienation of the individual, no matter what the milieu.

Neely, Jessica. "Personal Allegiances." *Belles Lettres: A Review of Books by Women* 7 (Winter, 1991-1992): 11-12.
Discussion of *The Night Travellers* and *Jack of Diamonds*. Sees in both the novel and the short stories a recognition of conflicts involving allegiances, whether personal or ideological. Spencer also writes about the distrust engendered by prejudice, whether in Montreal or in Tyler, Mississippi. Neely calls both books works "of depth and grace and enormous humanity."

Nettels, Elsa. "Elizabeth Spencer." In *Southern Women Writers: The New Generation*, edited by Tonette Bond Inge, pp. 70-96. Tuscaloosa: University of Alabama Press, 1990.
Probably the best brief study of Spencer. Skillfully draws from biographical details, statements in interviews, critical insights, and the evidence of the works themselves. Concludes that Spencer's central theme is that life cannot be separated into categories such as "life and death, health and sickness, sanity and madness," or past and present. As a modern Southern writer, Spencer is producing "new forms and meanings" out of the materials of the past. The bibliography includes a list of published interviews.

Park, Clara Claiborne. "A Personal Road." *The Hudson Review* 34 (Winter, 1981-1982): 601-605.
Spencer's use of her Southern background is unique. She does not emphasize the memory of the Civil War or the lives of the poor, whether black or white. She does dramatize, however, the consciousness of place in the social scale, which preoccupies the middle and upper classes in the South and which propels Spencer's characters into plans for escape. The need to walk a "personal road" and the fact that one must pay a price for doing so are seen by Spencer as a universal dilemma.

Phillips, Robert. "The Art of Fiction CX: Elizabeth Spencer." *The Paris Review* 31 (Summer, 1989): 184-213. Also in *Conversations with Elizabeth Spencer*, pp. 113-133. Jackson: University Press of Mississippi, 1991.

Based on three interviews with Spencer, along with questions that she answered in written form. The emphasis is on her theoretical and practical approach to her craft. Among writers she admires, Spencer includes Willa Cather, Herman Melville, and Mark Twain; however, she does not agree with critics who believe that her Italian works suggest dependence on Henry James. Like other Southern writers, she sees herself as approaching the truth not abstractly but through concrete characters and incidents. A one-page typed draft of a short story, with handwritten corrections, is printed opposite the initial page of the article.

Prenshaw, Peggy Whitman, ed. *Conversations with Elizabeth Spencer*. Jackson: University Press of Mississippi, 1991.

A collection of eighteen conversations, thirteen of which have been published previously. Three others are transcriptions from television or radio programs, and two were conducted for this book. The conversations are unedited and are arranged in chronological order. A biographical chronology is included, as well as an invaluable index of titles, proper names, and topics.

_____. *Elizabeth Spencer*. Boston: Twayne, 1985.

The first book-length study of Spencer. Based on numerous interviews with the author and checked by her for factual accuracy. The first chapter, "A Life of Storytelling," is biographical. A full chapter is devoted to each of seven novels, discussed in chronological order. A separate chapter deals with the novella *Knights and Dragons* and the related story "Ship Island." Her other short stories are discussed in chapter 9. In her conclusion, Prenshaw praises Spencer for her artisanship and for the range and variety of her work. The conflict that can be traced throughout Spencer's fiction is that between individuality and conformity; although she understands the need for independence, Spencer sees "the danger posed by a society or a fiction dominated by self-obsessed, self-enclosed persons." Contains a detailed chronology, as well as a primary and secondary bibliography. Sound, readable, and perceptive.

_____. "Elizabeth Spencer." In *The History of Southern Literature*, edited by Louis D. Rubin, Jr., pp. 497-500. Baton Rouge: Louisiana State University Press, 1985.
Brief biographical summary and chronological discussion of Spencer's works. While her themes and subject matter suggest William Faulkner and Robert Penn Warren, her treatment is original and often powerful. She combines modernist devices with traditional, effective plot development and characterization.

_____. "Mermaids, Angels, and Free Women: The Heroines of Elizabeth Spencer's Fiction." In *Women Writers of the Contemporary South*, edited by Peggy Whitman Prenshaw, pp. 146-164. Jackson: University Press of Mississippi, 1984.
Argues that in Spencer's later fiction, women protagonists begin as figures tormented by uncertainty about their own nature. They are torn between consciousness of an individual identity and the world's requirement that they assume expected roles. These roles may be expressed in images of "seductive but evasive mermaids" and "passive angels," as well as in references to isolation and captivity. Although almost all of these women are Southerners, they are already cut off, emotionally or physically, from the sense of place that could have sustained them. They struggle toward freedom, but in the process, they find that they must pay a price for it.

Pugh, David G. "*The Voice at the Back Door*: Elizabeth Spencer Looks into Mississippi." In *The Fifties: Fiction, Poetry, Drama*, edited by Warren French, pp. 103-110. Deland, Fla.: Everett/Edwards, 1970.
An analysis of Spencer's early novel *The Voice at the Back Door*, as a realistic picture of the pattern of hypocrisy evident in Mississippi in the 1950's. Pugh explains the subtext of much of the dialogue and even the significance of "costume or gesture or setting," which might be lost on a reader unfamiliar with Southern society. Many of his examples involve the women characters, who are shown as motivated not by real feelings but by their desire to fulfill the expectations of society.

Reisman, Rosemary M. Canfield. "*Jack of Diamonds and Other Stories*." In *Magill's Literary Annual: Books of 1991*, edited by Frank N. Magill. Vol. 1, pp. 405-408. Englewood Cliffs, N.J.: Salem Press, 1992.
Although many of her short stories do not take place in the South,

Spencer's preoccupations are those of Southern writers, such as the influence of the past in the present, the desire for stability in a world dominated by transience, and the conflict between the individual and the community. The persistence of a few themes, however, does not make her stories repetitive. They vary greatly not only in setting but also in plot and in the cast of characters.

_____. *"The Night Travellers."* In *Magill's Literary Annual: Books of 1991*, edited by Frank N. Magill. Vol. 2, pp. 573-576. Englewood Cliffs, N.J.: Salem Press, 1992.
Interprets the novel as an account of the heroine's search for freedom, which ironically is threatened both by her conservative parents and by her equally adamant husband, an activist in the fight against the Vietnam War, who for the sake of his own passion is willing to sacrifice his child, his wife, and his wife's career as a dancer. The essay also stresses Spencer's theme of the universal need for home and stability, which typically conflicts with the drive to attain independence of thought and action. Differs from reviews that ignore the flaws of the antiwar activists.

Smith, Amanda. "Elizabeth Spencer: The Southern writer Optimistically Explores the Almost Impenetrable Mysteries of the Human Heart." *Publishers Weekly* (September 9, 1988): 111.
An interview emphasizing Spencer's Southern roots, which Smith calls "the central influence on her fiction." Spencer believes that Southerners, especially Southern women, have a unique sensibility; although she has lived in many places, she still possesses this sensibility. The Gulf Coast is especially appealing to her. The stories in the *Jack of Diamonds* collection, like her other works, emphasize the fact that human relationships are basically mysterious.

Spencer, Elizabeth. "Emerging as a Writer in Faulkner's Mississippi." In *Faulkner and the Southern Renaissance*, edited by Doreen Fowler and Ann Abadie, pp. 120-137. Jackson: University Press of Mississippi, 1982.
A talk given by Spencer at the 1981 Faulkner and Yoknapatawpha Conference in Oxford, Mississippi, in which she explains why although her family and friends read widely, they did not read William Faulkner. After she went to Vanderbilt and discovered Faulkner, Spencer, like others of her generation, had to struggle against his influence on her own writing, especially in style. Despite

her admiration of Faulkner, she is concerned about some of his attitudes: his nihilism, his depiction of women, and his assumption that only the group he calls Snopeses are capable of villainy. She urges that in admiring him as a folkhero and his later works as redemptive, readers remember the element in Faulkner that is "complicated, wild, passionate, dark and dangerous—the real thing."

_____. "On Writing Fiction." *Notes on Mississippi Writers* 3 (Fall, 1970): 71-72.
A brief statement about Spencer's motivation in writing. Although she still does not know what her major pattern or theme may be, she believes that her work succeeds in "stirring the deep serious roots of life."

_____. "Revisiting Teoc." In *Family Portraits: Remembrances by Twenty Distinguished Writers*, edited by Carolyn Anthony, pp. 219-236. New York: Doubleday, 1989.
Memoir of Elizabeth Spencer's childhood visits to Teoc, the plantation home of her lovable uncle, Joseph Pinckney McCain. Deep in the Mississippi countryside, Teoc became a refuge for the two Spencer children, a place where they could feel free. An unconventional man who was intolerant only of "hypocrisy, or churlishness," or failing to keep one's word, McCain was responsible for making Teoc a place of harmony and joy. The most complete explanation of McCain's importance to Spencer during her formative years.

_____. "Storytelling, Old and New." *The Writer* 85 (January, 1972): 9-10, 30.
Spencer's writing came naturally from growing up in a society that "believed in stories." Her own inspiration comes from actual events that puzzle her and stimulate her imagination; in writing a story, she searches for an answer. The author concludes by expressing her boredom with modern self-exploration and her conviction that writers find richer material in "group stories," which are told, retold, and expanded within a community. Such stories would bring people together instead of locking them into private isolation.

Sullivan, Walter. "The Continuing Renascence: Southern Fiction in the Fifties." In *South: Modern Southern Literature in Its Cultural Setting*, edited by Louis D. Rubin, Jr., and Robert D. Jacobs, pp.

376-391. Garden City, N.Y.: Doubleday, 1961.

Praises Spencer as a writer who gives "new life" to the Southern Literary Renaissance through her "exploration of the social and political tensions" in the South, as seen in *The Voice at the Back Door*. The novel is technically "faultless"; furthermore, it is admirable in that Spencer refuses to oversimplify but "allows humanity to all" of her characters. Its only flaw is a somewhat contrived ending.

_____. "Love in a Bad Season." *The Sewanee Review* 99 (Summer, 1991): 80-82.

In this review of *The Night Travellers*, a longtime admirer suggests that Spencer's art can triumph even over bad timing. Although her novel about Vietnam War protesters appeared when Americans were celebrating their victory over Iraq, fortunately Spencer's emphasis was not on political issues but on the description of a difficult historical period and on its results in the lives of those who lived through it. The central interest of this distinguished book is not in ideas or events but in the "enduring and loving" heroine.

Welty, Eudora. "Foreword." In *The Stories of Elizabeth Spencer*, pp. xvii-xix. New York: Doubleday, 1981.

Welty's description of her first meeting with her fellow Mississippian, Elizabeth Spencer, then a student at Belhaven College in Jackson, Mississippi. The older writer recalls her impression of Spencer as a mannerly, giggly Southern girl who was already dedicated to her art. Welty praises Spencer for her skill in evoking a sense of place and in capturing the nuances of human relationships, along with her "capacity for cool detachment" and her "deliberateness to pull no punches," a combination of qualities that is reminiscent of Katherine Mansfield. An illuminating and important essay.

Winchell, Mark Royden. "A Golden Ball of Thread: The Achievement of Elizabeth Spencer." *The Sewanee Review* 97 (Fall, 1989): 580-586.

During the years that Elizabeth Spencer spent outside of her native South, she retained a consciousness of home, which was reflected even in works set in Italy or in Canada. In *The Salt Line*, she has returned to a Mississippi setting. Since the publication of that novel and of her collected stories, Spencer has received increased critical attention. While critics continue to mention her fine artisanship, they now are becoming more aware of Spencer's analytical power. Although a moralist, she is not didactic, for she recognizes the complexity of the moral decisions with which human beings are faced; although a Southerner who left home in order to attain independence, she has come to recognize that the identity of an individual depends on the recollection of home and a recognition of one's attachment to family.

ANNE TYLER

Betts, Doris. "The Fiction of Anne Tyler." In *Women Writers of the Contemporary South*, edited by Peggy Whitman Prenshaw, pp. 23-37. Jackson: University Press of Mississippi, 1984.

An important essay previously published in *Southern Quarterly* (Summer, 1983). Succinctly and simply sums up some of the predominant images and themes in Tyler. Sees Tyler dealing with "a Reality which changes very little, but waits for its runaways to come home and learn at the dinner table how to tolerate even their next-of-kin." Gives particular attention to photography as metaphor (and to links to Welty). See also in this same volume Laurie L. Brown's "Interviews with Seven Contemporary Writers" (pp. 3-22). Tyler answers by mail (as usual) but with some slightly longer answers than usual.

Binding, Paul. "Anne Tyler." In *Separate Country: A Literary Journey Through the American South*, pp. 198-209. New York: Paddington Press, 1979.

Based on a visit to Tyler's home in Baltimore (and part of Binding's "tour" of other literary figures). Not so much an interview as an essay on her works with occasional notes on Tyler's own comments. Perhaps a few important ideas here, among them that Tyler "disowns" her first two novels and that Binding can think of "no woman writer who writes more sympathetically about men."

Bowers, Bradley R. "Anne Tyler's Insiders." *Mississippi Quarterly* 42 (Winter, 1988-1989): 47-56.

Bowers finds Tyler's irony and humor particularly expressed by the way in which "we become 'insiders' who understand the implication of a particular phrase, who watch the characters verbally run toward each other with loving and open arms, sometimes connecting but all too often running past." Thus, character is revealed by verbal interplay in which characters are often unaware of the revelations. Concludes that technique is one of Tyler's most effective skills.

Brooks, Mary Ellen. "Anne Tyler." *Dictionary of Literary Biography: American Novelists Since World War II*, edited by James E. Kibler, Jr. 2d ser. Vol. 6, pp. 336-345. Detroit: Gale Research, 1980.
Covers her life and work up through *Morgan's Passing*. Includes useful biographical notes and critical review of her works. Sources are not given for the numerous quotes from Tyler herself that are well worked into the discussion of her writing. Bibliography of Tyler's short-story publications attached.

Cook, Bruce. "New Faces in Faulkner Country." *Saturday Review* (September 4, 1976): 39-41.
Article on the whole idea of what constitutes post-Faulkner Southern writing. Tyler is considered, according to a quote by Reynolds Price, "the nearest thing we have to an urban Southern novelist." Tyler is quoted as denying any indebtedness to Faulkner, instead claiming Eudora Welty as her greatest influence. Good essay for understanding the context of Tyler's writing.

Eckard, Paula Gallant. "Family and Community in Anne Tyler's *Dinner at the Homesick Restaurant*." *The Southern Literary Journal* 22 (Spring, 1990): 33-44.
Using comparisons to Faulkner and McCullers, Eckard argues that *Dinner* is in the Southern tradition of portraying the powers of family and community. "Through the Tulls, Tyler shows that while families can be a source of anguish and pain, they also can provide a touchstone for remembering common pasts and for finding a sense of place, belonging, and, ultimately, oneself."

English, Sarah. "Anne Tyler." *Dictionary of Literary Biography Yearbook: 1982*, edited by Richard Ziegfeld, pp. 187-194. Detroit: Gale Research, 1983.
Includes brief interview (conducted in writing in July, 1982). The extreme private nature of Tyler is revealed in such comments as, "I've never felt my real life had that much to do with my writing life," and by the brevity of her answers (markedly shorter than the questions). Good review of works. Short bibliography.

Gibson, Mary Ellis. "Family as Fate: The Novels of Anne Tyler." *The Southern Literary Journal* 16 (Fall, 1983): 47-58.
Gibson reads the works up through *Dinner at the Homesick Restaurant* as sharing a common philosophy in which "the familial becomes

metaphysical." According to Gibson, "Tyler works an intricate commentary on the nature of fate and on the importance of family to individual understandings of fate and responsibility." Also calls for greater academic attention to Tyler. Has helpful footnotes.

Gilbert, Susan. "Anne Tyler." In *Southern Women Writers: The New Generation*, edited by Tonette Bond Inge, pp. 251-278. Tuscaloosa: University of Alabama Press, 1990.
This thoughtful essay focuses on the proposition that in twenty years of writing, Tyler's concerns have deepened, not widened. The novels pry apart the world of the family and the burdens of history, dealing with the desire to escape followed by the inevitable return. "There is the repeated emphasis on movement without change, on change without movement," Gilbert posits. Notes and bibliography.

Jones, Anne Goodwyn. "Home at Last, and Homesick Again: The Ten Novels of Anne Tyler." *The Hollins Critic* 23 (April, 1986): 1-14.
Jones unifies Tyler's works by positing that her "texts concern themselves, through metaphor of home and wandering, with the issue of personal psychic growth." Jones finds tensions between the search for home's perfect comfort and the inevitable failure of that search throughout Tyler's fiction. Most notable in resolving the dilemma, according to Jones, is Macon in *The Accidental Tourist*, who returns "home" while choosing "to abandon his illusions that home means either safety or imperishable bliss."

Michaels, Marguerite. "Anne Tyler, Writer 8:05 to 3:30." *The New York Times Book Review* (May 8, 1977): 13, 42-43.
A detailed account of Tyler's writing routine based on a visit with the author. Also has lengthy quotes from Tyler on the importance of her family and the prime motivators in her fiction. Tyler says her "interest is character. The real joy of writing is how people can surprise one."

Morrow, Mark. *Images of the Southern Writer*. Athens: University of Georgia Press, 1985.
A full-page photograph and a brief informal interview, in which Tyler reflects on her need for privacy, family, and the difficulty in defining her as a Southern writer. According to Tyler, "I grew up in the South, but I always looked enviously at Southern families and

wished I could be a part of one of them." Morrow's discussion of Tyler is as sensitive as his photographic study.

Nesanovich, Stella. "Anne Tyler." In *Critical Survey of Long Fiction*, edited by Frank N. Magill. Vol. 7, pp. 2671-2685. Englewood Cliffs, N.J.: Salem Press, 1983.
Covering up through *Dinner at the Homesick Restaurant*, this essay looks in some depth at Tyler's achievements, biography, and critical reception. Nesanovich also analyzes each novel, with frequent allusions to other reviews. Overall, Nesanovich believes "the truth of her characterizations and her eye for details" will win her an increasing national public, including academic attention. Brief bibliography.

_____. "An Anne Tyler Checklist, 1959-1980." *Bulletin of Bibliography* 38 (April-June, 1981): 53-64.
An impressive bibliography of works by and about Tyler, including extensive lists of reviews about the novels through *Morgan's Passing*. Unfortunately, little critical discussion of Tyler had taken place by time Nesanovich compiled this list. Brief introduction with a plea for more serious attention to Tyler.

_____. "The Individual in the Family: Anne Tyler's *Searching for Caleb* and *Earthly Possessions*." *The Southern Review* 14 (January, 1978): 170-176.
Review of both novels. *Searching for Caleb* is seen as being "about the various ways in which people respond to life, the curiosity and involvement of some, the removal and caution of others." *Earthly Possessions* has a narrower focus in which "growth is limited more by the paradoxical and contrary nature of life itself than by human choice." Nesanovich concludes that these novels are evidence that "important work is coming."

Parini, Jay. "The Accidental Convert." *The New York Times Book Review* (August 25, 1991): 1, 26.
Review of *Saint Maybe*. "Only Anne Tyler could make an arresting novel out of material like this." He finds certain flaws in the work, including insufficient motivations for the main character, Ian. "Nonetheless, I adored *Saint Maybe*," he concludes, calling the book in many ways her "most sophisticated work."

Petry, Alice Hall. *Understanding Anne Tyler.* Columbia: University of South Carolina Press, 1990.
A nonacademic (for the most part) study of Tyler and her works. Very useful for an overview. The introduction is clearly written and contains many reliable observations about general critical responses to Tyler, such as writers claimed to have influenced her (Hawthorne to Faulkner) and her seemingly chaotic worldview. Each novel (up through *Breathing Lessons*) is considered in order. Notes are at the end of each chapter. Annotated bibliography and index also attached.

Robertson, Mary F. "Anne Tyler: Medusa Points and Contact Points." In *Contemporary American Women Writers: Narrative Strategies,* edited by Catherine Rainwater and William J. Scheick, pp. 119-152. Lexington: University Press of Kentucky, 1985.
A complex analysis of Tyler's narrative patterns, especially as they regard traditional expectations of the "family novel." "Rather than the mounting feeling of inevitability to which we are accustomed in family narratives, Tyler's plots impart the feeling almost of random branching." Robertson attempts to explain why. Lengthy bibliography of works by Tyler (short stories, essays, reviews—compiled by Elaine Gardiner and Catherine Rainwater).

Ross-Bryant, Lynn. "Anne Tyler's *Searching for Caleb*: The Sacrality of the Everyday." *Soundings: An Interdisciplinary Journal* 73 (Spring, 1990): 191-207.
Asserts that Tyler has an important role to play in helping readers explore "an uncharted region." For Ross-Bryant, Tyler's "fiction challenges our theological and ethical assumptions by offering a nondualistic experience of the sacred and an ethic of empathy and care, found within the everyday world of family."

Shelton, Frank W. "The Necessary Balance: Distance and Sympathy in the Novels of Anne Tyler." *The Southern Review* 20 (October, 1984): 851-860.
Shelton examines the pull in Tyler's works toward separation and distance for the characters. Simultaneously, she is said to portray the return to family and the familiar for healing and acceptance. "Her heroes, then, resemble her in their ability to give others distance to be themselves and also relate to others with genuine sympathy."

Stephens, Ralph C., ed. *The Fiction of Anne Tyler*. Jackson: University
Press of Mississippi, 1990.
Probably a starting point for in-depth research. The essays collected
in this book represent the first compilation of critical discussion of
Tyler. All argue at some level for more academic attention to her
writings. See Doris Betts's essay, especially for a foundation of
critical thought. Other essays explore interdisciplinary approaches to
Tyler, such as tracing sociological or psychoanalytical factors in her
writing. Each essay includes notes for further sources. Note: Most of
the essays were from papers presented at a national symposium on
Tyler in Baltimore, in April, 1989. Two essays were previously
published: Mary J. Elkins' *"Dinner at the Homesick Restaurant*:
Anne Tyler and the Faulkner Connection," *Atlantis* 10 (Spring,
1985): 93-105; and Margaret Morganroth Gullette's "Anne Tyler:
The Tears (and Joys) Are in the Things," chapter 5 of her book *Safe
at Last in the Middle Years*, Berkeley: University of California Press,
1988.

Tyler, Anne. "Because I Want More than One Life." *The Washington
Post* (August 15, 1976): pp. G1, G7.
A lyrical essay in which Tyler speaks simply of her writer's life of
wandering through the imagined lives of others. The familiar refrain
of interruptive kids and confused neighbors does not mar her
moments of escape. She comments on her distant response to critics
and the important shared solitude of writer to reader.

_____. "Still Just Writing." In *The Writer on Her Work*, edited
by Janet Sternburg, pp. 3-16. New York: W. W. Norton, 1980.
Poignant, humorous essay on "the effect that being a woman/-
wife/mother has upon my writing." Traces the chaos Tyler must
navigate in order to find precious few concentrated moments for her
fiction. Many biographical notes on her Quaker upbringing and its
impact on her perceptions. Also notes the importance for her of
discovering Eudora Welty's writings as well as the "mist of irony
that hangs over whatever I see."

Updike, John. *Hugging the Shore: Essays and Criticism*, pp. 273-299.
New York: Alfred A. Knopf, 1983.
Collects four important *The New Yorker* reviews by Updike of
Tyler's novels. "Family Ways," "Loosened Roots," "Imagining
Things," and "On Such a Beautiful Green Little Planet" cover,

respectively, *Searching for Caleb, Earthly Possessions, Morgan's Passing*, and *Dinner at the Homesick Restaurant*. Updike is pivotal to Tyler's increased public and academic attention. The essays are more than reviews, speaking continuously of Tyler's place in the literary world.

_____. "Leaving Home." *The New Yorker* 61 (October 28, 1985): 106-112.
Updike seems to enjoy *The Accidental Tourist* while not proclaiming it a masterwork. Some of the slapstick family elements push too far, in his view. Updike notes, however, the skill with which Tyler "persistently concerns herself with the moral evolution of male characters."

Voelker, Joseph C. *Art and the Accidental in Anne Tyler*. Columbia: University of Missouri Press, 1989.
This book analyzes most of Tyler's novels. Chapters consider elements at work in different books, from her "pattern-building imagination in *The Clock Winter*" to "Tyler's use of idealization" in *Dinner at the Homesick Restaurant*. All are unified, according to Voelker, by "the central dynamic of Tyler's fiction, a shuttling of the imagination between inner and outer worlds, a series of impossible or at least impermanent choices." Generous notes throughout the book. Bibliography and index at end.

Zahlan, Anne R. "Anne Tyler." In *Fifty Southern Writers After 1900*, edited by Joseph M. Flora and Robert Bain, pp. 491-504. New York: Greenwood Press, 1987.
An excellent summary from which to begin work on Tyler. Covers the biography, major themes, and critical response pertaining to Tyler. Zahlan predicts the end to academic neglect of this author, especially after the continued praise for her by such critics/authors as Doris Betts and John Updike. "Tyler has at last been recognized as an important contemporary writer," according to Zahlan. Brief bibliography attached.

ALICE WALKER

Adams, Timothy Dow. "Alice Walker." In *Critical Survey of Long Fiction*, edited by Frank N. Magill. Vol. 7, pp. 2746-2757. Englewood Cliffs, N.J.: Salem Press, 1983.
Announces Walker as "a major contemporary American writer" and goes on to enumerate the publications and honors warranting the label. Adams traces Walker's growth in her writing, focusing on the metaphor of her own childhood scars. The essay concludes by discussing *The Color Purple*, quoting one reviewer who calls the book "an American novel of permanent importance." Useful bibliographies attached.

"Alice Walker: A Special Section, Literary Criticism." *Callaloo* 12 (Spring, 1989): 295-345.
Collects a diverse group of essays on Walker. Included are "Alice Walker's *The Third Life of Grange Copeland*: The Dynamics of Enclosure"; "All Saints Should Walk Away': The Mystical Pilgrimage of *Meridian*"; "Desire and Alice Walker: The Quest for a Womanist Narrative"; "Sifting Through the Controversy: Reading *The Color Purple*"; "Alice Walker: A Selected Bibliography, 1968-1988."

Awkward, Michael. "*The Color Purple* and the Achievement of (Comm)unity." In *Inspiriting Influence: Tradition, Revision, and Afro-American Women's Novels*, pp. 135-164. New York: Columbia University Press, 1989.
Using Jean Toomer's *Cane* and Zora Neale Hurston's *Their Eyes Were Watching God* as points of comparison, Awkward explores the theme in *The Color Purple* of the black woman's struggle to maintain and express her creative spirit "that has survived despite racist and sexist efforts to suppress it and a general devaluation of its products." Awkward argues that in the novel, Celie's letters are her outlet, as well as Walker's argument, against the critics who, for example, claim Hurston's narrative voice to be a major "weakness."

Banks, Erma Davis, and Keith Byerman. *Alice Walker: An Annotated Bibliography, 1968-1986*. New York: Garland, 1989.

A book-length bibliography with relatively short yet somewhat more evaluative annotations than those of other bibliographies. Well-organized breakdown of categories such as "General Books and Reference Sources," "Criticism of Individual Works," and "Bibliographies." The "Introduction" provides a substantial review of Walker's biography and critical reception. Indexed.

Bell, Bernard W. "The Contemporary Afro-American Novel, 1: Neorealism." In *The Afro-American Novel and Its Tradition*, pp. 259-270. Amherst: University of Massachusetts Press, 1987.

After a brief biographical sketch, Bell summarizes Walker's works and labels her a "critical realist." The discussion looks at Walker's portrayal of men who are seen as "traditional black male chauvinists of both the lower and middle class who stereotypically vent their hatred of exploitation by whites on their families." The women, however, announce "the emergence of a new generation of radical black heroines."

Bloom, Harold, ed. *Alice Walker*. New York: Chelsea House, 1989.

Part of the "Modern Critical Views" series. Collects important essays from the history of Walker criticism (1979-1988). Some of the essays might be difficult to find in the original publications, while at least three appear for the first time in this volume. They are: "'Show Me How to Do Like You': Didacticism and Epistolary Form in *The Color Purple*" (Tamar Katz); "Clytemnestra's Children: Writing (Out) the Mother's Anger" (Marianne Hirsch); and "Writing the Subject: Reading *The Color Purple*" (Bell Hooks). Bloom's short "Introduction" offers some pointed challenges to the traditions of Walker criticism (especially feminist criticism). Ends with a chronology of Walker's life and works, a substantial, if selected, bibliography, and a full index.

Butler-Evans, Elliott. *Race, Gender, and Desire: Narrative Strategies in the Fiction of Toni Cade Bambara, Toni Morrison, and Alice Walker*. Philadelphia: Temple University Press, 1989.

"Drawing largely on narratology, feminist cultural theory, semiotics, and Neo-Marxist concepts of ideology, this study explores the relationship between two conflicting discourses—one an inscription of race, the other focused on gender—within the fictional narratives

of three Afro-American women writers." Butler-Evans makes a
pointed study of Walker's *The Third Life of Grange Copeland* and
Meridian as examples of the tension between texts "on the broad
racial experiences of American Blacks," on the one hand, and those
more focused on "the histories of Black women," on the other hand.
Long bibliography. Much textual discussion of other critical works.

Byerman, Keith E. "Women's Blues: The Fiction of Toni Cade
    Bambara and Alice Walker." In *Fingering the Jagged Grain:
    Tradition and Form in Recent Black Fiction*, pp. 104-170. Athens:
    University of Georgia Press, 1985.
    Both Bambara and Walker are credited with feminist ideologies,
    especially in telling "stories of the initiations of black girls into
    womanhood, defining in the process the complex meaning of being
    black and female in a culture that has denigrated both qualities,"
    according to this essay. Both hope for political change. In Walker's
    case, Byerman sees greater use of historical context with, ironically,
    political constructions "that run counter to the thrust of that very folk
    history."

Callahan, John F. "The Hoop of Language: Politics and the Restoration
    of Voice in *Meridian*." In *In the African-American Grain*, pp. 217-
    255. Urbana: University of Illinois Press, 1988.
    Callahan examines Meridian Hill as a flawed revolutionary struggling
    to find a voice that is not only correct for her beliefs but also right
    for the political realities. "But to her, possession of a true personal
    voice is bound up with the creation of an authentic public and
    political voice." Walker's larger goal, Callahan says, is the restora-
    tion of a revolution based on true voices, not rhetorical tricks and
    false selves. Notes. Walker is alluded to numerous other times
    throughout the book.

Christian, Barbara. "Alice Walker." In *Dictionary of Literary Biogra-
    phy: Afro-American Writers After 1955, Dramatists and Prose
    Writers*, edited by Thadious M. Davis and Trudier Harris. Vol. 38,
    pp. 258-271. Detroit: Gale Research, 1985.
    A substantial entry tracing Walker's biography, writings, and critical
    reception. Christian summarizes Walker's most controversial and
    persistent themes as "the relationship between black women and
    men, black parents and children." Her drive for social/political
    change is rooted in her quest for appreciating the spirit of the

individual, Christian notes. Includes primary and limited secondary bibliographies.

_____. *Black Feminist Criticism: Perspectives on Black Women Writers*. New York: Pergamon Press, 1985.
Collects Christian's essays on writers, including four that discuss Alice Walker as a primary topic. "The Contrary Women of Alice Walker: A Study of Female Protagonists in *In Love and Trouble*," "Alice Walker: The Black Woman Artist as Wayward," and "An Angle of Seeing: Motherhood in Buchi Emecheta's *Joys of Motherhood* and Alice Walker's *Meridian*" may be especially helpful. Other essays allude to Walker. Many of the essays have been printed elsewhere. Includes notes and index.

_____. "Novels for Everyday Use: The Novels of Alice Walker." In *Black Women Novelists: The Development of a Tradition, 1892-1976*, pp. 180-238. Westport, Conn.: Greenwood Press, 1980.
Talks of "the repressed creativity of black women" as a theme in Walker's works, especially *The Third Life of Grange Copeland* and *Meridian*. Through the terrors and abuse, black women are shown collecting fragments of their creative selves and stitching them into memorable survival quilts, Christian notes. Ultimately, however, Christian sees in Walker's writing a charge to society to change so that individual struggles for expression need not be so arduous.

Coetzee, J. M. "The Beginnings of (Wo)man in Africa." *The New York Times Book Review* (April 30, 1989): 7.
Review of *The Temple of My Familiar*. Representative of (if gentler than) some other reviews. Coetzee finds the book flawed in narrative, history, and character. Walker seems to be reading beyond normal expectations of reality, according to Coetzee. The book is not really a novel so much as "a mixture of mythic fantasy, revisionary history, exemplary biography and sermon. It is short on narrative tension, long on inspirational message."

Collins, Gina Michelle. "*The Color Purple*: What Feminism Can Learn from a Southern Tradition." In *Southern Literature and Literary Theory*, edited by Jefferson Humphries, pp. 75-87. Athens: University of Georgia Press, 1990.
Using Walker's affirmation of the label "mules of the world" for

black women, Collins attempts to show the virtues of proudly carrying such a title. Walker's direct language in *The Color Purple* is praised as a model for breaking down the "will to silence" that oppressed groups often reinforce within their own race or gender out of fear of perpetuating stereotypes. Even as Southerners have tried to display their faults and differences in a context of pride, so should feminists not fear honesty in portrayals such as Walker's, Collins argues.

Cooke, Michael G. "Intimacy: The Interpenetration of the One and the All in Robert Hayden and Alice Walker." In *Afro-American Literature in the Twentieth Century: The Achievement of Intimacy*, pp. 133-176. New Haven, Conn.: Yale University Press, 1984.
Put in the context of changes in the civil rights goals and methods, Walker is studied as one representing the synthesis of differing attitudes summed up by Cooke as "intimacy." Thus, Cooke submits, Walker's approach to social change is not single note, neither militant nor passive; rather, it tells (in *Meridian* especially) that personal truths are at the core of social intimacy. Meridian is an eccentric in order to remind us that movements must accommodate all individuals, not merely a certain type of individual.

Davis, Thadious M. "Alice Walker's Celebration of Self in Southern Generations." In *Women Writers of the Contemporary South*, edited by Peggy Whitman Prenshaw, pp. 39-54. Jackson: University Press of Mississippi, 1984.
According to Davis, "Walker grounds her fiction and poetry primarily in the experiences of the South and Southern blacks." He identifies her themes of community and individual struggle for identity as linking her to Southern literary traditions. Her voice, however, defines a unique vision and perspective, especially in the portrayal of the black woman's abused life.

DuPlessis, Rachel Blau. "Beyond the Hard Visible Horizon." In *Writing Beyond the Ending: Narrative Strategies of Twentieth-Century Women Writers*, pp. 142-161. Bloomington: Indiana University Press, 1985.
Comparing narratives by Walker, Dorothy Richardson, and Zora Neale Hurston, DuPlessis finds them sharing a view of the hero as "a representative of a striving community, breaking with individualism in her rupture from gender-based ends." Walker uses Meridian

as "a multiple individual, who articulates social and spiritual questions." Walker's refusal of the martyr's ending for the book indicates that the history of the individual is not written by death but continues in the spirit and political body of the community.

Ensslen, Klaus. "Collective Experience and Individual Responsibility: Alice Walker's *The Third Life of Grange Copeland* (1970)." In *The Afro-American Novel Since 1960*, edited by Peter Bruck and Wolfgang Karrer, pp. 189-218. Amsterdam: B. R. Gruner, 1982. Explores the tensions between Walker's belief in an individual moral code of responsibility and the need for social reforms aimed at supporting, rather than tearing down, individual ethics—particularly in the black community. The triangle of Grange, Josie, and Brownfield represents the level of sacrifice needed of some individuals in securing some hope for future generations, Ensslen posits. Bibliography.

_____. "History and Fiction in Alice Walker's *The Third Life of Grange Copeland* and Ernest Gaines' *The Autobiography of Miss Jane Pittman*." In *History and Tradition in Afro-American Culture*, edited by Gunter H. Lenz, pp. 147-166. Frankfurt: Campus Verlag, 1984. Ensslen explores the narrative tools used in evoking historical content. In *The Third Life*, Walker is first seen as "presenting change as a result of socio-cultural experience," according to the essay. Closer examination, however, reveals that the individual is driven to self-awareness and personal historical perspective by some inner moral engine, Ensslen concludes. See also the essay by Anne Koenen and Sabine Brock, "Alice Walker in Search of Zora Neale Hurston: Rediscovering a Black Female Literary Tradition" (pp. 167-180).

Evans, Mari, ed. *Black Women Writers (1950-1980): A Critical Evaluation*, pp. 453-495. Garden City, N.Y.: Anchor Press/Doubleday, 1984. The "Alice Walker" section collects one essay by Walker and two others about her, along with a short biography/bibliography. In "Writing *The Color Purple*," (originally published in *In Search of Our Mothers' Gardens*, by Walker), Walker relates much of the seeming haphazard process that led to her novel. Barbara Christian contributes "Alice Walker: The Black Woman Artist as Wayward." That essay traces the themes of her writings, concluding that the one unifying element seems to be Walker's "contrariness." "There is a sense in which the 'forbidden' in the society is consistently approached by Walker as a possible route to truth," Christian summarizes. Bettye J. Parker-Smith's "Alice Walker's Women: In Search of Some Peace of Mind" delves into the "claim that Black women's conditions result from an intrinsic weakness" in Walker's fiction.

Fifer, Elizabeth. "The Dialect and Letters of *The Color Purple*." In *Contemporary American Women Writers: Narrative Strategies*, edited by Catherine Rainwater and William J. Scheick, pp. 155-171. Lexington: University Press of Kentucky, 1985.
Explores the power of language and writing to free and transform Celie in the novel. Fifer contends that "without language, silence would have ensured madness or, as in her mother's case, an early death." Nettie's letters are especially important in effecting Celie's transformation, Fifer adds, having a power, merely through their words, to affirm Celie's existence. Includes a substantial bibliography of works by Walker (including articles and reviews).

Fisher, Jerilyn. "From Under the Yoke of Race and Sex: Black and Chicano Women's Fiction of the Seventies." *Minority Voices* 2 (Fall, 1978): 1-14.
Particularly examines *The Third Life* as a study of lower-class women forced to submit to male dominance and to abandon "traditional female responsibility." "In Walker's novel the Black family suffers, victimized by misdirected anger," Fisher concludes. The essay also alludes to *Meridian* and the story "Everyday Use."

Gates, Henry Louis, Jr. "Color Me Zora: Alice Walker's (Re)Writing of the Speakerly Text." In *The Signifying Monkey: A Theory of Afro-American Literary Criticism*, pp. 239-258. New York: Oxford University Press, 1988.
Gates finds Walker's narrative voice a synthesis of and expansion beyond the pioneering works of Hurston's *Their Eyes Were Watching God* and Rebecca Cox Jackson's *Gifts of Power*. The efforts Walker makes in *The Color Purple* to delineate the letters from normal epistolary forms wherein a correspondent writes about events is evidence of the struggle to make the letters themselves the main events of the book. As Gates puts it, "[W]e read Celie reading her world and writing it into being."

Harris, Norman. *"Meridian:* Answers in the Black Church." In *Connecting Times: The Sixties in Afro-American Fiction*, pp. 98-119. Jackson: University Press of Mississippi, 1988.

Harris connects the novel to three aspects of the Civil Rights movement: the socialization process that alienates the black person from his or her history; the conflicts between black men and women; and the rise of nationalism (and, thus, separation) against integration. The characters in *Meridian* face the crisis of personal history versus political activism, Harris says. The contradictions of the two can best be soothed, at least in the person of Meridian, by the black church.

Harris, Trudier. *Exorcising Blackness: Historical and Literary Lynching and Burning Rituals*. Bloomington: Indiana University Press, 1984. Allusions to Walker throughout this book. *The Third Life of Grange Copeland* is examined in some depth (pp. 35-39) as a study of men "who have been psychologically, socially, and politically emasculated." *The Color Purple* and a few short stories are also considered, especially in the context of "symbolic castration of black males."

_____. "Three Black Women Writers and Humanism: A Folk Perspective." In *Black American Literature and Humanism*, edited by R. Baxter Miller, pp. 50-74. Lexington: University Press of Kentucky, 1981.

The essays in this book were originally presented at a conference in 1978. Harris' contribution examines works by Sarah Wright, Paule Marshall, and Alice Walker. *The Third Life of Grange Copeland* presents, for Harris, an example of African-American writing in which folk tradition and religion mix with humanism. It is Grange's reconnection to human relationships "not motivated by any externally imposed set of values," values such as those that a church imposes, that comes closest to saving him, the essay argues. Even facing death, he is unable to pray because "to do so would deny his entire life of independent action and free will."

Hernton, Calvin C. "Who's Afraid of Alice Walker?" In *The Sexual Mountain and Black Women Writers*, pp. 1-36. New York: Anchor Press/Doubleday, 1987.

An impassioned defense by a black male writer "against the red bricks of slander and bigotry that are hurled at black women and the literature they produce." Hernton examines *The Color Purple* as a slave narrative, defining the genre as "a black-invented art form."

While making some differentiations between book and movie, Hernton lauds the true portrayal of black male sexism, as well as the racism and sexism of whites, in both media. The essay also speaks directly to the campaign against the movie.

Hite, Molly. "Chapter 3: Romance, Marginality, Matrilineage: *The Color Purple.*" In *The Other Side of the Story: Structures and Strategies of Contemporary Feminist Narrative*, pp. 103-126. Ithaca, N.Y.: Cornell University Press, 1989.
An extended reexamination of the chief narrative problems of *The Color Purple*. Hite suggests that critics faulting "the violations of realist conventions" in plot and in the nature of the letters may be missing some important African-American traditions that redefine the criteria of "realist." Hite discusses Hurston's *Their Eyes Were Watching God* as a precursor to the same "faults" attributed to Walker.

Hogue, W. Lawrence. *Discourse and the Other: The Production of the Afro-American Text*. Durham, N.C.: Duke University Press, 1986.
The numerous references to Walker throughout the text are most concentrated in chapter 5, " History, the Feminist Discourse, and *The Third Life of Grange Copeland*" (pp. 86-106). "A product of the feminist movement, *The Third Life* (1970) works upon and transforms the same raw material, the same American and Afro-American historical past, as Gaines's *Miss Jane Pittman*," Hogue contends. Above all, the essay says, Walker's narrative helps replace the old myths of black womanhood with new constructs giving greater depth, meaning, and future to black women.

Johnson, Charles. "The Women." In *Being and Race: Black Writing Since 1970*, pp. 105-109. Bloomington: Indiana University Press, 1988.
Johnson includes Walker in a chapter-length survey of other African-American women writers of the 1980's. *The Color Purple* "stands at the crest of black women's fiction in the 1980's," according to Johnson, even though her earlier novels are considered "stronger artistic achievements." Overall, Walker is praised for her devotion to "the priority of freedom" in expressing artistic and social truths, no matter how challenging or dark.

Karl, Frederick R. "The Female Experience." In *American Fictions, 1940-1980*, pp. 417-443. New York: Harper & Row, 1983.
This chapter surveys women's literature, especially from 1960 to 1980, and makes reference to Walker's impact as a black female writer "in the strange situation of feeling both a social and political commitment and a commitment to her sex." *Meridian* has, at its core, the metaphor of the "wild child," the black woman's potential fate in society. Becoming a whole individual is not enough, Karl sees Walker saying; rather, the black woman must work to make the social order whole, as well.

Mickelson, Anne Z. "Winging Upward, Black Women: Sarah E. Wright, Toni Morrison, Alice Walker." In *Reaching Out: Sensitivity and Order in Recent American Fiction by Women*, pp. 112-174. Metuchen, N.J.: Scarecrow Press, 1979.
Looks specifically at *Meridian* and *In Love and Trouble* as examples of writing on "the astringencies of the situation of both black men and women" in a white society. Readings of the works are general, emphasizing the struggle for "wholeness" among characters, especially black women, who seem to have few, if any, choices. Mickelson praises Walker's dialogue and narrative techniques.

Miller, Jane. "Women's Men." In *Women Writing About Men*, pp. 227-263. London: Virago, 1986.
Miller considers *The Color Purple* to have "a celebratory and almost ecstatic quality" beyond the brutalities it portrays. One of its most interesting aspects is the multiplicity of examples for escaping the situation of the African-American woman, according to Miller. While it may be impossible to call Walker's men role models, "she provides the possibility for a miraculous redemption for men, as a by-product of women's laughter, creativity and delight in themselves."

O'Brien, John. "Alice Walker." In *Interviews with Black Writers*, pp. 185-211. New York: Liveright, 1973.
An interview from relatively early in Walker's career. The introductory note traces her accomplishments up to that time. Walker wrote her answers in full, well-chosen prose. She discusses at length her suicidal tendencies, her process of writing poems and fiction, her admiration for Zora Neale Hurston, and *The Third Life of Grange Copeland*, among other topics. Walker identifies her greatest feeling

to be for "young black women whose rocky road I am still travel-
ing."

Porter, Nancy. "Women's Interracial Friendships and Visions of
Community in *Meridian, The Salt Eaters, Civil Wars,* and *Dessa
Rose.*" In *Tradition and the Talents of Women,* edited by Florence
Howe, pp. 251-267. Urbana: University of Illinois Press, 1991.
Using a "feminist psychoanalytic perspective," Porter discusses "how
race, class, and cultural experience affect the dynamics" of friend-
ships between black and white women in various authors' works.
According to Porter, the relationships of Truman, Lynne, and
Meridian "deconstruct" the Civil Rights movement by exposing
discrepancies between its ideology and practice. See other references
to Walker throughout the book.

Pratt, Louis H., and Darnell D. Pratt. *Alice Malsenior Walker: An
Annotated Bibliography, 1968-1986.* Westport, Conn.: Meckler, 1988.
Primary and secondary sources provided with short, descriptive
annotations. Has a section on "Book and Movie Reviews" that may
provide sources not collected elsewhere. The "Introduction" is a clear
and simple essay on Walker's characteristics as a writer, especially
as a portrayer of black men. Index.

Shapiro, Laura. "*Possessing the Secret of Joy.*" *Newsweek* (June 8,
1992): 56-57.
A short review of the novel. The dedication ("To the Blameless
Vulva") may be of questionable judgment, but the book is not,
Shapiro says. *Possessing the Secret of Joy* is an "amazing feat."
Walker has "written a powerful novel about brutal misogyny, and
she's made it both horrifying and readable, angry and warm-hearted,
political and human."

Spillers, Hortense J. "The Permanent Obliquity of an In(pha)llibly
Straight': In the Time of the Daughters and the Fathers." In
*Changing Our Own Words: Essays on Criticism, Theory, and
Writing by Black Women,* edited by Cheryl A. Wall, pp. 127-149.
New Brunswick, N.J.: Rutgers University Press, 1989.
Looking specifically at Ellison's *Invisible Man* and Walker's "The
Child Who Favored Daughter" from *In Love and Trouble,* Spillers
contemplates the handling of father-daughter incest in African-
American literature and society. Using complex language and thought

structures, the essay attempts to define differences among imagined, actual, and literary versions of incest. See this same book for allusions to Walker in other essays. Notes and index.

Steinem, Gloria. "Do You Know This Woman? She Knows You: A Profile of Alice Walker." *Ms.* (June, 1982): 35, 37, 89-94.
Extensive interview-based essay on Walker, with a companion piece, "Her Mother's Gifts," by Mary Helen Washington (p. 38). Steinem describes the power of *The Color Purple* one month prior to its publication and predicts it will make Walker a national figure. Walker speaks of her fantasies of revenge against so many who had wronged her and her people. She also comments on the role of her husband in supporting her work and personal growth.

Tate, Claudia. "Alice Walker." In *Black Women Writers at Work*, edited by Claudia Tate, pp. 175-187. New York: Continuum, 1983.
This interview covers much of Walker's writing, especially *Meridian*, yet curiously barely mentions *The Color Purple*. Walker is concerned with the lack of substantive critical work done on *Meridian*. She feels few readers have dealt with the whole of the work, in part because of its "crazy quilt" narrative form and also because of "the whole sublayer of Indian consciousness." A short biographical sketch opens the interview.

Wade-Gayles, Gloria. "Black, Southern, Womanist: The Genius of Alice Walker." In *Southern Women Writers: The New Generation*, edited by Tonette Bond Inge, pp. 301-323. Tuscaloosa: University of Alabama Press, 1990.
A general appreciation of Walker's accomplishments. Wade-Gayler attempts to weave a pattern of personal growth affecting narrative growth. For example, *The Third Life of Grange Copeland* belongs to a "stage of Walker's consciousness that sensitized readers to the truths of black women's pain." In contrast, the later *Meridian* is more concerned with "teaching readers about the meaning of liberation." Primary bibliography and notes.

_____. "Giving Birth to Self: The Quests for Wholeness of Sula Mae Peace and Meridian Hill." In *No Crystal Stair: Visions of Race and Sex in Black Women's Fiction*, pp. 184-215. New York: Pilgrim Press, 1984.
Compares and contrasts Walker's portrayal of women in *Meridian*

to Morrison's in *Sula*. Wade-Gayler sees "devotion and sacrifice rather than alienation and hostility" as Walker's themes in *Meridian*. The sense of community is strong. Also notes the abusive role of black men in the novel, although not as strongly as in *The Third Life of Grange Copeland*. Other allusions to Walker throughout the book.

Walker, Alice. "*One* Child of One's Own: A Meaningful Digression Within the Work(s)." In *The Writer on Her Work*, edited by Janet Sternburg, pp. 121-140. New York: W. W. Norton, 1980.
Walker defends at great length her determination never to have more than one child. The essay is interspersed with supposed quotes from Walker's mother, who tries to persuade her to have more. Sifting the essay does produce some comments directly pertinent to Walker's role as a writer.

Washington, Mary Helen. "An Essay on Alice Walker." In *Sturdy Black Bridges: Visions of Black Women in Literature*, edited by Roseann P. Bell, Bettye J. Parker, and Beverly Guy-Sheftall, pp. 133-149. Garden City, N.Y.: Anchor Press/Doubleday, 1979.
Focuses primarily on Walker's overriding concern for the role of black women. Her most distinguishing trait is her vision of black women's struggle "from women totally victimized by society and by the men in their lives to the growing developing women whose consciousness allows them to have control over their lives." References to fiction and non-fiction, novels and short stories.

Williams, Carolyn. "'Trying to Do Without God': The Revision of Epistolary Address in *The Color Purple*." In *Writing the Female Voice: Essays on Epistolary Literature*, edited by Elizabeth C. Goldsmith, pp. 273-285. Boston: Northeastern University Press, 1989.
Celie's evolving views of God, as displayed in her letters, reveal her growing understanding of herself. The initial God she rejects is really based on a male image of the divine, Williams argues. "Recognizing the bitter irony of Pa's recommendation of God as a correspondent depends on seeing Celie's simultaneous exclusion from and implication within the male network of power relations." Eventually, the "womanist revision of God" affects Walker's own narrative authority. Notes.

Willis, Susan. "Alice Walker's Women." In *Specifying: Black Women Writing the American Experience*, pp. 110-128. Madison: University of Wisconsin Press, 1987.

Going back to the character "Wile Chile" in *Meridian*, Willis traces a common element among Alice Walker's female characters—the imprisonment by "social and sexual categories ascribed to all women, and black women in particular." In the case of Meridian, Walker makes clear "that mothering, as it has been defined by heterosexual relationships in racist society, is the single most insurmountable obstacle to a black woman's self-affirmation," Willis conjectures.

MARGARET WALKER

Baytop, Adrianne. "Margaret Walker." In *American Women Writers: A Critical Reference Guide from Colonial Times to the Present*, edited by Lina Mainiero. Vol. 4, pp. 315-316. New York: Frederick Ungar, 1982.

Biographical entry and brief comments on Walker's works. *Jubilee* can be classified in several genres, "Civil War epic, historical fiction, and the slave narrative." It breaks new ground by having an epic heroine, not an epic hero. Despite her strong convictions, Walker manages to deal objectively with her historical materials.

Bell, Bernard W. "The Contemporary Afro-American Novel, 2: Modernism and Postmodernism." In *The Afro-American Novel and Its Tradition*, pp. 281-338. Amherst: University of Massachusetts Press, 1987.

Jubilee is skillfully crafted, moving chronologically like a slave narrative, but including such literary refinements as epigraphs that reflect the movement of the book from repression and despair to liberation and hope. "Vyry's commitment to freedom" is the central theme of the novel. The characterization is superb; in Vyry, Walker has created "one of the most memorable women in contemporary Afro-American fiction," not the stereotypical loyal slave, but a compassionate human being with a strong ethical sense. The story is realistic; however, because Vyry is not concerned with politics except as her family is affected, she represents black women of previous generations, rather than those of the present. Bell's brief sketch of Walker's life emphasizes literary and intellectual influences.

Carby, Hazel. "Ideologies of Black Folk: The Historical Novel of Slavery." In *Slavery and the Literary Imagination*, edited by Deborah McDowell and Arnold Rampersad, pp. 125-143. Baltimore: The Johns Hopkins University Press, 1987.

Although both Margaret Mitchell and Margaret Walker based their accounts of Southern life before the Civil War on oral history, the novels are very different. In fact, *Jubilee* is a realistic response to the romanticism of *Gone with the Wind*. Unlike Mitchell, who merges her slaves and her rural whites into an undifferentiated pastoral people, Walker shows how an oppressive white society categorizes people as white and black, not as rich and poor or rural and urban. *Jubilee* is an important novel that merits greater attention from the critics.

Chapman, Abraham. "Negro Folksong." *Saturday Review* 49 (September 24, 1966): 43-44.
Chapman admires the technical sophistication of *Jubilee*, as evidenced in the use of chapter headings, which come from folk experience but are also integrally related to the structure and theme of the novel. The chief weakness of the novel is the "stilted prose of the narrator." *Jubilee* is, however, the first novel concerning slavery and the Civil War written about a black protagonist and from the black point of view.

Christian, Barbara. *Black Women Novelists: The Development of a Tradition, 1892-1976*, pp. 71-79. Westport, Conn.: Greenwood Press, 1980.
Walker structured *Jubilee* from folklore elements,intending it to have a mythic or an epic quality, but critics have found the novel disappointing. It is suggested that there was an insoluble problem in her work, the fact that her epic characters, the slaves themselves, were kept too isolated to have a sense of history. When Walker remedied the deficiency with her own comments, the effect was a lack of unity. The real achievement of *Jubilee* is its images of women, who are not stereotypical, but complex and convincing. Walker shows that strong black women of the nineteenth century created and preserved a valuable culture.

Daniel, Walter C. "Margaret Walker's Brother Ezekiel: Priest-Prophet of the "Invisible Church." In *Images of the Preacher in Afro-American Literature*, pp. 225-239. Washington, D.C.: University Press of America, 1981.
Traces the importance of Brother Ezekiel, a character in *Jubilee*. As "poet of his people," this Baptist plantation preacher plays two conflicting parts, comforting the slaves by emphasizing the happiness that awaits them in the next world, while secretly using biblical references to encourage them in the struggle for earthly freedom.

Trusted by masters who heard only their public statements, Brother
Ezekiel and other preachers like him were in fact not only "the
source of vital information" but also the political leaders of slave
society. Although he is a relatively minor character in the novel,
Brother Ezekiel is important to Walker's realistic creation of
antebellum black society.

Davis, Arthur P. *From the Dark Tower: Afro-American Writers, 1900
to 1960.* Washington, D.C.: Howard University Press, 1974.
Notes the change in Walker's intellectual position; from moderation
and integrationism in the 1950's, she moved in the 1960's toward
black nationalism. Davis writes at length about her poetry, which he
considers far better than her prose. Walker seemed unable to control
the family materials on which *Jubilee* was based. Instead, she
utilized too many stock plot devices without establishing a clear
direction for the book. Many of the characters are merely unconvincing, poorly developed stereotypes.

Emanuel, James A. "Margaret (Abigail) Walker." In *Contemporary
Novelists*, edited by D. L. Kirkpatrick. 4th ed., pp. 846-847. New
York: St. Martin's Press, 1986.
Biographical data and a critical essay on *Jubilee*. Interesting
discussion of the major characters' thematic importance. Emanuel
points out details, gleaned during Walker's years of historical
research, that make the novel an accurate picture of life during the
period, as well as an affirmation of the spiritual triumphs of black
people, celebrated in the figure of Vyry.

Evans, Mari, ed. *Black Women Writers (1950-1980): A Critical
Evaluation*, pp. 497-526. Garden City, N.Y.: Anchor Press/Double-
day, 1983.
Margaret Walker is one of the fifteen black women writers considered in this ambitious work. The section devoted to her includes two
essays. Eugenia Collier's "Fields Watered with Blood: Myth and
Ritual in the Poetry of Margaret Walker" explores a number of
themes that can also be applied to her novel *Jubilee*. Eleanor
Traylor's "Music as Theme: The Blues Mode in the Works of
Margaret Walker" devotes considerable space to the pattern of the
novel, illustrating with musical references its movement from a kind
of annihilation to a new birth. Brief biographical data and some
bibliographical references at the end of the section.

Freibert, Lucy M. "Southern Song: An Interview with Margaret Walker." *Frontiers: A Journal of Women Studies* 9 (1987): 51-56. Emphasizes the influences upon Walker's thought and style. Walker agrees with Minrose Gwin that *Jubilee* reflects a special relationship between black and white women, a bonding that developed as a result of male domination and brutality. Because the patterns of their lives differed greatly, however, black and white women have taken different paths as they move toward freedom.

Giovanni Blotner, Nikki, and Margaret Walker. *A Poetic Equation: Conversations Between Nikki Giovanni and Margaret Walker.* Washington, D.C.: Howard University Press, 1974.
A transcription of informal conversations arranged after both African-American women writers had appeared together at a conference. Although they are informal and unstructured, the talks naturally address the central issue of the future of black people in the United States. Partly because of the difference in generation, which they discuss, Walker is far more moderate than Giovanni on the assessment of whites' intentions and on the appropriate response of blacks to violence from whites. In the third chapter, "Content and Intent: Some Thoughts on Writing, Criticism and Film," Walker indicates her own at least partial dissatisfaction with *Jubilee*. The chapter called "Notebook" is primarily Walker's account of her relationships with black writers of her generation, especially her close friendship with Richard Wright, and therefore is of special biographical interest.

Goodman, Charlotte. "From *Uncle Tom's Cabin* to Vyry's Kitchen: The Black Female Folk Tradition in Margaret Walker's *Jubilee*." In *Tradition and the Talents of Women*, edited by Florence Howe, pp. 328-337. Urbana: University of Illinois Press, 1991.
Unlike earlier white novelists, even those such as Harriet Beecher Stowe who were so sympathetic to blacks, Margaret Walker presents black women not as stereotypes but as complex individuals, who to a large degree are responsible for preserving and transmitting their cultural heritage. The novel was unjustly criticized for being too full of incident and even of trivia. Actually, such specific details of daily life as Vyry's "herbal medicines, her cooking, her needlework, her songs and sayings," and even her possessions are "signifiers of the black female folk tradition." Goodman suggests that *Jubilee* has been overlooked because its tone was too moderate for a militant era. It

should be included in the canon as a fine novel with an unforgettable protagonist and as "a celebration of the black female community."

Gwin, Minrose C. "*Jubilee*: The Black Woman's Celebration of Human Community." In *Conjuring: Black Women, Fiction, and Literary Tradition*, edited by Marjorie Pryse and Hortense J. Spillers, pp. 132-150. Bloomington: Indiana University Press, 1985.
Jubilee reflects Walker's synthesis of humanism and religion, which emphasizes reverence for human life and is therefore antipathetic to any form of racism. The work is a synthesis of folklore and imagination, of realism and mystical vision. The story of Vyry symbolizes the nurturing powers of women, as well as their capacity to rise above racial differences, recognizing their common experience as members of the same sex. Walker's vision is of a redemption of society, based on the recognition of common humanity and the value of all human beings.

Jones, John Griffin. "Margaret Walker." In *Mississippi Writers Talking*, edited by John Griffin Jones. Vol. 2, pp. 120-143. Jackson: University Press of Mississippi, 1983.
An important interview conducted on March 13, 1982. After an extensive discussion of the influence of her family on her own view of life, Walker talks about her college years, her friendship with Richard Wright, the difference between his philosophical position and hers, and the problems faced by black men and women in contemporary American society. Walker makes a significant distinction between the genesis of *Jubilee* and the creative impulse that produced her poetry.

Klotman, Phyllis Rauch. "Oh Freedom"—Women and History in Margaret Walker's *Jubilee*." *Black American Literature Forum* 2 (Winter, 1977): 139-145.
Jubilee was based not only on the oral tradition of Walker's family but also on her research in slave narratives. In structure, *Jubilee* closely parallels a number of such accounts. Although most of these narratives were written by men, rather than by women, black women did function as preservers of history. Often stories of past events were transmitted from mother to daughter, from woman to woman. In the novel, it is Aunt Sally, the cook at the Big House, who relates such stories to her adopted daughter, Vyry, stories that then go to

Vyry's daughter and from her to a female grandchild, Margaret Walker herself. A well-documented and interesting study.

McDowell, Margaret B. "The Black Woman as Artist and Critic: Four Versions." *The Kentucky Review* 7 (1987): 19-41.
Insightful discussion of four prominent African-American writers who are also critics: Margaret Walker, Audre Lorde, Alice Walker, and Toni Morrison. All have brought new excitement to criticism; all go beyond mere interpretation of texts to relate them to black culture. Each of them, however, has her own viewpoint. Walker sees black literature as part of a broader humanistic heritage. Knowledge of that heritage enables black artists to attain inner freedom.

Miller, R. Baxter. "The 'Etched Flame' of Margaret Walker: Biblical and Literary Re-Creation in Southern History." *Tennessee Studies in Literature* 26 (1981): 157-172.
Points out biblical echoes and references in *For My People*, which themselves were derived from the black American environment in which Walker was nurtured. From that culture came "the solemn nobility of religious utterance, the appreciation for the heroic spirit of Black folk, and the deep respect for craft." Among the African-American leaders compared to biblical heroes are Benjamin Mays, Adam Clayton Powell, and Martin Luther King, Jr. Although Walker may be seen as a romantic, above all she "reaffirms the faith of the spirituals" in hoping for a better future.

Morrow, Mark. "Margaret Walker." In *Images of the Southern Writer*, pp. 82-83. Athens: University of Georgia Press, 1985.
A full-page photograph and brief informal interview, in which Walker reflects on the pattern of her life, in particular on her debt to her parents for inspiring her lifelong love of reading, and her thoughts about the changes that have taken place in the South. Morrow's verbal study of Walker is as sensitive as his photographic study.

Pettis, Joyce. "Margaret Walker: Black Woman Writer of the South." In *Southern Women Writers: The New Generation*, edited by Tonette Bond Inge, pp. 9-19. Tuscaloosa: University of Alabama Press, 1990.
Margaret Walker should be classified as a contemporary writer because, although her first work appeared in the 1930's, she

anticipated many concerns and themes that preoccupy the present generation of young black women writers, and in her ongoing work she continues to influence and to be influenced by them. As the first realistic novel of its kind by a black author, *Jubilee* established a tradition in historical fiction. The book is also significant as a refusal to be defeated by the "silences" that threaten all women writers.

Powell, Bertie J. "The Black Experience in Margaret Walker's *Jubilee* and Lorraine Hansberry's *The Drinking Gourd.*" *CLA Journal* 21 (December, 1977): 304-311.
  Jubilee dramatizes what it meant to be black in the South before, during, and immediately after the Civil War. Although three important characters, Master John Dutton; his wife, Big Missy; and the overseer Ed Grimes differ in their treatment of blacks, all are obviously committed to the prevailing view, that they are subhuman, created for the use of whites. Walker's novel also shows, however, how, through their family life and through religion, blacks found the strength to endure their lot. Lorraine Hansberry's play differs from *Jubilee* in that it includes some whites who defy their society, treat blacks as human beings, and thus maintain their own humanity.

Rowell, Charles. "Poetry, History, and Humanism: An Interview with Margaret Walker." *Black World* 25 (1975): 4-17.
  An interview focusing on Walker's perceptions of her own works and her assessments of other writers. Walker explains the genesis of her own work, beginning with her exposure both to poetry and to the folk tradition in childhood. Later influences included the Harlem Renaissance poets, especially Langston Hughes, and African-American fiction writers such as Zora Neale Hurston. Walker discusses her own views of her novel *Jubilee* and responds candidly to comments made by critics. Concludes with a definition of what Walker calls "Black humanism" and a lengthy discussion of trends in black literature. A revealing interview that elicits a great deal of helpful information.

Schraufnagel, Noel. "Accommodationism in the Sixties." In *From Apology to Protest: The Black American Novel*, pp. 121-145. Deland, Fla.: Everett/Edwards, 1973.
  In a decade when the best novels by African-Americans were militant, *Jubilee* must be categorized as one of the lesser "nonprotest or accommodationist" works of fiction, which assume that blacks can

survive only by adjusting to the standards of white society. Like other protagonists of "accommodationist" fiction, Vyry turns inward for solace, passively preserving her personal integrity. Unlike the heroic, "race conscious" Randall Ware, Vyry is "a female version of Uncle Tom." Despite echoes of Faulkner, a "relatively competent historical study."

Tate, Claudia. "Margaret Walker." In *Black Women Writers at Work*, pp. 188-204. New York: Continuum, 1983.
An interview in which Walker discusses her worries about *Jubilee* during the three decades when she was researching and writing it. Actually, she feels that it was a better book because it was not completed until she had experienced a great deal more of life than she had at age nineteen, when it was begun. Walker also discusses her supposed rivalry with Gwendolyn Brooks and her relationship with Richard Wright and touches on her problems with Alex Haley. In response to a question on images of black women in American literature, she quotes at length from an unpublished manuscript, dealing with the way in which black writers picture black women. Unfortunately, they imitate white male writers, showing women as "evil, disreputable and powerless." By and large, only black women writers have created black women characters who are admirable.

Walker, Margaret. "How I Wrote *Jubilee*." Chicago: Third World Press, 1972.
In this monograph, Walker sought to answer persistent questions about the relationship between her novel *Jubilee* and the real life experiences of her great-grandmother, the protagonist of the novel that the author says was a life's work. Although she had enough faith in the oral tradition to be certain that her grandmother's account was accurate, she substantiated it with years of reading, research, and interviews. In an introduction, Gloria Gayles comments that this brief essay is also significant as a portrait of an amazing woman, Walker herself, who combined dedication to her roles as "mother, wife, and teacher" with that of artist.

_____. *How I Wrote "Jubilee" and Other Essays on Life and Literature*, edited by Maryemma Graham. New York: Feminist Press at City University of New York, 1990.
A volume of fourteen representative essays and speeches by Walker, ranging in date from 1943 to 1988. Although the editor divided them

into two groups—"Growing out of Shadow," primarily autobiographical and "Literary and Other Legacies," more critical in nature—she
points out that because thought, imagination, and action are inextrica-
bly intertwined in Walker's life and work, this distinction is
essentially artificial. Considering that, Graham, in her introduction,
ascribes the neglect of Walker to critics' discomfort with her
intellectual position, which combines social radicalism with Christian
humanism, Walker's essays on "Rediscovering Black Women
Writers in the Mecca of the New Negro" and on "The Humanistic
Tradition of Afro-American Literature" are both particularly
significant. Both the introduction and the collection itself are
excellent.

_____. "On Being Female, Black, and Free." In *The Writer on
Her Work*, edited by Janet Sternburg, pp. 95-106. New York: W. W.
Norton, 1980.
A candid personal essay, stressing the writer's joy in her art but also
noting the difficulties she has faced not only because of poverty and
racial discrimination but also because of the sexual bias that pervades
American society. Points out that in addition to the difficulty of
finding time for creativity when they must support themselves and
tend their families, black women writers must deal with the "pressures of a sexist, racist, violent, and most materialistic society." As
women, however, they have an opportunity to understand, to nurture,
and to heal, both in their lives and in their works.

_____. "Willing to Pay the Price." In *Many Shades of Black*,
edited by Stanton L. Wormley and Lewis H. Fenderson, pp. 117-130.
New York: William Morrow, 1969. Also in *How I Wrote "Jubilee"
and Other Essays on Life and Literature*, edited by Maryemma
Graham, pp. 15-25. New York: Feminist Press at City University of
New York, 1990.
Explains how her parents helped her to overcome the obstacles of
being black, poor, and a woman by instilling an appreciation of
education, a sense of obligation toward God and other human beings,
and a desire to excel. As an adult, she was motivated to write
realistic fiction and poetry, and she was "willing to pay the price" to
do so. She also makes clear her position on "Black Power." While
she does not believe in hatred or violence, she feels that political and
social action are essential if blacks and whites in the United States
are to learn to live together and thus to preserve the country.

Ward, Jerry W., Jr. "A Writer for Her People: An Interview with Dr. Margaret Walker Alexander." *Mississippi Quarterly: The Journal of Southern Culture* 41 (Fall, 1988): 515-527.

In this interview, conducted in 1986, Margaret Walker speaks of her strong ties to Mississippi and to the Southern landscape, which is a part of her and from which her images almost always come. Unlike Alice Walker and other Gothic writers, Margaret Walker belongs to "the Sentimental tradition." Because of her religious background, she is also an optimist. Walker outlines some possibilities for future publications and concludes with an explanation of her feelings about black activism: She is "black, woman, writer," "very Black Nationalist."

Williams, Delores S. "Black Women's Literature and the Task of Feminist Theology." In *Immaculate and Powerful: The Female in Sacred Image and Social Reality*, edited by Clarissa W. Atkinson, Constance H. Buchanan, and Margaret R. Miles, pp. 88-110. Boston: Beacon Press, 1945.

In *Jubilee*, Vyry and her mother, Sis Hetta, both illustrate the "communal life-support model" of black women's experience. Unlike Zora Neale Hurston's Lucy and Alice Walker's Celie, Margaret Walker's characters fulfill their needs through serving as preservers of both the black and the white communities within which they live. Both of them suffer because of their status as slaves; however, Vyry gains spiritual strength and survival skills that make it possible for her to be transformed into a person, a free woman and a leader of her family and of her people.

SYLVIA WILKINSON

Buckner, Sally. *"Cale."* In *Survey of Contemporary Literature*, edited by Frank N. Magill. Rev. and enlarged ed. Vol. 2, pp. 1041-1044. Englewood Cliffs, N.J.: Salem Press, 1977.
"A perceptive examination of the individual's interaction with a narrow, provincial culture," is how this review summarizes *Cale*. Buckner applauds Wilkinson's portrayal of the sociology of Cale's world, especially the way issues of race are dramatized rather than merely sermonized. The reviewer does note an incomplete or inconsistent development of Cale's psychology.

Chappell, Fred. "Unpeaceable Kingdoms: The Novels of Sylvia Wilkinson." *The Hollins Critic* 8 (April, 1971): 1-10.
Chappell uses some of his own descriptive powers in describing the way Wilkinson paints her literary worlds, both rural and urban. He is particularly concerned with exploring Wilkinson's portrayal of farm life, in which "every inch is filled up with an organism going about its own purpose, and yet fretfully entangled with the lives about it." Also considers the treatment of sex in her first three novels.

Dillard, R. H. W. *"Moss on the North Side."* In *Survey of Contemporary Literature*, edited by Frank N. Magill. Rev. and enlarged ed. Vol. 8, pp. 5094-5097. Englewood Cliffs, N.J.: Salem Press, 1977.
Dillard sees *Moss* as a mature first novel with "all the care and conscious analysis that a writing school requires without ever losing its own distinctive voice and approach." What literary extremes it shows are forgivable to the reviewer given the overall power of this dark "novel of initiation" of the young girl, Cary. Calls Wilkinson a talented writer with great potential.

Dykeman, Wilma. "Taking Life as It Comes." *The New York Times Book Review* (August 14, 1966): 26.
Favorable review of *Moss on the North Side*. "This is a work of high quality. Its flaws may be found in its virtues occasionally carried to

excess." Dykeman lauds the immediacy of the senses in Wilkinson's writing. She is also attracted to the strong narrator, "a girl wonderfully tough and tender who meets life as it comes."

Graham, John. "Sylvia Wilkinson." In *The Writer's Voice: Conversations with Contemporary Writers*, conducted by John Graham, edited by George Garrett, pp. 200-213. New York: William Morrow, 1973.
Garrett provides a short biography and impressionistic "Snapshot" of Wilkinson before the two-part interview that Graham conducted in June, 1970. Wilkinson speaks initially of the process for *Cale*, "a transitional book" in her writing. She also comments on the validity of men writing through female characters and women writing through male characters, especially as she did in *Cale*. Other topics include Wilkinson's obsessions with natural and historical detail and *A Killing Frost*.

Kearns, Katherine. "Sylvia Wilkinson." In *Dictionary of Literary Biography Yearbook: 1986*, edited by J. M. Brook, pp. 356-366. Detroit: Gale Research, 1987.
A relatively full discussion of Wilkinson's background, writings, and critical reception. Kearns notes the importance of outside enthusiasms (especially car racing) as contrasts to the version of Wilkinson as a writer. They are "the dual energies that have formed her as an artist." Many references to reviews within the text, along with a list of publications by her at the front and a few secondary sources at the end.

Kersh, Gerald. "A Closing of Old Wounds." *Saturday Review* (October 7, 1967): 44.
Review of *A Killing Frost*. Takes a great deal of space criticizing the marketing aspects of the novel—the title, the dust jacket art, the author's picture. Finally able to concede that Wilkinson "has conveyed here as solid a portrait of a thirteen-year-old girl at a certain season as has ever been written." Predicts a masterpiece from the author within seven years.

Kincheloe, Henderson. "A Killing Frost." In *Survey of Contemporary Literature*, edited by Frank N. Magill. Rev. and enlarged ed. Vol. 6, pp. 3998-4000. Englewood Cliffs, N.J.: Salem Press, 1977.
This review warns against the perils of a young girl narrator, then seems to find Ramie an acceptable version in *A Killing Frost*.

Kincheloe claims the narrator "has the artist's ability to see with her mind or imagination, to create what her eyes never saw," attributes that are also claimed for Wilkinson as an author. Ultimately, however, it is Miss Liz who is the most memorable character, according to the essay.

Levin, Martin. "Reader's Report." *The New York Times Book Review* (November 12, 1967): 68.
A short review of *A Killing Frost*. Levin summarizes the book's plot, then contends that "Miss Wilkinson has a touch of the poet that gives her autumnal memoir a gentle radiance." Emphasizes the power of nature to unite the girl and her grandmother.

Morrow, Mark. *Images of the Southern Writer*. Athens: University of Georgia Press, 1985.
A full-page photograph and brief informal interview in which Wilkinson reflects on her writing habits and life-style, particularly her obsession with racing cars. Wilkinson avoids too much contact with other writers or academics. "My work is serious and that's enough seriousness and intellectualism for me." Morrow's presentation of Wilkinson is as sensitive as his photographic study.

"*Moss on the North Side*." *Time* (August 12, 1966): 79-80.
Brief review of her first novel in the context of reviews of the year's other first novelists. Considers *Moss* "a lyrical evocation of childhood by one of the most talented Southern belletrists to appear since Carson McCullers." Also places Wilkinson's book as one of the "season's three most flagrantly gifted first novels."

Quammen, David. "The Bildungsroman That Didn't Build." *The New York Times Book Review* (February 21, 1982): 13.
Primarily negative review of *Bone of My Bones*. Quammen praises the fine language of the novel while mourning the lack of structure. "For all its honesty, for all its decent writing, at just 272 pages, 'Bones of My Bones' seems interminable, even to a reader partial to Southern country subjects." Quammen wonders at Wilkinson's narrative choices given her writing history.

Rubin, Louis D., Jr. "Foreword: A New Edition of *Cale*." In *Cale*, by Sylvia Wilkinson, 2d ed., pp. vii-xix. Chapel Hill, N.C.: Algonquin Books, 1986.

Rubin writes as Wilkinson's publisher and former teacher and as one "disappointed at what seems to me the failure of American literary critics, reviewers, and readers in general to recognize and to honor one of the most remarkable writers who have been publishing fiction during the last several decades." Gives much on the biographical and publishing background of Wilkinson. Considerable insights into the strengths and difficulties of her narrative tendencies. This edition of *Cale* has been edited "to cut back severely on Falissa's presence, and to allow her son Cale to occupy the centrally prominent role he was meant to fill."

Swink, Lottie H. "Sylvia Wilkinson." In *Southern Writers: A Biographical Dictionary*, edited by Robert Bain, Joseph M. Flora, and Louis D. Rubin, Jr., pp. 489-490. Baton Rouge: Louisiana State University Press, 1979.
A short summary of Wilkinson's education and writings. Also includes honors and awards as well as a limited primary bibliography up through *Shadow of the Mountain* (1977). Makes special notes of her background in painting and avid interest in sports-car racing.

Vance, Jane Gentry. "Fat Like Mama, Mean Like Daddy: The Fiction of Sylvia Wilkinson." *The Southern Literary Journal* 15 (Fall, 1982): 22-36.
Vance explores Wilkinson's "dominant theme" of "the development of the female psyche in the mid-twentieth century South" through her five novels. Vance finds growth in complexity, especially in confronting sex and the woman's role in the Southern world. Major recurring weaknesses include narrative technique and the difficulty in articulating mental reality for her "non-literate secondary characters," according to Vance. Important critical essay.

_____. "An Interview with Sylvia Wilkinson." *The Kentucky Review* 2 (1981): 75-88.
From the 1980 University of Kentucky Women Writers Conference. An introductory biographical sketch leads into a lengthy interview. Wilkinson begins the discussion by speaking of the power of the natural world in her life and the way she needs to alternate vigorous outdoor activity with the withdrawal necessary to write. She also describes the nonverbal ways her mother influenced her to write. About fiction, Wilkinson says, "I think it serves to ground us, to give us something to come back to that is basic: human love, human change, human tragedy."

_____. "Sylvia Wilkinson." In *Critical Survey of Long Fiction*, edited by Frank N. Magill. Vol. 7, pp. 2889-2896. Englewood Cliffs, N.J.: Salem Press, 1983.
Notes that for Wilkinson's characters, "nature is still a living symbolic force, and her considerable powers of description bring nature alive for the urban reader." Reviews the major movements of Wilkinson's career and considers her novels in turn. While her last three novels failed to get the kind of critical attention the first two did, Vance still sees them as evidence of continued growth. Short bibliographies (primary and secondary).

Wilkinson, Sylvia. "Growing up in America: South." *Mademoiselle* (April, 1969): 208, 298-302.
Moving essay on what a Southern childhood means to her. "At first, to remember a childhood is to remember only the hurts," Wilkinson begins. She goes on to record the contradictions of life in the South, especially the respect for nature's power along with a seeming constant betrayal of it. Wilkinson also talks of her early desires to write.

_____. "I Like That Eustacia Vye." *Writer* 91 (August, 1978): 9-12, 28.
An extended and colorful discussion on character creation. Wilkinson uses examples from her writing students along with her own works to show various paths for arriving at character traits. One can begin with autobiographical material but must be willing to leap into the imagination to complete the character, according to Wilkinson. Includes an excerpt from a letter by Wilkinson on how she balances teaching with writing.

_____. "Three Teachers." In *An Apple for My Teacher*, edited by Louis D. Rubin, Jr., pp. 132-138. Chapel Hill, N.C.: Algonquin Books, 1987.
With humor and poignancy, Wilkinson recounts the impact of three teachers on her decision to write. She notes how one stern young matron virtually guaranteed her writing career after chastising her for "disgusting" writing about pulling ticks. Also includes the impact of a biology teacher on describing the natural world.

_____. "A Time to Live, a Time to Write." *Writer* 81 (July, 1968): 9-11, 44.

Written soon after her second novel. Wilkinson describes the important contributors to her literary output. Journals are especially useful, both as receptacles for "undisciplined outbursts" and as "seeds" for other writing. For Wilkinson, the process also requires careful consideration of memory, place, and character. Finally, she relates some of the tricks she uses to keep the writing fresh and exciting for her as the author.

Woodlief, Ann M. "Sylvia Wilkinson: Passages Through a Tarheel Childhood." In *Southern Women Writers: The New Generation*, edited by Tonette Bond Inge, pp. 236-250. Tuscaloosa: University of Alabama Press, 1990.
Comments on the regional autobiographical foundation of Wilkinson's writings, yet finds that "the novels are also universal portraits of the maturing child who reaches for knowledge and wisdom embedded in nature and in people, especially the aged." Traces this idea through the various works. Woodlief admits Wilkinson's status has slipped since the early acclaim but finds reason for hope of a resurgence of attention with future writing. Bibliography and notes.

Yardley, Jonathan. "Her Aching "Bones': On Being Young and Female in the Old South." *The Washington Post* (February 10, 1982): pp. C1, C9.
A respectful if hesitant review of *Bone of My Bones*. Yardley believes Wilkinson has gone to the well of girlhood experience once too often. The novel, according to Yardley, lacks narrative coherence and "suggests that she has now explored the rites-of-passage novel for all it is worth and then some."

JOAN WILLIAMS

Blotner, Joseph. *Faulkner: A Biography*. Vol. 2, pp. 1291-1293, 1301-1303, 1429-1435. New York: Random House, 1974.

Excerpts from the biography provide one version of events transpiring between Williams and Faulkner (parts of which are contested by Williams). Primary allusions are listed above in the page references, while more incidental ones can be found from the biography's index. Little in the way of critical discussion of Williams' writings here.

Boroff, David. "The Trouble with Jake." *The New York Times Book Review* (May 21, 1961): 4.

Boroff's review of *The Morning and the Evening* describes it as "written in a neat, orderly, judicious prose without a trace of Faulknerian amplitude." Boroff admires Williams' restraint in avoiding obvious horrors and focusing on the horrors of general human insensitivity. Williams is "a gifted writer in superb control of her craft."

Bray, Rosemary. "*County Woman.*" *The Village Voice Literary Supplement* (February, 1982): 4.

Exasperated review of the novel as a well-intentioned but failed moral treatise. Bray bemoans the moralizing of a white woman explaining the ills of racism. The book itself is "Peyton Place meets the Civil Rights Movement." She finds little credibility in the supporting characters or in Allie's transformations. Notes Williams' capacities as a writer who is "too capable to be dealing in silly plots like this."

"*County Woman.*" *The New Yorker* (March 15, 1982): 143.

Brief review. Calls *County Woman* "a rare beauty: Joan Williams' ear for the nuances in Southern dialects . . . is as keen as her eye for the changing seasons." The reviewer finds the depiction of Allie's questionings and transformations credible and affecting. The plot "twists and turns with the vigor of a real, if exceptional, life."

Hicks, Granville. "Sorrow Without Horror." *Saturday Review* (May 13,
1961): 20.
Hicks places Williams in the company of Southern women writers
such as Welty, McCullers, Grau, and O'Connor in this review of *The
Morning and the Evening.* Hicks finds the material—but not the
treatment—Gothic. "I think Miss Williams has deliberately turned
her back on Gothic terrors. What can be brought about by ordinary
people, people with a fair share of good will, is terrifying enough for
her." Williams' simple, straightforward voice strikes Hicks as well
suited for her task, especially in its avoidance of clichés.

Milton, Edith. "Worlds That Dwindle and Change." *The New York
Times Book Review* (September 18, 1983): 14, 28.
Milton finds some of the tales in *Pariah* dated and haunted by the
image of Williams' mentor, Faulkner. Beyond style, the review faults
their tone. "What undermines these stories is their explicit and facile
moral judgments." Milton does find effective writing in two stories:
"No Love for the Lonely" and "Vistas."

Morrison, Gail M. "Joan Williams." In *Dictionary of Literary Biography: American Novelists Since World War II,* edited by James E.
Kibler, Jr. Vol. 6, pp. 367-370. Detroit: Gale Research, 1980.
One of the few sources for lengthy discussion of Williams' biography and works combined. Morrison notes the lack of attention to
Williams (outside her role as a significant footnote to Faulkner
studies). Her novels, according to Morrison, "deserve attention more
serious than has been accorded them thus far." Only the first four
novels (including an allusion to the then forthcoming *County
Woman*) are addressed. Short primary and secondary bibliographies.

Neff, Richard E. "Jake and the Others." *The Christian Science Monitor*
(May 18, 1961): 7.
A review of *The Morning and the Evening* that speaks glowingly of
the delicate touch with which Williams portrays her world and
characters. Neff is less impressed with the plot elements, where
"Miss Williams' firm grasp weakens." While much of the tone is
evocative of her Southern elders (Faulkner), "there is a substantial
residue that is wholly her own," the review concedes.

"*Pay the Piper.*" *Publishers Weekly* (March 25, 1988): 52.
This review of the novel finds some redeeming depth at the end

when Laurel finally realizes how much she has wasted her life. Overall, though, Williams "seems here to have muted a potentially engrossing story." The main character is largely unappealing: "Laurel's passivity and life-long subservience to men make her a rather colorless character, lacking the animation that might inspire empathy in readers."

Rubin, Louis D., Jr. "Life and Death of a Salesman." *Saturday Review* (May 21, 1966): 32-33.
Review of *Old Powder Man*. Rubin finds more in the book than Williams would have him believe she intended. "Miss Williams has created a less reprehensible, and more representative and universal, character than even she apparently perceives." While Southern in heritage, Williams does not fall prey to the young writer's frequent syndrome of mimicry, according to Rubin. Williams "does not write imitation Faulkner."

Scafidel, Beverly. "Williams, Joan." In *Lives of Mississippi Authors, 1817-1967*, edited by James B. Lloyd, pp. 470-471. Jackson: University Press of Mississippi, 1981.
This largely biographical sketch of Williams also refers to critical issues in her writing. Scafidel assesses Williams' major theme as related to "a sense of domestic tragedy. Her characters are lonely people who, for the most part, are unable to communicate with those nearest them." Scafidel also quotes from Williams on the Faulkner relationship, saying that while he did not teach her much about writing, she "served as a catharsis which started him writing again."

Scholes, Robert. "Fictional Facts as Factual Fiction." *The New York Times Book Review* (May 15, 1966): 40-41.
Scholes, who praises Williams' first novel, considers her second, *Old Powder Man*, "neither dramatic nor imaginative." Particularly bothersome to the reviewer is the novel's tendency to read like a biography, thus circumventing the potential emotional powers of the story. Scholes guesses "this story may have a personal significance for its author which is lost on the reader." The ending section confirms Scholes's belief in Williams' talent as a writer, even if misspent in this attempt.

Warren, Robert Penn. "Death of a Salesman—Southern Style." *Life* (May 20, 1966): 10, 18.

There is high praise for *Old Powder Man* (and *The Morning and the Evening*) in this review. Warren likens Williams to a water witch who "can walk over the most unpromising territory, and suddenly her willow wand bends toward the spot where the live spring lies hidden." The simple, direct style strikes Warren as a risky "anti-technique" approach at which Williams succeeds. He places her firmly in the Southern tradition.

Williams, Joan. "In Defense of Caroline Compson." In *Critical Essays on William Faulkner: The Compson Family*, edited by Arthur F. Kinney, pp. 402-407. Boston: G. K. Hall, 1982.
Williams' defense of Mrs. Compson may shed some light on characters in her own works. The essay attempts to correct the notion that Caroline Compson is "a whiner and complainer . . . responsible for the downfall of the Compson family." Williams finds respect for Mrs. Compson among the other characters of the novel and also argues that her limitations were all women's limitations of that time and region.

_____. "Remembering." *Ironwood* 17 (1981): 107-110.
A memoir of poet Frank Stanford that also serves to illuminate the research Williams was doing for *Old Powder Man* when she met Stanford. Stanford's adopted father had been a customer of Williams' father, the central character of the novel. Williams wonders if her role as literary confidant of the young Stanford could have prevented his suicide.

_____. "Twenty Will Not Come Again." *The Atlantic Monthly* (May, 1980): 58-65.
A moving account of Williams' years with Faulkner. She speaks from the mid-century vantage point of her naïve beginnings with Faulkner—both romantically and artistically. Williams details some of the exchanges they had about writing, including the revisions he offered to her short story "The Morning and the Evening." Williams corrects Joseph Blotner's assertion that Faulkner helped expand the story into her first novel. Of Faulkner, Williams says, "I felt protective of him, though, because he was neglected as a writer and deserved better."

_____. "You-Are-Thereness' in Fiction." *Writer* 80 (April, 1967): 20-21, 72-73.

"It is my inclination to write as if the reader were standing beside me," begins this short essay. Williams gives examples from her own and others' writings of what makes description memorable. The biographical note on Williams quotes her as saying she had "absolutely no discipline as a writer" prior to her husband's influence. Williams talks about repetitive images in *Old Powder Man*.

"The Wintering." The Virginia Quarterly Review 47 (Summer, 1971): R96.
This very short review of the book fails to mention the Faulkner connection while praising "its carefully modulated understatement of deeply experienced emotion." The reviewer seems deeply hopeful of a return to romantic traditions that are the foundation of Williams' treatment in the novel.

Wittenberg, Judith Bryant. "The Career of Joan Williams: Problems in Assessment." In *Women Writers of the Contemporary South*, edited by Peggy Whitman Prenshaw, pp. 273-282. Jackson: University Press of Mississippi, 1984.
Wittenberg traces the pattern of Williams' inconsistent career and points to the difficulties her inconsistencies offer critics. Relates comments from an exclusive telephone interview. Wittenberg believes Williams' sporadic writing pace and her persistent link to Faulkner keep Williams from standing apart in critical attention. Williams comments that staying in the South would have helped her: "I would have written a lot more because all that Southern flavor would have kept turning me on as I was exposed to it." A more recent return to the region, however, proved to Williams that the real South has changed drastically from her written versions.

_____. "Joan Williams: The Rebellious Heart." In *Southern Women Writers: The New Generation*, edited by Tonette Bond Inge, pp. 97-113. Tuscaloosa: University of Alabama Press, 1990.
Critical and biographical essay with allusions to an interview done by the author. Wittenberg explores the tangle of Williams' life as someone too often known as merely a one-time protégé of William Faulkner. "There are obvious challenges in properly assessing the corpus of this particular writer," Wittenberg observes, "haunted by a powerful male mentor, struggling to keep working through the difficulties of a somewhat turbulent personal life." She also struggles with being female, with being a Southerner living in the North, and

with the promise she has yet to fulfill, according to the essay. Still, it concludes, the difficulties of study should not discourage much-needed critical work on this author. Bibliography, notes.

INDEX

Note: Entries appearing in boldface direct reader to authors featured.

INDEX

INDEX